C000076074

Dear Iain,

I thought this looked the most boring book ever until I started to read it — can I borrow it when you've finished?!

Much love,

Jo x..

ROADS TO OBLIVION

ROADS TO OBLIVION

Triumphs & Tragedies of British Car Makers 1946-56

CHRISTOPHER BALFOUR

BAY VIEW
BOOKS

ACKNOWLEDGEMENTS

This book would not have been possible without access to the efforts of earlier generations. My particular thanks to Simon Taylor and Charles Pierce at Haymarket magazines, who have allowed me to quote from *The Autocar* and *The Motor* and use copies of archive pictures. Also to David Dyster and colleagues at the Society of Motor Manufacturers and Traders (SMMT) who located the forms on which production figures had been sent to the Society in the late 1940s and early 1950s. I was able to study the relevant SMMT Yearbooks with their tables of export figures at the National Motor Museum Library at Beaulieu. Christine Lalla and Karl Ludvigsen encouraged me to peruse the Rodolfo Mailander collection of photographs in the Ludvigsen Library, Collier Street, Islington. Kim Hearn and Cathy Sarrell were their usual patient and helpful selves at the Quadrant Library in Sutton, bringing out so many plates and negatives to find the most appropriate prints. John May's photographic skills produced useable copies from rather old material. Thomas Farley, Ed DeBrecht, Phil Green, George Mason, Gordon Wilkins and John Terry were generous with their time in providing specific information. I'd like to single out Ken Middleton, whose crystal-clear memories of Rootes and his personal contribution to the Isuzu Minx in Japan, and his earlier years at the Daimler, are almost enough subject matter for another book. Talking to Giles Chapman, David Hodges (who also provided photographs), Mark Hughes and Jon Pressnell, and reading their work, stimulated thought. In the text I have acknowledged the more recent books and articles which have been consulted. Finally, my publisher would not have received a typescript without Ann's unstinting efforts at deciphering my handwriting and at the typewriter.

Published 1996 by Bay View Books Ltd
The Red House, 25-26 Bridgeland Street
Bideford, Devon EX39 2PZ

© Copyright Christopher Balfour 1996

Type and make-up by Chris Fayers and Sarah Ward

ISBN 1 870979 82 6
Printed in China

CONTENTS

INTRODUCTION

In the years after 1946, (when I was 11), there were 25 separately-owned British marques listed in *The Autocar Buyer's Guide*. Until 1953 there were no imports into the UK, but even the thought of the purchase of a foreign car by the family or relatives to replace their Armstrong, Humber, Lanchester, Morris, Singer or Triumph would have been regarded as idiosyncratic and unpatriotic. The British manufacturers offered an extensive choice. The problem was getting hold of cars on the home market, but it was presumed that supplies would in time be available again. There was no thought that vehicles from other countries would ever supplant them.

Yet as I write, 50 years later, only AC, Bristol, Morgan, Rolls-Royce and Rover remain, joining later arrivals Caterham, Lotus, Marcos, Reliant, TVR and Westfield. With childhood memories of "imperial pride and national greatness" it has been painful to witness this transformation in my own lifetime, especially where personal experiences helped me to see something of what was coming. I remember the relief, as a teenager visiting the family in India in 1947, when we were allocated a softly sprung American Ford or Mercury for cross-country journeys over rough dirt roads, in place of the normal issue Hindustan (Morris) or Lanchester Ten for office duties round Jamnagar. Back in England, schooldays drew to a close and the business of making a living loomed. I wanted to be involved in making better cars but made the mistake of yielding to prevailing pressure not to train as an engineer or (still more undesirable!) mechanic. Gentlemen, I was told (though my aspirations were not in that direction), do not get their hands dirty, and I had to present mine for inspection after every expedition in the Morgan three-wheeler! Because my parents were abroad, I had more contact with the older generation and tasted their antipathy to matters mechanical. How many aspiring English engineers were dissuaded from their initial career choice in the first half of this century?

National Service intervened and took me to North Africa. A timely legacy meant that the Morgan could be replaced by a new Fiat Millecento which was waiting for me in Tripoli in the summer of 1952. I experienced the benefits of the latest European design, with high top gear and low piston speed. The Fiat seemed to glide along the straight Libyan roads where British offerings like the Minor and Mayflower buzzed. In 1955, when at Cambridge, we achieved the loan of an early Land Rover station wagon for the summer vacation. Over appalling roads, far worse than the Indian or African experience, we drove to the north east corner of Afghanistan. Letters to other manufacturers suggesting a survey of agents and service facilities en route had met with no response. Naively, I hadn't understood that the almost overwhelming everyday problems of manufacturers were far too wearisome for them to bother about an offer from an unknown outsider. But on our subsequent journey through the Middle East we were the recipients of numerous complaints about faults in new British cars, and our own tally of leaf spring and chassis breakages did not please the Solihull engineers when we returned the Rover. It was many years before that vehicle was equipped with the current coil spring suspension.

My own efforts in the motor industry were unsuccessful. After BMC had made it clear they had no place for Arts graduates, I presented myself as a trainee at the Humber in Stoke. I have not forgotten the initial comments of the training officer: "We do not want enthusiasts here. You must accept that making cars is just like making pots or pans". Over the years I have come to understand what he meant. They did not want the sort of enthusiasm that feeds off exciting activity and wanes when faced with boring repetitive tasks. But at the time it seemed an inappropriate beginning which might not have befallen, say, a Mercedes trainee. We were sent into the workshops and onto the production lines at Ryton acutely aware of our nuisance value to busy employees all with their targets to achieve. It was a never-to-be-forgotten experience of the realities of manufacture, but there was no formal training structure, and I began to wonder whether Rootes would survive long enough for me to achieve a "proper job". Eventually I turned to other things and resolved to take every opportunity to research and read about that first postwar decade, for it was the decisions and events of those years which played a significant part in the demise of British companies even though some of them continued to sell cars after 1956. The idea of a book took root when I was working in the Motoring Archives of Haymarket Magazines. I was able to fill the gaps in my knowledge and Haymarket kindly agreed that I could both quote from contemporary issues of *The Autocar* and *The Motor* and make use of their photographs.

Whilst there were common factors which affected the industry, the more I delved the more I realized that for each company there was a different tale to be told, with its individual mixture of chance, circumstances, decisions, mistakes and success. I also wanted to write of the diverse products and discovered a rich seam amongst the ten thousand or so letters sent in to the magazines during those years. These personal comments from owners point to the truths behind the coded sentences of road test reports. British cars were exported worldwide and many of them provided basic, reliable transport over vast areas of still undeveloped land. To demonstrate this fitness of purpose to the world's customers they were entered in many rallies and trials, driven across continents and taken on long-distance record attempts. The accounts of these manifold endeavours were another colourful source of information. Subsequent publicity did promote sales, and the resultant earnings, if less than the country needed, were still a vital contribution at a difficult time. If every example of the better designs had been correctly assembled with fault-free components, if economic and marketing difficulties had not proved so obdurate, and if it had been possible to provide better overseas service facilities, there might have been a happier ending to this story. The roads of the world might still be populated with Austins, Hillmans, Morrises and Standards, and UK roads not filled with French, German, Italian, Japanese and Swedish vehicles.

I have purposely not written of MG, whose cars are now available again from Rover, or of HRG, who turned to light engineering in 1956 and then continued for another ten years. Both makes have been well described in other books. Neither Gordano nor Kendall had complete cars effectively in use (the Gordano prototype was using an MG engine). Nor have I more than touched on "industrial relations", the name given to the complicated issues of human relationships, particularly between employer and employee, in industry. These issues are also the subject of many comprehensive studies. In fact, driven by common needs, the partnership did work during that first decade. It seemed more valuable to concentrate on the other aspects of those years.

Christopher Balfour
March 1996

Pre-war Background

A Singer Six in Nyasaland in 1936.

The Motor Industry was not created by committees. This was as true in Britain as in other countries. The discovery of the power released when a mixture of air and petrol was ignited in an enclosed space (to be christened the combustion chamber) was to change the world. It is not surprising that only single-minded, forceful personalities were able to seize this elementary discovery and use it to provide employment and factories producing self-propelled machines. Religions, which can take over the human brain and body, do not grow without struggle and suffering! Most of the founding fathers were born in the middle years of the 19th century, having begun their working lives in the cycle and similar trades. Man's short working span is still shorter when his major endeavour does not begin until he is nearly 40, and part of our story is how in each company the succession was handled or came about.

Herbert Austin, William Hillman, Thomas Humber, and Siegfrid Bettman and Reginald

Maudslay (of Standard and Triumph) were, or would have been, over 80 in 1945. The comparative success of their companies in the following decade stems in part from the accession of towering, many would say ruthless, second-generation leaders who were all in place with untrammelled power by the end of the war. Leonard Lord at Austin, William Rootes, and John Black at Standard-Triumph were all young enough to vigorously tackle the multitude of problems. Was it chance or shared vibrations from late Victorian confidence that led to their conception between 1894 and 1897? Miles Thomas, William Morris's Vice-Chairman and Managing Director, was also born in 1897. The tragedy of Nuffield Products (MG, Morris, Riley, Wolseley) stems from their founder's birth between the two generations, some 12 years after Herbert Austin and some 19 years before Lord and Thomas. In 1945 Morris was 68 but still insufficiently wearied by his years to be forced to hand over the reins. Or did Thomas's failure to depose Morris show he lacked the ruthlessness and commitment required for those arduous years? When the bust-up came it was the older man who stayed. The trio of middle-aged industry leaders did not become a quartet.

Dudley Docker and Percy Martin of BSA and Daimler, Benjamin and William Jowett, Richard Lea and Graham Francis, George Singer and John Siddeley were also no longer alive or no longer involved in 1945. Their companies' comparative decline was in part because no super-humans had emerged to take their place, and the later 20th-century management structures, which at best take care of succession without resort to personality cults, had not evolved. The dedication and hard work of the ordinary beings who beavered away in these firms did not replace the single-minded determination of their founders.

The third group are the builders of the younger companies who came on the scene in 1945. Each found different routes to success or failure.

So much for the people, what of the products? British design had unfortunately been circumscribed by taxation policy. As Chancellor of the Exchequer, Lloyd George had introduced a formula for rating engine power in his 1909 Budget. The higher the rating measured as "horse-power", the higher the tax paid. The formula (evolved in discussion with the RAC, hence RAC rating) was a combination of the number of cylinders and the measurements of the bore, but not the stroke of each cylinder. This tax on "horse-power" remained till the 1940s and consequently the major British manufacturers had to concentrate on small engines with the minimum of narrow, tall cylinders to achieve a low horse-power rating. When the cars themselves cost less than £150, a few extra pounds a year in tax influenced buyers. Where larger engines were made, they had the same configuration.

Engines of the small British cars weighing around 15½cwt (Austin, Morris, Standard)

had cylinder bores of less than 60mm and strokes between 90 and 100mm to fit the 8hp rating and an annual tax of £6. In contrast the cylinder dimensions of the 16cwt Italian Fiat were 68×75mm. Tax in England was £9 but the car was much more athletic and 10mph faster than the UK product. In the middle range it is also instructive to compare two vehicles providing similar interior room; a conservative, RAC rating-influenced British design and a more advanced European counterpart.

	Wolseley12	Front wheel drive Citroen 15
Front leg room (inches)	46in	48in
Rear leg room (inches)	48in	46in
Front seat width (inches)	48½in	48in
Cylinder bore (mm)	69mm	78mm
Cylinder stroke (mm)	102mm	100mm
Cubic capacity (cc)	1548	1911
RAC rating (hp)	12hp	15hp
Road Tax	£9	£11 5s
Weight (cwt)	26½cwt	21¼cwt
Brake horsepower	44	57

The Citroën engine was still a long-stroke design but, because there was no worry about the RAC rating, it could have wider cylinders and a higher capacity. The Citroën was also 5cwt lighter, so with a bigger engine pulling less weight (and FWD) it's not surprising that performance was far ahead of the Wolseley's.

Other European designers finding that wider, shorter, stumpy cylinders, the opposite to a low RAC score, produced more power for the equivalent volume and permitted a more compact and therefore lighter cylinder block. There was some campaigning against the horsepower tax but no massive outcry. The average UK motorist, delighted to be mobile at all, didn't know what he was missing because there was also a 33⅓% duty on all motor imports between 1915 and 1939. The few who brought in a big French Hispano or the like weren't too concerned; they had the money anyway. It was only in the late 1930s when the ex-factory prices of the Americans were coming down so that, for instance, a 4020cc Packard Six was on

A Humber Snipe at
Scutari, Albania in
1931.

the British market at £515 duty paid compared with big Austins and Standards at £325 and Humbers at £400, that more UK drivers comprehended what was happening.

It was increasingly realized that the low-powered heavy English saloon, with stiff springs and low ground clearance to maintain stability on the winding but comparatively well-surfaced English road, wouldn't be that attractive to overseas motorists faced with long distances over poorly-surfaced roads and tracks when they knew there were more suitable alternatives at a not much higher price. The majority of Australians and many buyers in India, Kenya, Rhodesia and elsewhere preferred the vehicles with large, unstressed engines, strong flexible springs, and high ground clearance, which were spewing off the US assembly lines in vast numbers. Because they were cheap and suitable they sold almost everywhere and local mechanics could keep a Chevrolet or American Ford mobile in Eldoret, Peshawar or Umtali. The unfortunate Lord Errol was murdered on the road to Karen in an American Buick, not a British Humber or Wolseley.

The larger UK manufacturers knew they were not producing good export machines but what could they do? How could they build up that volume if there had to be different designs for home and export? In many ways it had been easier in the 1920s, when

the then current designs had higher ground clearance and bigger engines anyway. The Australians liked the old sidevalve export Armstrong 14, which John Siddeley produced for that era, and the Alvis 12/50 was well regarded in Africa. When travelling in the 1950s I remember encountering 25-year-old vintage Bentleys and the like, kept because they were still best on the local tracks. There was a US Aid official in Kabul who used his 4½-litre Bentley in preference to the organization's Jeeps.

The British motor industry still managed to ship increasing numbers throughout the 1930s – by 1937 78,000 of a total production of 379,000. The Export issues of the magazines help to explain how it was done. First there was Empire Preference. Faithful Colonial motorists paid lower duties on Imperial products and it was reckoned that 90% went to those markets. There were still legions of Colonial administrators. The pages depict Armstrong-Siddeleys used by the British Legation in Jeddah, a Humber in Albania, a "Flying" Standard with pipe-smoking, trilby-hatted owner on the North-West Frontier, a Singer Six in Nyasaland, the Wolseley of the British C-in-C in Delhi, and many more.

Second there was that particular Englishness, emphasized by the smaller companies producing more expensive cars. Good handling, higher quality engineering and materials, sculptured grilles, leather upholstery and wood trim still appealed to some motorists, particularly the more affluent, all over the world. There are pictures of the Maharajah of Nawanager with his Lanchesters, the Crown Prince of Denmark with his Siddeley Special, Mr Stanley, "an Australian magnate", with his Daimler, Mr Nomura in Japan with his supercharged Lea-Francis. They, and their chauffeurs, coped with the less suitable aspects in order to enjoy other delights. An Alvis or Lagonda looked splendid at Melbourne Races or on a Cape Town boulevard, but often shared its garage with a Plymouth or Pontiac for the serious rough stuff.

Third, we produced different types. Our small cars, which the Americans didn't attempt, were more economical and easier to park if motoring was mainly on urban streets. There were those who preferred our light small tourers outside the towns because they were easier to push and didn't sink in mud! South African AA Scouts used Austin Sevens. The Trojan pictured coming out of its packing case on Thursday Island was the best bet for a prospecting expedition. Our sports cars gave value for money. For Réin Loring, the Spanish aviator, with his Le Mans Singer, for Captain Abdullah with his Talbot Ten in India, there were no cheap alternatives.

However, two letters in the correspondence columns, both from Army officers,

sum it all up. An RE Captain wrote: "Wherever one goes, even in remote villages, there will be a local mechanic who can do most things to an American and he'll have spares on the spot. With distances so vast it means a good deal to know you are not likely to be stranded for long." And from an RASC Captain: "The average British car is a sound engineering job designed and built to last, and meant for use on reasonably good roads. On the other hand the American is a mass-production affair, comparatively inefficient but, in view of its low cost, probably the ideal to knock to pieces on tracks. Neglect seems to have little effect on them."

A study of world registration figures in 1938 would reveal that of 35 million cars on earth, 27 million were in America and only 520,000 in Africa and 390,000 in Asia. Now the argument is about reducing pollution with fewer vehicles, but in 1939 there was an industrial opportunity for those who cared to see. The pity of it was that our engineers and designers were not given a clear run and then we Europeans turned to making weapons to kill each other. For five and a half long and exhausting years British companies were not in a position to take up this opportunity.

The very rich were not deterred by the 33⅓% import duty on cars like this 1925 37.2hp Hispano-Suiza. In 1957 the author's half share in this car cost him £45.

"EVEN VICTORS ARE BY VICTORIES UNDONE"

(DRYDEN)

When peace came in 1945, the markets of the world, largely deprived of vehicles for five years, were desperate to purchase any form of mechanized transport. Who could supply the longed-for goods? America, whose factories had transferred to war production, preferred to concentrate on domestic needs and, anyway, the poorer countries did not want their petrol-guzzling machines. In mainland Europe factories were flattened ruins. Japan, also battered, had hardly started on car manufacture before the war so there was little to rebuild.

This left exhausted Britain, uninvaded and with at least some of its bombed factories repaired, as virtually the only provider for the worldwide market. The problem was that as well as its people, the country's finances were showing signs of exhaustion. Germany may have been beaten but the cost had been prodigious. National expenditure had exceeded national income, overseas investments had been sold, and both dollar and gold reserves had been depleted. Britain needed financial assistance and the only people in a position to help were the Americans. Unfortunately Roosevelt, wartime comrade-in-arms, had died and successor Truman was no soft touch. Vinson, US Treasury Secretary, drove a hard bargain over the loan to Britain's supplicant negotiators led by Lord Keynes. Exporting industries would have to get on and earn money in any way they could. Well may the wartime pages of the magazines have had articles discussing the most suitable postwar war export car with engines freed from the shackles of the horsepower tax. Well may the official sub-committee on postwar reconstruction of the motor industry have written in March 1945: "Too many companies, too many models, not enough standardisation of production and parts to ensure low cost, failure to design vehicles that could defeat the competition in overseas markets, limp export marketing and poor service and spares organisation." In practice the only way of earning that money in double-quick time was to grab all the materials that could be allocated under the still continuing wartime system of state control, re-start assembly of the pre-war designs and get them straight to the docks. It was a happy ideal to improve spares and service facilities, but was it ever practical when cars were sent anywhere in the world where buyers could produce the cash? It is so much easier to set up an efficient back-up organization when specific areas are targeted for sales. Reginald Rootes, as president of the Society of Motor Manufacturers & Traders, reminded his colleagues that there were: "Two years of golden opportunity to achieve a solid base; anyone can achieve a brief flashy success in a seller's market". But the real achievement was to have loaded vehicles, which did actually function, onto the ships, 970 of them before the end of 1945, and then over 86,000 in 1946.

If there had not been this desperate need for earnings from overseas, and if there had been a far-seeing and understanding government with money available to put the whole operation on hold whilst ideals were considered, a more solid foundation might have been laid. Instead, in July 1945, in the first General Election for ten years, the British people, still remembering the unemployment and stagnation of the 1930s, gave Labour 393 seats and the Conservatives only 213. The priority of the new Attlee Government, as had been made clear in House of Commons debates, was its commitment to

Packing C.K.D. Austins at Longbridge in late 1946.

the Beveridge Report. The Conservatives had questioned whether a nation impoverished by war could afford such largesse, but the Labour Party was determined to raise sufficient tax revenue to provide the National Health Service and national system of social security insurance which Beveridge had recommended. It was a classic case of putting the cart before the horse, of spending before the money had been earned from production. Labour was also determined to allocate money to housebuilding. These were all worthy aims but the spin-off was that there were no resources, and no inclination, for a positive State-spearheaded campaign to win world markets, a peacetime equivalent to the recapture of Europe. To quote from Correlli Barnett's *Audit of War*: "There were not the glimmerings of the post-war Japanese concept whereby the state, through a single ministry, positively led industry and the banks in collaborative long-term development of particular sectors of the economy."

The motor magnates were left to do it their way. There was not even a joint attempt to

hammer out the most appropriate tax and fiscal policies for the industry's long-term future. In the November 1945 Budget Chancellor Dalton at least announced the coming end of the horsepower tax, but it would be another two years before a new £10 flat rate tax was in place in January 1948. In the same Budget it was confirmed that purchase tax on cars would continue for the forseeable future. Industry leaders were united in their adverse reactions: "Mr Dalton is quite wrong when he says that purchase tax on home sales is a stimulus to exports. The reverse is the case because a reduction in factory 'through-put' because of this tax means that the full economies of quantity production are not realised in home or export markets." (Miles Thomas, Nuffield); "All extra costs and taxes prevent the steady growth of a sound home trade only upon which a substantial export business can be built up and maintained. Car factories expanded during the war and managers are anxious to retain the wartime workers. The Government proposals give little encouragement." (George Hally, Daimler).

They did not realize there were even

A desolate scene at Meopham in Kent gives ample evidence of the rigours of the winter of 1947.

higher taxes ahead, that there would be steel shortages, that even "priority" home motorists would have to wait three years for a vehicle and that the time would come when there was no petrol at all for British private motorists. For the next few years, when they needed maximum support, manufacturers had to export with the background of an almost non-existent home market. Government and industry relations improved in March 1946 with the formation of the Motor Industry Advisory Council (two civil servants, two trade unionists, two from the SMMT and eight industry figures), but there was little that they could do to change the facts of life. Ten years later *The Motor*'s Lawrence Pomeroy was to provide a graphic summary during a Detroit lecture: "The high level of UK exports immediately after World War II was artificially stimulated by a combination of national needs and Socialist economics at a time when the need for foreign currency was paramount. This need led to the sale of large numbers of pre-war or untried post-war designs in countries for which service and spares left much to be desired. Hence, although successful in the primary purpose of securing currency, the export-first policy has left 1½ million pre-1939 cars (about 50% of the total) on British roads, and a legacy of sales resistance in other parts of the world."

Meanwhile aspiring British purchasers took what comfort they could from the Motor Industry Jubilee cavalcades. In August 300 vehicles set out from Hyde Park. They were led by the 1875 Grenville steam coach, paired with an 1898 Benz, followed by veteran, vintage and post-vintage cars. *The Autocar* captured the spirit of the occasion: "By 4 o'clock crowds were massed four or five deep the whole length of Shaftesbury Avenue. A roar of astonished delight went up as the Grenville steam coach came chuffing round the corner with steam pouring from its safety valve and the stoker very busy on his rear platform." The London event was followed by other cavalcades in Belfast, Birmingham, Cardiff and Edinburgh during the autumn. For a few hours the British public were able to forget their carless state and gaze on both past achievements and the new models which were being despatched overseas.

Any euphoria did not last. Winter 1947 brought Arctic weather (some reports say the worst since 1881). Insufficient coal had been stockpiled so that power supplies to the factories were cut. At this vital time production was suspended and export orders lost. Writing now it's as if "The Gods" had set themselves to chasten the victors at every opportunity.

COMPETITORS & MARKETS IN THE FIRST DECADE

I: EUROPE

FRANCE

If British motorists felt hard done by, it was far worse in France. If you had chanced by some petrol and managed to ship your vehicle to St Malo in summer 1945 to motor in Normandy or Brittany, you might have thought you were back in the 19th century. The horse was paramount again. Occasionally an ancient Citroën or Renault would come wheezing along with what looked like a boiler attached to bumpers or running boards. These were the "gazogènes", the rural equivalent of the urban vehicles which used cylinders of town gas. Their basic fuel was wood and they had the appearance of an 1880s steamer! Throughout France there were perhaps 70,000 cars still functioning. Petrol, tyres and batteries were in short supply. Factories had been bomb-damaged and machine tools pillaged or destroyed.

"The horse was paramount again." Paris, at least its buildings still intact, in spring 1945.

The authorities, as well as sorting out all the problems stemming from the issue of who had and had not collaborated in the war, were at first more positive than the British Government about motor industry matters. Minister Pons planned to form companies into groups which would each concentrate on a single model, with steel supplies then assured. In practice the individual firms fought for freedom and some, like Mathis, lost out with no steel forthcoming for their promising three-wheeler. Then came a punitive tax for cars of 16CV and over (CV equals *chevaux* but is measured differently to UK hp). 16CV was around 2.9 litres, so the pre-war successes – Delahaye, Hotchkiss, Talbot – were dealt a death blow. On balance early postwar state action was as unhelpful

Two 4CV Renaults outside the Madeleine, Paris in the late 1940s, with a Citroën van, Salmson, Peugeot, Citroën, Peugeot and Renault also visible.

By the end of 1946 10,000 cars of all types had been exported, principally to Belgium, Sweden, Switzerland and the colonial territories. Such quantities were no threat to UK exporters. The threat was to come from French work on new designs which were to be sold in far greater numbers than British creations.

French manufacturers also contrived not to compete with each other at home. By 1949, if you wanted a 2CV it was Citroën, if a 4CV Renault, if a 9CV Peugeot, and the home market was protected from imports. These were the ways to provide a stable base from which to plunge into long-term exporting.

GERMANY

For the conquered there were hardly any horses, let alone "gazogènes". *The Autocar*'s Editor Geoffrey Smith toured Germany in August 1945 and reported devastation everywhere: "Bridges down, railways unusable, no telephones. In Cologne the manufacture of hand carts was the priority. At Fallersleben Volkswagen sometimes managed 17 Kubelwagens (a jeep-type machine) a day for the relief organisations."

Partition didn't help. BMW and Auto-Union factories were both in East Germany. The West Germans took the only possible course and set themselves to tackle the chaos under the control of the British and American Military Commission. They survived the Russian blockade of Berlin in 1948, helped by the Allies' 324-day air lift of supplies. Adenauer became the first postwar Chancellor in 1949 and Economics Minister Erhard then

as UK state inaction. Despite making only 1,413 cars in 1945, most of which went for export (it was almost impossible for a private motorist to obtain a permit to purchase), the industry bravely mounted the 33rd Paris Exposition in the battle-scarred Grand Palais as early as 1946. The coming 2CV Citroën was a rumour in the aisles. Actual stars of the show were the rear-engined Renault 4CV and the Grégoire-based Panhard twin amongst the shoals of minicars from Julien, Rovin and others. Somehow the old-established coachbuilders had produced enough materials to create beautiful bodies on modified 1939 chassis like Delahaye to tempt overseas buyers.

BRITISH EXPORTS TO EUROPE										
	1946	1947	1948	1949	1950	1951	1952	1953	1954	1955
Belgium	3,880	12,214	15,006	13,083	15,187	12,606	14,228	12,034	14,997	14,937
Denmark	5,021	1,172	1,247	2,558	4,073	2,694	4,603	10,871	12,664	7,399
France	239	593	391	434	986	1,550	2,465	3,215	2,995	2,763
Germany	435	905	712	2,411	3,033	2,464	2,371	3,071	3,159	3,852
Netherlands	3,158	4,430	5,079	6,454	9,646	7,893	7,443	9,032	12,439	12,688
Portugal	2,340	4,499	7,130	4,067	2,831	2,427	2,961	1,655	1,958	1,837
Sweden	3,553	5,708	3,343	3,566	23,892	16,425	13,827	22,355	39,677	19,268
Switzerland	2,706	5,985	4,889	5,468	5,234	3,379	3,293	2,719	3,143	3,074

ABOVE The 34th Paris 'Exposition' in 1947, with a Figoni Delahaye. RIGHT At Fallersleben Volkswagen sometimes managed 17 Kubelwagens a day.

scrapped controls over industry. By February 1950 petrol was no longer rationed. In May 1951 The Autocar wrote: "It needed a visit to bring home to outsiders the background of destruction and dislocation against which the recovery process is being carried on. In Frankfurt and Mainz, for example, whole districts have simply been abandoned. The ruins lie as the bombers left them, the streets blocked by rubble. This sombre background throws into sharper contrast the increasing number of shiny new cars on the road. There is no purchase tax and the greater part of output still goes to the home market." As in France, there was little competition for British exporters during the 1940s whilst the German companies carefully hatched their plans.

By the 1950s they were on the move again. Mobility at home was restored with the help of the Volkswagen and other economy machines like DKW and Lloyd (Goggomobils, Heinkels and Messerschmitts came later in the decade). Then VW opted for America, and they did it thoroughly, first building up good service and spares facilities. Mercedes took their time. There was no question of throwing together improperly developed

vehicles to appease eager buyers. First it was the improved pre-war 170, particularly diesel versions, to satisfy the taxi market. Next in 1951 it was the big 300 designed for the likes of Swiss and Argentine customers and offering much better suspension and roadholding than the American alternatives. Then came the start of the march towards European executive hegemony with the arrival of the 220 Series. Borgward flourished for a while but were undercapitalized when stormier times were encountered. Opel and Ford were moving towards their present positions. BMW stumbled and did not get their act together until the 1960s. By 1953 a limited trade agreement had been signed between Britain and Germany. Borgward, BMW, Mercedes, Porsche and VW had stands at Earls Court. Conversation in the aisles hinted that home buyers were unlikely to rush to buy "enemy" cars. The detractors might have done better to study and digest.

"In Cologne the manufacture of hand-carts was the priority."

Three years later, in 1956, the German Republic produced more cars than Britain and was challenging in most export markets.

ITALY

Italy had to cope with having fought on both sides. Steel, tyres and petrol were, if anything, in shorter supply than in France, but at least Fiat's Mirafiori factory had not been flattened. The car population was tiny, reported to be less than one car for every hundred Italians. Gradually new editions of the pre-war 500 (Topolino) and 1100 were delivered to farmers, merchants and small-holders, and the peninsula was on its way to mobilization by Fiat. In the next ten years the Agnelli organization carefully researched the design and set about the production of two worldwide sellers which were to be assembled in Austria, Belgium, Germany, Spain and Yugoslavia, and later in Argentina, India and Poland. The 600 was rear-engined and the new 1100 was a light unitary structure with short stroke and low piston speed (see Triumph Mayflower for comparison). A 1400 was less successful on account of very high gearing and soft suspension, though these features were appreciated in countries like Spain where there were then long distances to be travelled on poor surfaces. None of these products (or the smaller-volume Lancias and Alfa-Romeos) were serious rivals to British exporters in this first decade,

but, all the time, the way was being paved for future success.

SWEDEN

There was little thought that another European volume producer might emerge from Sweden. SAAB were known as aircraft manufacturers and Volvo produced just a few thousand cars alongside their commercial vehicles, so Swedish buyers lapped up the available British cars. SAAB and Volvo observed their weaker features and settled down to design and build a better product. Paul Dubois, writing from Uppsala in 1952, summed up: "Your products have to stand comparison in quality with German and Swedish products and that comparison is often likely to be to the disadvantage of the English products. A car has to stand up to a cruel beating on Swedish gravel roads in temperatures ranging from 86 degrees F to far below freezing for at least four months. We therefore need our vehicles to be tight, heated and very well insulated, and most English types do not fulfill these requirements. Why did you not make better use of your car industry after the war? You started production with mostly pre-war models and that is where you lost the initiative."

Exactly. Paul Dubois' criticism was right on target from the Swedish viewpoint (he also wrote that the Minor's engine was not powerful enough for safe overtaking in their conditions), but he did not know of the other constraints under which British firms had been forced to operate.

OTHER EUROPEAN COUNTRIES

Countries like Belgium, Denmark, Norway, Portugal and Switzerland were a free market in which the vehicles of different nationalities could be seen competing on equal terms.

The Americans had set up assembly plants in Brussels and Antwerp in the 1930s, but components were not shipped across the Atlantic directly after the war. The British took their chance and pre-war types were transported across the Channel in old tank landing craft. Over 12,000 were sold in Belgium in 1947 but this happy situation did not last. In January 1948 there were new import taxes, 24% for complete cars but only from 6% to 18% for separate components, and at the same time the American plants began to receive supplies. This led to the situation where an imported Singer Ten cost more than a Belgian-assembled Chevrolet

"The Brussels Exhibitions were showcases for the world." Note contrast between US cars and pre-war type Morris and Wolseley over on the right.

with twice the power. Partners who could assemble were sought. Imperia built Standard Vanguards and Minerva put together a run of Armstrong-Siddeleys. Cars from Holland did not have to pay the 24% duty and J.J. Molenaar produced 120 Morris Minors a week at Amersfoort. At the 1948 Brussels Exhibition, out of 52 separate makes, 34 were British.

Switzerland was another example of the free market and in 1946 we were top of the list with 2,706 cars sold. Like Brussels the 1948 Geneva Show was a showcase for the world. Amongst the record of 72 different exhibitions there are names which evoke memories of hopes unfulfilled: Cisitalia, Claveau, Gatsonides' Gatford, Britain's Invicta, Isotta-Fraschini and Tucker. Volkswagen and Opel were the sole German exhibits. As in Belgium and the other countries our cars had done well at first but were not always trouble-free and buyers transferred to other European makes when they became available.

A trickle of British cars went to impoverished, civil war-wracked Spain in the 1940s. However SEAT was established in 1953 with finance from Fiat and thereafter dominated sales with imports controlled by high duties.

II: THE WORLD

Before turning to the difficulties encountered in some more distant markets, there were other problems which faced all manufacturers. Mr Shipley's report on the deterioration of motorcars during shipment overseas spoke of the humidity and temperature variations in the holds of vessels like the *Rippingham Grange* and the *Pacific Stronghold*, "which were ideal breeding grounds for rust and mould as they tramped from the damp northern climate through the tropics to Australia and South America. In some cases vehicles have had to be cleaned down to bare metal and the interior trim completely removed and cleaned."

AUSTRALIA

The voracious demand of Australian customers played its part in the decision to put production before new design development in the UK. But the purchasers of the late 1940s and early 1950s proved fickle friends. Whilst they flocked to buy when there was nothing else, the Australian aim, right from 1945, was to produce an Australian car. Even better designs would not have been guarantors of success.

The future lay with those who could become full partners in the Australian endeavour. This is where British companies lost out. It was General Motors who took up the challenge with the first GM-Holden, developed in America expressly for Australian conditions, and on sale at the end of 1948. By 1956 a quarter of a million had been sold, with cars exported to Malaysia, New Zealand and Thailand. At least Lord Nuffield had foreseen the position and purchased Sydney's Victoria Park racecourse in 1947. This did not endear the company to all locals but, together with the later purchase of Fisherman's Bend, Melbourne, laid the basis for future BMC assembly from both locally made and imported components and thus countered the import restrictions when they came. These had been temporary in 1952 but from 1st April 1955 the permitted figure for assembled cars from non-dollar countries was dropped to only 40% of imports achieved in 1950. Rootes and Standard also had their own assembly plants, whilst companies like Singer encouraged their distributors to set up assembly lines on which cars were virtually hand built to order from

Redex Round-Australia Trials. At the Madura control point British cars visible include: Standard Vanguard I & II (Spacemaster), Humber Super Snipe, Austin A40 Devon, A70 Hereford and Jowett Javelin.

BRITISH EXPORTS TO THE WORLD

	1946	1947	1948	1949	1950	1951	1952	1953	1954	1955	1956
Australia	15,149	19,176	53,384	84,670	122,162	107,342	57,033	60,595	90,977	99,213	55,878
British W Africa*	882	2,075	2,453	3,225	3,099	4,564	3,972	4,396	3,778	5,321	6,030
British E Africa**	883	1,494	4,225	4,254	3,551	5,478	3,838	3,088	4,063	5,608	4,724
Canada	730	1,951	14,479	31,227	76,278	27,393	21,332	28,811	16,449	14,155	20,545
India	5,490	11,215	12,885	5,574	10,391	11,821	6,456	2,936	2,049	1,680	1,921
Japan	-	11	15	106	501	1,152	1,921	4,521	3,810	5,040	3,859
New Zealand	7,658	14,327	9,241	11,553	19,723	32,992	27,262	21,086	38,828	37,650	30,646
South Africa	4,921	9,513	16,239	18,632	19,532	24,123	19,719	20,397	18,020	27,921	22,519
South America											
Argentina	2,056	3,508	1,033	279	109	1,070	348	45	47	36	705
Brazil	802	2,429	7,101	7,901	7,627	9,214	7,770	814	19	36	41
Chile	625	586	91	374	190	599	312	7	23	24	33
Peru	238	195	36	340	1,887	618	222	122	9	114	194
Uruguay	949	1,899	1,124	1,519	3,076	2,954	2,008	495	1,147	618	93
Venezuela	232	515	781	870	1,382	1,007	940	1,449	1,328	1,395	1,507
USA	1,128	1,127	24,497	6,716	19,980	19,808	31,328	25,337	26,347	19,464	38,205

* Gambia, Gold Coast, Nigeria, Sierra Leone   ** Kenya, Nyasaland, Somaliland, Tanganyika, Uganda, Zanzibar

imported components. In 1956 Harold Hastings wrote in *The Motor*: "Success in the next few years will depend more and more on the Australian content in the cars. This process will continue until all the cars sold in real quantity will not just be assembled but totally manufactured in the country."

BMC and their successors made considerable efforts and, after some uncertain hybrids like the Lancer and the Major, did produce vehicles which were progressively more Australian. It was not until the 1970s that production was suspended because of the Leyland parent's difficulties in the UK.

New Zealand

New Zealand motorists remained as loyal to British manufacturers as they had before the war. However, the country's balance of payments was poor so that from the start there were restrictions on the number of imports and duties had to be paid. As the regulations favoured unassembled goods, small assembly

BELOW The site of Fishermen's Bend, Melbourne, which was to become **BMC's** main Australian assembly plant. **BELOW RIGHT** Royal Automobile Club, Sydney, in the late '40s. Most of the vehicles are American, but Triumph 1800, Austin and Morris are visible.

plants were set up, often using distributors. The result, with local labour costs and both sales tax and import tax was expensive, but demand still remained higher than the number of cars that could be brought in. It was particularly difficult to obtain licences for higher performance machines like Lea-Francis and Healey because there was no "consumer need" in a country where the overall speed limit was 50mph in 1949, raised from 40mph in 1948. British imports increased in the 1950s and were the most common sight on the roads, increasing the countryside's "Englishness". This continued for many years until the Japanese arrived.

AFRICA

Britain would have become a rich nation if it had been able to supply Africa's vehicle needs. Unfortunately the doors to the continent's more affluent region, South Africa, were not always fully open. In the immediate postwar years the Americans, many with

Raymond Flower and "a lady from the Flower stable (his mother)" wins highest award at Cairo Concours d'Elegance with Mulliner Silver Wraith.

their own assembly plants, were well established, but by 1948 British manufacturers had still managed to double 1939 sales. Then, just when the new generation A70s and Vanguards were beginning to prove their abilities on hot gruelling runs like the 975 miles from Johannesburg to Cape Town over the Karoo, South Africa introduced a ban on assembled cars. Austin had purchased a site at Blackheath near Cape Town but no factory had been built. Arrangements were made for Morris and Standard to be assembled from components at the Chrysler plant, Motor Assemblies near Durban; Austin at both the Studebaker plant near Port Elizabeth and the Hudson/Willys establishment at Johannesburg; and Rootes at Atkinson Oates of Cape Town. Meanwhile plans went ahead for Blackheath with a capacity of 150 cars per week. It was producing A50 saloons and pick-ups by 1955, the year when import restrictions were eased, and went on to produce other BMC vehicles like the Oxford. These models had adequate suspension and dust sealing and British effort was well rewarded. Harold Hastings wrote up one journey to Port Elizabeth: "We drove the Oxford absolutely flat out for mile after mile, and I could not help reflecting on the enormous strides that have been made in British cars in recent times."

It was a different story in Central Africa. Road conditions were worse and it was a giant task to provide service and spares facilities from British West Africa to Southern Rhodesia. There is an argument that some companies should have paid less attention to American difficulties or to the fickle Australians and gone flat out for Central Africa. In fact the British gradually lost ground, not helped by product deficiencies (insufficient ground clearance, inadequate power, see Morris section); and Fiat, Mercedes, Peugeot, Skoda and Volkswagen established their hold on the market until the Japanese came.

Egypt was a bright spot. Colonel Flower had established the Cairo Motor Company between the wars and lived at the sumptuous Château de Fardous on the banks of the Nile.

The Committee for the British Motor Show in New York's Grand Central Palace, April 1950. From left to right: Sir William Welsh (North American Director SMMT), Brian Rootes (Rootes), C W Baker (Nuffield), W G Owen (Lucas) and Joseph Dudley (Austin).

With sons Raymond and Neville, the family were ambassadors for British cars, particularly Alvis, Nuffield products and Rolls-Royce. Raymond saw to it that a British vehicle was seen as the correct wear for the highest social occasion and film stars of the moment were photographed in MGs and Riley roadsters. He also organized Concours d'Elegance and often contrived that the highest prize was gained by a Flower Rolls-Royce conducted by a lady from the Flower stable!

NORTH AMERICA

The difficulties of selling in the United States are described in individual sections (see Austin and Morris). 18,000 British cars were registered in 1948, a further 14,000 in 1949. Sir William Welsh, the enterprising American representative of the SMMT, led the way in organizing a British Motor Show in New York's Grand Central Palace. When the doors were opened in April 1950 American motorists found that the widest possible display of goods had been shipped from Britain. A BRM chassis, John Cobb's record-breaking Railton, the Rover Turbo-car and a

1907 Rolls-Royce underlined British skills. Straight-eight Daimlers, drophead Lagondas and Bristols pointed, in the words of SMMT President Frederick Connolly, to the British offering of vehicles that were complementary rather than competitive. Numerous sports cars from Allard, Frazer-Nash, Healey, Jaguar, Jowett, MG and Singer were well received.

The harsh reality was that by 1950 US producers were back in full flow and it was no longer necessary to wait for their value-for-money vehicles on the home market. Despite these efforts and the interest shown by the 110,000 visitors to this New York Show, the objective of 50,000 sales for that year was not achieved. By 1954 sales had climbed to just over 26,000. Nearly 39,000 New Zealand sales in the same year underscored the comparative failure. It was later on in the 1950s that the sports cars were successful, and the Morris Minor was appreciated for a few years.

Canada was more fruitful. In 1948 and 1949 there was a Canadian campaign for saving American dollars and consequently US-assembled cars were not imported. The Canadian plants could not cope with demand and during 1950 British manufacturers sold over 70,000 vehicles in this other

The Rootes Group publicity machine! Sunbeam-Talbots and Hillman Minxes to the fore at the 1953 Miss Universe competition, Long Beach, California.

North American market. Of these 26,000 were Austins, mainly A40s, which benefited from Leonard Lord's expenditure on a large parts and rectification factory at Hamilton and spares depots at Winnipeg and Vancouver. In April of that year he spoke of long-term hopes for a Canadian assembly plant. Meanwhile there were extensive efforts to improve sealing against the dust of unsurfaced roads and to design locks and controls which would work in the extreme cold of a Canadian winter.

In August 1951 Austin organized their own exhibition in the armoury of the Seaforth Highlanders in Vancouver. By all accounts it was another praiseworthy effort with pre-war Austin 7s, an ambulance on the Sheerline chassis, and the latest A70 Hereford station wagon as well as the full range of A40s. Unfortunately, that year's Canadian budget both increased sales taxes and imposed severe restrictions upon hire purchase. Deposits had to be as high as 50%, with payments completed after just one year. Local dealers responded by cutting prices on the already cheaper and simpler Canadian-built editions of American cars. British manufacturers with their shipping and other costs were in no position to reduce prices, and at the end of that year both Austin and Morris had to ship surplus vehicles back across the Atlantic. However, Britain did not give up and by 1954 the SMMT was organizing an Earl's Court type event in Toronto. Austin (and Austin-Healey), Jaguar, Morris, Singer, Standard-Triumph and Rootes (teamed with Rover) all had separate stands, but the figures told their own story. Our exports to Canada that year were down to 16,449.

SOUTH AMERICA

Exporters were despatching cars, and at least some spares, from Alberta to Wellington and most places in between. Then, because every single opportunity had to be grasped in the national interest, they also had a go at the potentially vast South American market. There were still sizeable British colonies in Buenos Aires and Rio, and there was pro-British sentiment created by the old railway and trading dynasties. So, in 1946 and 1947, old-style Morris 8s and 10s were shipped out in their hundreds. With their adequate ground clearance and simple suspension they coped well with the traffic and tramlines of Buenos Aires and managed the shorter rural drives to places like the fabled Hurlingham Country Club.

The report by Rolls-Royce after a 5,000-mile tour with a development MkVI Bentley in December 1947 tells us much of market and road conditions outside the cities. Not only were there the familiar dust problems, but it was essential to have effective screens and deflectors so that radiators were not clogged by the carcasses of insects and butterflies. The Bentley was taken out to the *estancias* of wealthy Argentine families

The best of Britain? A survivor – a five year old Bristol 401 – on course for the 15,895 feet Ticlio Pass in Peru.

Hundreds of old-style Morris Eights were shipped to Buenos Aires, where they managed the drive to the fabled Hurlingham Club.

seeking alternatives to the powerful Cadillacs and Lincolns with their boasted 100mph averages over the open countryside. But then in 1948 Peron came to power and the imported car became a source of government revenue. Import licences were traded for money and other favours, with the successful making large sums on re-sale. Eric Forrest-Greene, an indefatigable agent for British companies, and who co-drove the Bentley on part of its trip, achieved a licence for 400 of Jowett's Bradford commercials but was unable to bring in any Javelins, which were

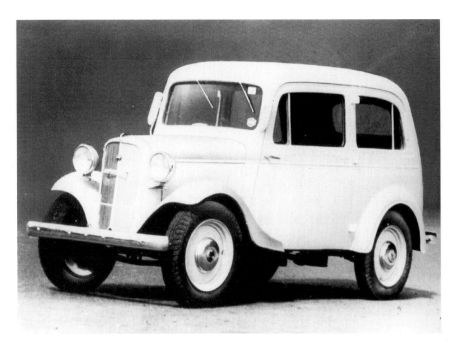

Nissan's 1949 offering – a developed version of the pre-war Austin 7 based Datsun.

later handled by a "favoured" Argentinian. It is reputed that the dictator himself had the concession for Mercedes. For eight years the normal market was closed and, even after Peron was ousted, nominally unrestricted imports were subjected to heavy surcharges. Rootes (see Hillman) had managed to get some cars in during the closed years and then sold many Minxes after 1956 in competition with Opel, Volkswagen, Peugeot and even Skoda and SAAB. The surcharge of £800 for this class was acceptable when the only home-based product was still a development of the pre-war German DKW. Once again British efforts were thwarted by events beyond their control. If the arrival of Peron or a similar government had been delayed a year, there could have been some profitable trading with little competition.

The MkVI was driven to Uruguay, then "a tourist's paradise, excellent food, superb beaches, clean hotels", and was exhibited in Montevideo's Casino. It was noted that there were large numbers of Austins and other British cars in use and most of the buses were AEC or Leyland. For its last expedition the uncomplaining Bentley was pointed west and cruised at 80mph (not 100!) for 500 miles across the plains towards Mendoza. Then it was up into the Andes, over the

12,600 feet Cristo Pass, and down the other side to Santiago in Chile. The descent "was considerably steeper than an Alpine Pass with second gear being used almost continuously." There was less obvious wealth than in Uruguay, with horse-drawn cabs still the main source of transport. Some British cars were in evidence, the big Humber being in demand for lengthy journeys in that long narrow country. The concluding snap-portrait of South American conditions concerns Peru, where the government favoured Sterling purchases in the late 1940s. Home-produced petrol was just a few pence per gallon so a large income was not required to run an economical car. The challenge was accepted and Alvis, Jowett, Morgan and Singer joined the larger manufacturers at the British Motor Show in Lima in 1950.

JAPAN

Japan's first postwar concern was reconstruction, with help from the victorious Allies. Next they had to struggle to make or purchase sufficient steel. By 1949 Nissan was producing a developed version of the Austin 7-based Datsun, and Toyota the more modern 995cc Toyopet, with a simple form of all-independent suspension. Taxes were high

The world needed new cars. TOP Pre-war Austin, Fiat, Morris, Vauxhall in Singapore. ABOVE Tehran street scene, 1950, Hillman Minx in motion on left. All the rest are American. Quartet in the foreground are: Mercury, Buick, Pontiac, '30s Hudson.

except on cyclecars of less than 350cc, which encouraged machines like the eponymous Flying Feather. There were reckoned to be 150,000 cars in the whole country but many of these belonged to the British and American Occupation Forces.

After 1950 the new Japanese Ministry of International Trade and Industry led the banks and industrial giants to collaborate in a 20-year development plan for the motor industry. Japanese engineers visited Renault in France and Austin and Rootes in Britain. The Europeans agreed to help. Hino was to build the rear-engined Renault, Isuzu the Hillman Minx and Nissan the A40 Somerset. Nissan also used a developed A35 engine in its Datsun 1000. This cooperation reduced by years the timescale of the development process which has led to the modern Japanese vehicle. Kenneth Middleton (see Hillman) remembers that when he was dispatched from Coventry he was encouraged to give "unfettered help in every way to his counterparts at Isuzu". He writes that: "this was achieved by a massive effort to meet the deadlines set by the Japanese Government for a programme to show the Japanese everything about the design and production of high volume passenger cars."

In Correlli Barnett's words, "The Japanese Ministry masterminded a plan which transformed a workshop operation into the largest and commercially most successful motor industry in the world." It would not have been done without European assistance.

INDIA

Traditionally, tough and simple American cars like Fords and Chevrolets were appreciated in India, whilst Lanchester and Rolls-

Royce flourished in the Maharaja market, and Imperial servants, English and Indian, bought a Morris, Humber, etc. After partition in 1947 India wanted to make her own vehicles, and heavy import duties were imposed on completed goods. Fortunately Miles Thomas had already signed up with the Birla Brothers to make the Hindustan version of the Morris 10 (see Morris). This arrangement led on to the Oxford-based Ambassador which is still in production with locally produced components. In 1949 duties were reduced for smaller cars. Rootes did well with the simple sidevalve Minx and established service depots, but this did not lead to assembly.

By the end of our decade the pattern for the following years was established, with Dodge, Fiat, Standard and Studebaker cars also being assembled. The aim was to make 60% of the parts in India. It can be argued that Britain missed another industrial opportunity because India became independent so

soon after the war. On the other hand the industry which has evolved seems to have suited the country's needs and Britain has played a leading part in the development of the companies making components. Some larger cars have continued to be imported by wealthier Indians who were able to pay the duties.

There were yet other markets but this selection should convey an impression of the difficulties faced by British manufacturers. In 1948 Nuffield Exports Limited calculated that, in an average month, 66 different countries either refused to accept British imports or imposed currency conditions or licence requirements. Only six countries – Canada, Iran, Portugal, Sweden, Switzerland, the USA and parts of South America – allowed free access and paid in the hard currency which Britain so badly needed. There was more to the export drive than making and selling.

COMPARISON WITH OTHER EXPORTING COUNTRIES: 1949 & 1953

EXPORTS FROM:		UK	FRANCE	GERMANY	ITALY	USA	CANADA
To Australia	1949	84,670	1,725	-	1,813	958	8,461
	1953	60,595	549	29	16	740	15,814
To Belgium	1949	13,083	15,312	5,439	1,060	21,388	37
	1953	12,034	12,306	20,090	994	14,601	4,193
To Brazil	1949	7,901	2,036	1	386	7,537	118
	1953	814	1,728	2,296	75	11,194	6,047
To France	1949	434	-	-	16	1,488	38
	1953	3,215	-	3,418	232	1,330	314
To Germany	1949	2,411	1,039	-	1,361	411	30
	1953	3,071	1,845	-	6,814	87	23
To India	1949	5,574	91	-	9	1,460	275
	1953	2,936	7	12	51	889	123
To Netherlands	1949	6,454	8,826	3,188	1,069	4,367	15
	1953	9,032	2,346	9,641	715	2,358	14
To Switzerland	1949	5,468	5,748	3,601	2,848	4,720	473
	1953	2,719	3,784	11,746	2,754	2,554	541
To South America	1949	18,632	1,901	2	183	15,875	4,336
	1953	2,932	1,638	4,480	771	5,209	4,374

"EXPORT OR EXPIRE" & OTHER PROBLEMS

The year 1948 ushered in what has often been referred to as the "Export or Die" period. The phrase stems from Supply Minister George Strauss's speech to Birmingham industrialists in February, which followed on from Stafford Cripps' call in September 1947 for the motor industry to export 75% of production. The country was still not paying its way. Much of the American loan had already been used and then there had been a loss of exports because of the bad winter. It is worth quoting from the Strauss speech, which at the time was dubbed the "Export or Expire [not die] Policy": "A single average car sold abroad may bring enough meat for 25 families of 4 persons or enough bread for 46 families for a year. Sentiment could not stand in the way when economic survival was at stake and food supplies in peril. Materials must go to the firms who can export and do. If that results in some firms having to close down, this may be better than struggling on with low production and mounting overheads."

In practice the Minister was warning of steel sanctions against companies who did not export 75% of their production. The motoring press wrote of this as an unwarranted attack on the smaller manufacturers, who could be more flexible in their approach to design and development, and suggested that the Government would better serve the industry if it concentrated its efforts on investigating steel shortages.

There is no evidence that Labour ministers were specifically against the motor car, but they did expect it to both ease the trade balance and provide a ready source of revenue at home. Thus, when the flat rate £10 car tax was at last introduced in January 1948 and it was realized this would provide less money, purchase tax of 66⅔% was levied on cars costing more than £1,000. This was

double the existing 33⅓% figure (introduced in 1940), which was retained for cheaper vehicles. At first the double tax only affected the likes of Bentley and Daimler and newcomers like Healey and Invicta. Was this more an appeal to sentiment than fiscal calculation? It could not bring in large sums because cars were only sold to "essential" users on the home market. In 1949 and until April 1950, when it was removed in the Budget, the double tax was more of an imposition as it became increasingly difficult to keep basic prices below £1,000.

Another way of saving foreign currency was to reduce petrol imports. Fuel remained amongst the commodities which were rationed and whose distribution had to be laboriously and expensively administered. Coupons were divided into three categories: Essential, Supplementary (which could be negotiated with officials for special purposes if you had the time and the patience), and Basic for everyone else. The latter had been set at nine gallons a month for a small car and 15 for the largest at the beginning of 1947. Most of the relatively few who had the use of cars accepted these restrictions with good grace, but then at the end of that year Hugh Gaitskell, Minister of Fuel and Power, announced that the basic ration would be

Hugh Gaitskell and Stafford Cripps at a press conference about the abolition of the basic petrol ration.

Leonard Lord about to set out on another export tour (to Australia and New Zealand) in 1952. Left to right: George Harriman (Deputy chairman), Leonard Lord (Chairman), Colonel A R Waite (Deputy chairman Export Co) and J F Bramley (Chairman Export Co).

abolished altogether to achieve a potential saving of $40 million. This was not a popular move. The police had to check on legitimate car use, applications for 'E' and 'S' coupons poured into the regional petroleum offices which, in the words of *The Autocar*, represented the Mad hatter's tea party in *Alice in Wonderland*, petitions were sent to the House of Commons and a committee had to be set up to investigate the black market. In April Gaitskell relented, helped by the American decision to assist European recovery by means of the Marshall Aid Plan. From June 1948 a third of the previous basic allowance was restored. This allowed about 90 miles private motoring per month. Rationing continued in some form until 1950.

It was an extraordinary home background for all those who sweated away on the export assembly lines. Production increased in 1948 but still the "dollar deficit" grew and gold reserves were reduced. In September 1949 Sterling was devalued by 30%. Demand for British vehicles surged to the extent that 66% of cars made were exported (the 75% figure wasn't achieved and steel sanctions were not imposed). This tiny island, its own roads deserted by today's standards, became the world's biggest exporter, even overtaking the efforts of those vast factories in the United States. But no sooner had we won the day than problems piled up again! War broke out in Korea in June 1950. Prime Minister Attlee, elected again with a majority of five in February, was in close consultation with President Truman. The story goes that he was able to restrain some of America's more pugnacious plans (even the possible use of atomic weapons) but at the price of a continuing commitment of British troops. This led to rising defence costs and needs, which in turn meant less steel for motor car production. Next the bill had to be paid, and one of the chosen measures announced in the April 1951 Budget was to re-impose double purchase tax, this time on all cars available for the home market. An Austin A70 Hereford which cost £738 in March was up to £899 by May. The Singer SM 1500 was up from £863 to £1,052.

Continuing difficulties and his tiny majority led Attlee to call another election in October 1951. The Tories, still led by the 77 year old Churchill, returned to power with a majority of 17 and found a balance of payments deficit of nearly £700 million. Their squeezes on credit did not help the industry. In February 1952 restrictions on hire purchase facilities were introduced for the first time and it was not till April 1953 that they responded to the appeals to reduce purchase tax. Even then it was only down to 50%. It was at this time that the export momentum slowed as the seller's market ended. More cars became available for the home market and for a while the considerable pent-up demand mitigated the effect of credit restrictions. By 1954 the economy had improved and in July hire purchase deals were freed from Government control. But the good times did not last. The following year, 1955, another credit squeeze was ordained and hire purchase restrictions were again imposed. They may have given the Chancellor a convenient tool to regulate the economy, but this time demand was affected. Employees had to be laid off and there began the run of what became known as the "stop-

AA and RAC patrolmen march into the House of Commons with the petition against the abolition of the basic petrol ration which was signed by, amongst others, employees at Longbridge (below).

go" policies which were to make life so difficult for production planners as demand yo-yoed up and down. Nor did the Unions like the uncertainty: one week overtime, the next week a lay-off.

The consequences of these political decisions were more than enough for the industry to cope with, but then international events in the form of the Suez drama took a hand. Exports were affected when the canal was closed. The Government brought back petrol rationing and, in February 1956, the minimum hire purchase deposit was still further increased to a massive 50%. Demand plummeted and thousands of employees

were made redundant. Looking back now, the circumstances could hardly have been more unfortunate. The industry was shackled at just the time when France, Germany and Italy were getting back to full production and advancing their own export drives. Whilst British manufacturers were to steam ahead again in the later 1950s, 1956 was the year which marked the end of that initial postwar opportunity. Of course the different companies all made their mistakes, as will be described in the following chapters, but I hope that these last three chapters illustrate some of the manifold difficulties, not of their own making, which they also had to face.

ALLARD

Sydney Allard was over forty when he tri-
umphed in the 1952 Monte Carlo Rally.
However, by then the buyer's market had
returned and Jaguars were rampant with the
impressive MkVII saloon. Fate had also intervened. Just as Sydney got back to England
George VI, a much loved monarch, died. In
the consequent mourning period Allard
missed out on the publicity which it would
otherwise have received as the first British
victor in the Rally since Donald Healey in
1931.

If only this success had been achieved two
or three years earlier, the resulting press coverage and, hopefully, sales might have given
the company the clout to engineer their more
modern designs ahead of the established
manufacturers. The irony is that Allard so
nearly did it. In 1949, the first postwar Rally,
Allards showed their potential by finishing
4th, 8th, 11th and 24th. The next year, in a
Mercury-engined M1, with Tom Lush (who
managed the competition side) and Guy

**Monte Carlo 1950. After losing three minutes at
the last stage, Sydney Allard made a titanic effort
in the acceleration test – 2 seconds faster than
anyone else – but still only finished 8th.**

Warburton, Sydney was one of the very few
to reach the Mediterranean without loss of
marks. There had been heavy snow and fog
from Lyons, but they still had minutes in
hand. Then came that fateful fuel stop. They
had interpreted the regulations as forbidding
filling up before the final tests. As they accelerated away from the pumps, the car jolted as
a wheel caught the edge of a ramp and the
engine cut dead. It took them 6½ minutes to
discover and replace the lead that had come
off the distributor cap. Despite a spirited
attempt to achieve the impossible, they were
2½ minutes late at the finish.

Sydney flung the big V8 at the subsequent
acceleration and braking test to record a
staggering time: 19 seconds and no-one else
below 21. But it was no good: five finishers

had clean sheets. They alone would enter the test round the mountains and would, barring accidents, fill the first five places. Two others were less than 2 minutes late. It was only when the Rally was lost that Allard realized he had misread those regulations. Refuelling after finishing was permitted! The only consolation being that, if that lead was loose, it might have come off in a test.

Today, when we are surrounded by speed restrictions and traffic patrols, the idea of driving across Europe as fast as possible in the middle of winter may seem anti-social. The road is not the place for heroic displays like Sydney's 1952 win. But in the early 1950s there was enormous enthusiasm for the Monte, fuelled by the likes of Raymond Baxter's wireless bulletins from a competing car. Sydney's effort with the same crew as 1950 driving a P1, again with the Mercury engine, built by the company which he had created, ranks as one of the great postwar British sporting and industrial achievements. The weather was atrocious. Already by Bourges many of the Glasgow contingent had lost marks. That year the route was over the Massif Central – and in the dark. Thundering along after Montluçon they saw, still some way ahead, the red glow of massed taillights. The next hill was sheet ice. Dozens of drivers were scrabbling for grip, sliding this way and that, and into each other. The conversation of those three old friends in the Allard cabin is not recorded, but they knew they'd be late at the next control if they joined that queue. They couldn't take off, but they'd do almost anything else. Then they realized the verge was just a car's width. Guy Warburton was driving. Tom Lush writes that he did not hesitate. Foot still down, he pointed the heavy P1 at the grass, lights flashing, horn sounding, and their momentum carried them bucketing past all the other cars. Later, after Clermont in thick snow, Sydney's wife Eleanor's P1 was ditched. They could only slow to check there were no serious injuries. It would have been another 1950 if they had stopped, for they made the Valence control with just 1½ minutes in hand.

Well loaded K1 in the main street of Skibotn in the north of Norway, 1951.

Now they learnt they were the only Glasgow starter still on time. They were one of fifteen who still had clean sheets at the finish. There was still thick snow on the mountain circuit for the regularity test, but Sydney's driving, despite close encounters with walls, and Tom Lush's time keeping, finally brought victory.

The dedicated team who had developed the Adlards Ford dealership (not Allard, but taken over from the building firm Roberts, Adlard) and built the replicas of Sydney's trials car before 1939 had spread their wings. It wouldn't have been possible without the business, production and design skills of Reg Canham, Dudley Hume and Dick Read, and the support of Sydney's two brothers, the twins Denis and Leslie, (who also ran the family building company Allard & Saunders). During the war the contract to service Ford military vehicles increased their product knowledge. Then, in 1946, Allard Motors began manufacture in Clapham, initially using the Ford components and V8 engines which were in the stores. The different models can be grouped according to chassis and suspension development

FIRST GENERATION ALLARDS 1946-1949

These cars came in three chassis lengths cut from side rails provided by John Thompson of Wolverhampton. The shortest were the few J1s, mainly for competition use, sometimes with cycle-type wings. The two-seater

K1s were mid-length and then came the two longer cars, both four-seaters, the L tourer and the M1 drophead. The latter was advertised as "the ideal car whether you live in Scotland, the USA, China, Africa, Europe or anywhere in the world; for no other car combines the vivid acceleration, superb road-holding, high ground clearance, and unfailing reliability with world-wide service for the Ford engine and gearbox." The theme was taken up in road tests, which emphasized the light, precise steering and the feeling of safety over winding roads. The testers also underlined the flexibility – "The gearlever can be left in top gear almost throughout a day's motoring" – but showed they had not lost their critical faculties by commenting that the old-fashioned design, with engine set far back, meant limited passenger and luggage space. The saloon with separate rear wings in the original brochure was a non-starter. Instead, the first P1, with full-width rear bodywork, adorned the 1949 Show stand. This first generation all had what became known as the waterfall grille. If Godfrey Imhof had been a little less exuberant in the 1948 final test, they would have won three Lisbon Rallies.

Production: *1946* 7; *1947* 162; *1948* 359; *1949* 183

SECOND GENERATION ALLARDS 1949-1952

The four-seater L was not produced in a second series. In August 1949 a J2 was announced with coil springs all round and a De Dion rear axle developed on Sydney Allard's Steyr-engined single-seater sprint car. The standard J2 engine was now the larger Mercury V8, but chassis were exported with fittings for other American V8s. Gearbox strength was a problem. The 3rd place car at Le Mans motored the last thirteen hours with only top gear and Imhof's box broke in the final test of the Tulip Rally.

Towards the end of the year M1 dropheads were fitted with front coil springs but retained the rear transverse leaf. The P1

The rally-winning P1 saloon, driven by Allard himself, en route to Monte Carlo in 1952.

Sydney Allard and Tom Lush receiving their prizes from Prince Rainier at Monte Carlo in 1952.

J2X at Rattlesnake Point. Fred Hayes on his way to achieving fastest time.

saloon was now coming into production and would also soon be fitted with front coils. At the 1950 New York Show the new K2 two-seater was displayed alongside a J2. It too had coils at the front and wore a new shallow grille. The American Ardun ohv conversion was available for Ford and Mercury V8s. *The Autocar*, testing an Ardun-Mercury K2, commented that there was terrific top end urge, but the well-known flexibility was no more. They wrote that it was for the driver who liked his motoring "in the raw".

At the 1951 Geneva Show the M2 drop-head had the third generation front end grafted on to the P type. The join line in the middle of the doors looked unnatural and the replacement M2X at Earl's Court kept the new A-grille but reverted to separate front wings. The final manifestation of the box frame was also on parade in the shape of a J2X with radius arms projecting forward and engine moved forward to improve handling.

Production: *1949* 183; *1950* 293; *1951* 355; *1952* 155

Even the experts make mistakes! Sydney Allard with his personal Safari Estate whilst practising on the Digne-Grasse section before the 1953 Monte Carlo Rally. He was to finish 9th, and achieve fastest time in the acceleration and brake test, driving a P1 saloon with a 4.4-litre engine.

THIRD GENERATION ALLARDS 1952-1956

Thomson's tools for making the old-style chassis side rails wore out. Replacement tools were uneconomic so Dudley Hume designed a lighter rigid twin-tube frame which could be manufactured at Clapham in different lengths. It was to be the basis of all subsequent models, but became the chassis in search of an engine. With the Ford Pilot now out of production the supply of sidevalve V8s was drying up. The longest models were the A-grilled Monte Carlo P2 saloon and the Safari Estate, with bodies by independent designer Jimmy Ingram, both with engine forward and relatively more passenger space. They were impressive-looking creations but at £800 more (at £2,568) than the more meticulously finished and detailed Jaguar (£1,775) and Armstrong Sapphire (£1,728) – and this with the basic Ford engine – they were non-starters on the burgeoning home market. However, some of the few (less than 20) overseas purchasers who fitted Cadillac or Lincoln units, often with auto 'boxes, were warm in their praise, happy to endure a bit of "the raw" in return for a beefy large car which went and handled well. Would that a better American V8 engine had been available in the UK as for the later Bristols and Jensens.

Three J2s racing at Pebble Beach, California. Cal Steinmetz (Mercury engine) leads Bill Pollack (Cadillac). Third is Jack Armstrong (Cadillac).

A twelve-inch shorter frame produced the K3 tourer. It had Dudley Hume's full-width body with a wide bench seat. Most of them (around 60) went to America without engines, but the market for engineless touring cars was not large. The Palm Beach had a K3-length chassis, without the De Dion, and a choice of the four- and six-cylinder Ford engines from the Consul and Zephyr. Hume, at Sydney's request, deleted the bug-eye lights on Ingram's prototype. It was hoped that the Zephyr-engined car would fill the market gap between the four-cylinder sports cars and the XK120, but prospective purchasers preferred the cheaper Triumph, the Austin-Healey at the same price, or the more expensive Jaguar. One Palm Beach was built with a 4.4-litre Dodge engine, and at the 1954 Show there was an AC Aceca-like saloon.

The final development was the JR, with heavier twin tubes and body by Hume, designed from the start for the Cadillac V8 and therefore not available for the UK. In 1953 two were entered for Le Mans. Sydney thundered away, all those Cadillac horses on full song, made the De Dion axle really work round the corners and led the pack past the pits the first time round. Timed at 148mph over the measured kilometer, the chief tester was at work again. No one did it better! But by the fourth lap the welds locating the rear axle had broken away and he was out. Zora Arcus Duntov, midwife to the Ardun conversion, kept the second car in contest for 65 laps.

Production: *1952* 155; *1953* 132; *1954* 36; *1955* 5; *1956* 23

FINAL YEARS

This model line-up continued till 1956 when it was announced that the production would only be to specific order. A handful of cars followed. The Palm Beach became the MII with the body re-designed in America, new front suspension based on the Mcpherson lay-out and a Jaguar engine option. The J2R

The first "bug-eyed" Palm Beach, which Sydney Allard rejected.

followed the JR. Both had the letter A in the radiator aperture. Experiments with an economy three-wheeler were short-lived.

The company returned to its roots, the Adlards dealership and other contract work which is not part of this story. Sydney was a realist. He knew when to stop. Some employment was maintained and there was no floundering under mountains of debt. He had taken the postwar opportunity. He had earned vital dollars, given pleasure to his customers and achieved some glorious moments at an age when many had given up competitive driving. It is less well known that all of this was accomplished with minimal sight in his left eye, the consequence of a youthful airgun incident.

ALLARD ACHIEVEMENTS
(Not including J Series track successes in America)

1947
Lisbon J1 2-seater: (A) G. Imhof 1st.

1949
Monte Carlo M1 Drophead: L. Potter 4th, A. Godsall 8th, (A) G. Imhof 11th, S. Allard 24th.
Alpine K1 2-seater: L. Potter.
Lisbon M1 Drophead (A): G. Imhof 1st.

1950
Monte Carlo M1 Drophead: S. Allard 8th, L. Potter 31st, (A) G. Imhof 38th.
Le Mans J2 2-seater: S. Allard 3rd.
Circuit of Ireland M1 Drophead: D. Johnson, Premier Award.

1951
Monte Carlo Cars with non-proprietary engines not allowed.
Alpine J2 S-seater: (A) G. Imhof, Alpine Cup.
5,000 Mile Journey to the Arctic Circle K1 2-seater: "F.J.H.".

1952
Monte Carlo P1 Saloon: S. Allard 1st.
RAC J2 2-seater (A) G. Imhof 1st.
Leinster Trophy J2 2-seater: D. Titterington 1st.

1953
Monte Carlo P1 Saloon: S. Allard 9th
Tulip J2 S-seater: (A) G. Imhof 1st, over 2,000cc sports. Palm Beach 4-CYL: D. Scott 1st, under 2,000cc sports.

The third generation twin-tube Allard chassis displayed at Earl's Court. This is a Palm Beach MK II with McPherson layout and Jaguar engine option. No De Dion.

ALVIS

Alvis no longer makes cars but has not taken the road to oblivion. The company was bought by United Scientific Holdings after a sojourn with British Leyland via a merger with Rover and still makes vehicles. It has moved on from successful armoured cars to successful light tanks, now built in new factories. The parent group has taken over the name coined by G.P.H. de Freville from "Al", the aluminium symbol and "vis", the Latin for force, for his company Aluminium Alloy Pistons. (de Freville himself wrote to *The Autocar* in May 1920: "I obtained a trademark for the word Alvis in an inverted triangle. In consultation with Mr. T.G. John, when we started to design a light car, we decided on using it.") The out-of-town shopping centre built on the site of the old car factory is also known as the Longwood Alvis retail park. De Freville would have been surprised at the consequences of his inspiration.

Thomas John had been a marine engineer and then during the First World War became works manager at Siddeley-Deasey. In the 1920s he established his own company. Helped first by de Freville and then by G.T. Smith-Clarke and W.M. Dunn, the renowned 12/50 was created. Admirable cars, including the adventurous front wheel drive models, followed. Financial problems were overcome. In 1934 a bid was made for Lagonda, then in receivership. It was typical of the Alvis approach to business that they would only offer a low figure which, by their calculations, might lead to profit. The successful bidder, at a much higher price, did not achieve lasting success. It is tempting to wonder whether Alvis-Lagonda might have become the combine that did not make the mistakes of other manufacturers, but John himself did not seem too concerned about the outcome. He was already realizing that the market each year could only take a thousand or so of the cars he wanted to make. As

Alvis alone he did not want to mass-produce a cheaper machine. He had reached the conclusion that had eluded some of his rivals, that quality car manufacture needed to be supported by other engineering activities. Thus it was that John set out on those tortuous paths which eventually led to success making aero-engines and armoured vehicles. War brought additional projects and Alvis ended up managing 21 factories. It also exhausted John, who retired in failing health in 1944 and died two years later. Smith-Clarke took over and maintained the Alvis philosophy. It was realized that in the particular circumstances of the postwar years, and provided money was not poured away through development costs, profits could result from the sale of a well-built car whilst the investigation of other products continued.

TA/TB14 1946-1950

Historians have criticised Alvis for not introducing an advanced design after the war. They fail to take into account first that the factory was heavily bombed and second the company's determination not to imperil its then strong financial position. Other companies' inspired efforts, like Jowett's Javelin or Lagonda's 2½ litre, did not lead to long-term survival. Instead of starting from scratch, Alvis looked again at the pre-war 12/70, designed when George Lanchester was assistant chief engineer, and used the available money to achieve worthwhile modifications.

The rigid box-section chassis was changed to give a longer wheelbase, wider track and lower propeller shaft. This permitted a wider body without the 12/70's rear footwells and five inches more width in the rear seat. The improvements to the long-stroke engine represented the efforts of conscientious engineers to get the best out of a conventional design. Better exhaust valve cooling, automatic tensioning of the chain drive to the

Monte Carlo, 1953. Having finished with a male crew in 1951 (32nd) and 1952, Dorothy Stanley-Turner tried for the Coupe des Dames in a TA21 but was unsuccessful. Shown are Nancy Mitchell, Mrs Fotheringham-Parker and Dorothy Stanley-Turner.

camshaft, and improved engine mountings were the sort of details which improved reliability and efficiency. The car was available with sports saloon coachwork by Mulliner and dropheads from Carbodies and Tickfords. All were most carefully built and included comfortable leather seats and traditional wood cappings. The chassis was also used as the base for the "utilities" or "shooting brakes" of that era, which avoided purchase tax; and also for special efforts by the smaller coachbuilders like Airflow Streamlines, Duncan, Richard Mead and Riverlee.

On paper the specification was the same as the cheaper Austin or Wolseley with similar springing and engine capacities; the difference was in the quality of the engineering and construction. Alvis had set up and tuned the old-fashioned leaf springs and

Marles steering to provide a combination of response, control and comfort superior to some of the early efforts at independent front suspension. Owners all over the world seemed to have liked the cars, for example H.J. Hutteman writing from Kafr-el-Zayat, Egypt: "My TA14 has carried me home safely from a 940-mile holiday tour which included such historic sights as the Pyramids and the El Alamein battlefield. I look forward to reading more about these excellent cars which offer reliable and comfortable motoring in a country where distances usually run into these figures."

Over 3,000 were sold, more than any other Alvis model, which suggests that the directors were right in their judgement on the needs for the postwar years. There are records of cars which were driven well over 100,000 miles. Unfortunately many of those which remained in England were then seized on with joy by UK scrap merchants for their metal content.

The 1948 Brussels Show demonstrated the

Ronnie Adam's TC21 being checked before the Blackpool final test of the 1954 RAC Rally. Adams (second from right in sweater) and Rawlinson won their class and were 6th in the Rally, not far behind the TRs and lighter saloons.

value of offering a separate chassis. Carrosserie Franco-Belge had constructed a wood framed and panelled drophead similar to the American town and country style. The other creation was a two-seater designed by an Italian for the firm of F.J. Bidée with headlights behind a low-set grille, and twin carburettors. This was taken over by Alvis and with higher headlights became their TB14. Not everyone liked the looks but the result was a tough reliable open car with all the driver appeal of the saloon. *The Autocar* wrote of the TB: "The outstanding impression was the pleasure of getting it on the road, where one could enjoy its capability to take everything a driver could give it."

A hundred or so were bodied by A.P. Metalcraft, most of them despatched to distant and sunnier climes.

Production: *1946* 100 (estimated); *1947* 833; *1948* 1,149; *1949* 730; *1950* 317

TA/TB/TC21 & TC21/100 1950-1955

At the beginning of 1950 Alvis was still only offering the 14, but at least this maintained the dwindling choice of marques which had not succumbed to bench front seats and imprecise column changes. In March the 3-litre 21 was announced, with much the same body from Mulliners (though alloy castings replaced part of the wood frame). It had a new six-cylinder engine and independent front suspension. From 1951 a Tickford drophead was available and a small batch of TB21s based on the two-seater 14 were completed by the end of 1952. Every report praised the feel and the handling of all the 3-litre cars. The company ran an inspired series of advertisements entitled: "For the sheer joy of driving I'd like to go there in an Alvis". There were pictures of the road across Balmoral Forest towards Lochnagar, the lakeside road from Lugano to Porlezza ("5½ hours in the bus, 4 hours in your Alvis"), while north-west of Hexham, "beside Hadrian's Wall the road runs arrow-straight under the wide skies of Northumberland. The pulsing power of your Alvis will speedily accept such an open invitation." *The Motor* wrote: "a car the eager character of which makes motoring a pleasure instead of merely a means of transport." *The Autocar*: "an experienced and critical driver will not fail to be impressed by the feel; handling qualities at both high and low speeds are much above average".

How was this achieved? Smith-Clarke

stressed the vital importance of carefully designed independent front suspension during a lecture to his fellow engineers in 1948. Alvis were not prepared to release the 3 litre until the suspension had been developed and tested to their complete satisfaction. There will always be some slack movement in an assemblage of bits of metal which both turns from left to right and goes up and down. It was realized that the best handling and steering came from minimising camber variation, in other words keeping the wheels as near vertical as possible (it was for this reason that Lancia had and Morgan still have the sliding pillar). Wishbones, springs and track rod were all conceived with this objective, even at the expense of some track variation when the steering neared full lock. As in the 14 the rest of the design was a thoughtful amalgam to achieve the desired character. Keen drivers, who had appreciated the 14,

J.W. E. Banks and Jack Sears on their way to 6th place in the 1954 Tulip Rally driving a TC21.

had wanted more power. Now, laid down with no tax constraints, the new short-stroke six permitted top gear pottering or a zoom up to 75mph in third gear.

Dorothy Stanley-Turner took 32nd place in the 1951 Monte Carlo Rally and would have scored in the Coupe des Dames if she had taken an all-female crew. In 1952 she was 149th, again with a mixed crew; and in 1953 she took Mrs Mitchell and Mrs Fotheringham-Parker but they were not placed. The best rally results came after the introduction of the TC21/100 Grey Lady in October 1953. Taking advantage of the better petrol that had become available, engine compression and rear axle ratio were both raised. The result was a machine which bettered 100mph in both *The Autocar* and *The Motor* tests and was travelling at 87mph at 2,500ft. per min. piston speed. Narrow chromium window frames improved visibility. Wire wheels and bonnet scoops were other recognition features. Ronnie Adams and Bill Banks forsook their more usual Jaguar and Bristol mounts,

Adams taking 6th in the 1954 RAC Rally and 4th in 1955, also achieving the fastest class time in three of the tests. Banks, driving with Porter, was 145th (out of 330 finishers) at Monte Carlo in 1954 and then in the same car (MTM1), with Jack Sears and Miss Sadler, achieved a respectable 6th place in the Tulip Rally the same year.

In January 1955 Michael Clayton and the other Bill Banks, photographer for *The Autocar*, had taken OWK605, the Grey Lady which Ronnie Adams subsequently drove in the RAC, to cover the Monte Carlo Rally. In bad weather conditions with sheet ice, blizzards and strong winds, "the Alvis demonstrated very forcibly the real value of safe handling characteristics". The only criticism, (in which they were not alone) was of the flat backrests to the split-bench front seats, an odd concession to fashion when the third passenger would have had to cope with the gearbox and the 14 had well-shaped separate seats. Private owners also appreciated their purchases. E.B. Watson-Smyth wrote from Welshpool: "Since the war I have concentrated on one make, Alvis. A year ago I took delivery of a 3 litre and words cannot express my admiration for this car. The company takes endless trouble to see that their customers have the very best possible treatment." H.W.O. Hornby from Renfrew enthused: "The TC 21/100 has now done many thousands of miles at speeds up to and exceeding 100mph, and has never given me a moment's anxiety under the worst of road conditions. The car has a magnificent gearbox and an engine which is a delight to sit behind."

Alvis had created a fine car but it was only to be available until the middle of 1955. Mulliner had been taken over by Standard, and Tickford, now owned by David Brown, was concentrating on the Lagonda. The wisdom of diversification was proved again. Production of the 3 litre ceased and effort concentrated on the Leonides aero engine and the six-wheeled armoured vehicles.

Production: *1950* 15; *1951* 628; *1952* 538; *1953* 279; *1954* 400; *1955* 177.

V8, GRABER AND WILLOWBROOK 3 LITRES 1955-1958

Alvis's continuing prosperity in the 1990s (unhindered by changes of ownership) confirms that sensible decisions were taken in the 1950s and '60s. Management did not reach their conclusions without expenditure and effort. Thanks to research by Jon Pressnell and John Williams, we now know that Alec Issigonis' sojourn with Alvis starting in 1952 after the BMC merger led to an advanced V8 saloon prototype with an early application of hydrolastic suspension. That prototype enabled the directors to get accurate quotations for bodyshells from Pressed Steel and others. It may have been a costly exercise (though Issigonis was the master of achieving results on the proverbial shoestring) but those quotations (and discussions with David Brown's organisation) led the company to conclude, like John in the 1930s, that making motor cars in greater volume was not the road to be taken. In December 1955 *The Autocar* reported Alvis chairman J.J. Parkes' official statement that "Due to the present high cost of capital equipment, the plans for the production of this vehicle on a larger scale than hitherto undertaken would be abandoned". Issigonis returned to BMC and success with the Mini.

Meanwhile Carrosserie Graber at Wichtrau, near Berne, had been building full-width coachwork on the TC21 chassis and exhibiting at Geneva. *The Motor* commented: "The Swiss concern have established a world-wide reputation. They rely on purity of line and scorn the use of chromium decorations. The beauty of their bodies is far more than just skin deep for underneath they are very well engineered." At Geneva in March 1955 there were three Graber Alvises including a close-coupled two-door four-seater saloon. Alvis liked this shape and had variants of the design on their own show stands later in the year. The Paris car had left-hand drive, disc wheels and rectangular built-in fog lamps either side of the grille. At Earl's Court there were wire wheels, separate

The 'road-test' 3 litre Alvis designed and in this case built by Graber (but soon to be built by Willowbrook) pictured on one of the flyover bridges above the new Ostend-Ghent road.

round fog lamps and right-hand drive. Response was favourable but Graber were not organised for series production. Willowbrook took over the design and made sixteen examples known as TC108G in their works at Loughborough before "financial problems" forced concentration on bus and coach bodies.

After our decade a development of the Graber with more room for the rear seats was built by Park Ward. The TD21 and the subsequent twin-headlamp TF21, still on the same 3-litre chassis, maintained the company's reputation and were the last Alvis cars. Twenty years and just two chassis: there was virtue in restraint.

Production: V8 1; Graber Approx. 100 which included dropheads and open cars; Willowbrook 16

ALVIS ACHIEVEMENTS

1951
Monte Carlo 3 litre: Mrs D. Stanley-Turner 32nd.

1952
Monte Carlo 3 litre: Mrs D. Stanley-Turner 149th.

1954
Monte Carlo 3 litre: J. Banks 145th.
RAC 3 litre: R. Adams 6th & 1st in class.
Tulip 3 litre: J. Banks 6th.
MCC Round-Britain TB 21: D. Laurence 1st in class.

1955
Monte Carlo 3 litre: M. Clayton. Coverage of Monte Carlo Rally for The Autocar.
RAC 3 litre: R. Adams 4th, 1st in class & fastest time in class at Goodwood, Oulton Pk. & Prescott Tests.
Tulip 3 litre: Boothroyd 3rd in class.

ARMSTRONG·SIDDELEY

An earlier competition foray. Tony Lago (of later Talbot fame) driving one of the 20hp Armstrong-Siddeleys in the 1932 Alpine Trial.

In the first chapter I wrote of man's short span and the problems of succession. Though still very much alive (as Lord Kenilworth) in 1945, John Siddeley was born back in 1866, now 130 years ago. He was a man who knew what he wanted and one of those rarer beings who had the self-confidence and self-discipline to achieve many of his objectives. Like other determined and far-seeing entrepreneurs he was not one to accept the restrictions and judgements of higher authority even when they were buttressed by the might of the armament makers. After five years as general manager of Vickers-owned Wolseley he concluded that the parent company directors were not going to support all his plans. In 1909 he transferred to Deasy which three years later became Siddeley-Deasy. These were the foundations of a manufacturing giant which contributed cars, engines and aircraft to the fighting services in the First World War.

When peace returned Siddeley, by then 53, was seeking a partner. Discussions with Daimler were inconclusive, but by the middle of 1919 Siddeley-Deasy had been purchased by the other armaments giant (and car maker since 1902), Armstrong Whitworth, with Siddeley himself remaining in charge of car (renamed Armstrong-Siddeley) and aircraft manufacture at Coventry. While the new parent struggled in postwar conditions, the Coventry factory prospered with models like the simple export 14, and pioneered with the innovative centre-steered, air-cooled, vee-twin Stoneleigh. It was typically Siddeley that when six years later he had decided that his new masters did not measure up to his own standards he persuaded the Coventry branch of the Midland Bank to lend him £1.5 million to buy back his company and his freedom. The deal included Armstrong-Whitworth Aircraft. A.V. Roe (Avro) and High Duty Alloys were other companies which came under the control of the new group.

Siddeley's bold action led to famous British aircraft and engines, to rail cars, to the manufacture of Wilson self-changing gears, and to another ten years of independent Armstrong-Siddeley cars sold under the slogan "cars of aircraft quality". 1932 brought a knighthood and the bank was repaid. The families who founded those northern industrial combines moved in the same circles. Were the Vickers directors influenced by Armstrong-Whitworth's surrender? In 1927 they too abandoned the motor industry (see Wolseley) and in the same year the two ex-car manufacturers amalgamated to form Vickers-Armstrong.

Their decisions need to be kept in mind when considering the postwar history of the industry. They had the technical knowledge, the access to capital and the diversity to counter economic cycles; yet their experience and inclination warned them against long-term commitment to large-scale car manufacture. Were they right to reach that conclusion at that stage of the motor car's development? Sixty years later Nissan have brought car manufacture back to north east England not so very far from where those boardroom deliberations took place. The difference is that Nissan come as heirs to all the technical, material and production advances of those sixty years.

If only Sir John had been 50 in 1935 but he wasn't. He was 69, had many other interests, and was not one to stay around because he could not conceive of life without his company. He had also long forseen the problems of the British transport industry which were to come to a head in the 1960s and '70s: the relatively small companies had to combine to face up to international competition. It is tempting to speculate on a successful outcome of those earlier Daimler negotiations. Would Sir John Siddeley have come to chair the BSA board and laid the foundations for a Mercedes-beating Daimler-Siddeley in our postwar decade? How would he have reacted to Lanchester? The reality was that Hawker Aircraft, the company of Frank Spriggs and Tom Sopwith, bought the Siddeley shares. We can now see that the consequences were predictable. Development pro-

gressed for the rest of the 1930s. In 1945, when men still wanted work as war production ceased and demand was worldwide, it obviously made sense to continue with the cars. But by the mid-1950s the complexion of the market had changed and sales were only achieved after battling with competitors. In 1959 the car and engine side became part of Bristol-Siddeley Engines, a subsidiary of Hawker-Siddeley. At that year's Apprentices' Dinner Tom Chapman, deputy chairman of the new company, said: "Let no-one think that the merger of these two powerful companies will do anything but strengthen our combined position in the motor industry". His optimism was misplaced.

With many other priorities (including engines for the Harrier jump-jet and the Concorde) and little profit from the Sapphires, it was decided in 1960 that production at Coventry should cease. It wasn't quite the end of car manufacture, as the Sunbeam Alpine was built for Rootes and the low-volume Bristol was still made at Filton. Today the part-Government owned Rolls-Royce are at Coventry, having taken over Bristol-Siddeley; other non-aviation Hawker-Siddeley companies have been purchased by BTR, and Vickers have returned to car manufacture with their ownership of Rolls-Royce Motors.

HURRICANE, LANCASTER, TYPHOON, WHITLEY AND LIMOUSINE 1946-1953

Armstrong-Siddeley announced their new car in May 1945. They were first in the field with a completely new model – it had to be new because drawings, jigs and tools had all been destroyed in those Coventry bombing raids. The intention was to produce well-engineered, reliable and durable transport using known design features rather than reaching for radical solutions. Planned production was around 2,000 a year, insufficient volume to consider an integral body and chassis unit which would also have limited the choice of body styles. Sidney Thornett's

Roger Barlow, a US importer, with his wife Louise and George Kirby, drove two Hurricanes to Los Angeles from New York in December 1945. This picture was taken en route in Delaware, in dreadful conditions. Barlow's accompanying Talbot is in the foreground.

chassis experience stretched back to the 1930s and his new separate frame had abundant strength to take the four different bodies, plus the two utility versions, without reinforcement. The two-door drophead Hurricane, and its sister the fixed-head Typhoon (announced in 1946), were built in Armstrong-Siddeley's own factory under the direction of Percy Riman. Costs were carefully controlled and the basic price was still below £1,000 – above which double purchase tax was then paid. There was also constant worry about supplies of appropriate materials – especially sheet steel. The resulting mixture of wood, aluminium and steel could not equal the durability of the chassis particularly in some export markets, but these bodies were still an ingenious achievement at that price in those difficult times. Mulliners of Birmingham were contracted to build the four-door six-light Lancaster saloon. They used traditional methods with much more wood in the frame and these bodies fared badly in the Australian outback. The four-light Whitley was introduced at the

1949 Show. Factory built, it was much stronger, with sheet steel or aluminium in most of the places where the Lancaster had wood. For 1952 there was also a six-light Whitley which replaced the Lancaster.

Having been conceived when the horse-power tax looked set to continue, the 1,991cc six still had a long stroke. It was a simple unstressed design, successfully (provided the relevant filters were regularly cleaned) using hydraulic tappets to operate overhead valves. It only achieved 70bhp, but components were so carefully machined and assembled that the unit is silky smooth even by today's standards. From 1948 a revised 2,309cc engine was available for export, and was introduced across the range (with the arrival of the Whitley) for 1950. Another 7bhp was obtained, at lower revolutions. There was a choice of manual or pre-selector gearboxes.

Robert Penn Bradley's fascinating book on Armstrong-Siddeleys from the Australian viewpoint alters one's perspective of the postwar cars. He tells of Hurricanes and

Mr Frank Brodie with his Hurricane in South Africa in 1951.

The Typhoon fixed head coupé. The body had a fabric-covered roof and was built by Armstrong in their own factory.

other styles which have survived (or been rebuilt – not too difficult with Thornett's chassis), have been fitted with gas shock absorbers, and are driven 600 miles in a day in Australia – admittedly on generally better roads. He makes the point that the lever arm shock absorbers, all that was available in the late 1940s, were the weakest point of the design. It was their ineffectiveness which gave the bodies such a hard time. The Citroën-like front torsion bars and conventional leaf rear springs coupled with modern shock absorber technology give ride and handling which makes a long journey still pleasurable without undue fatigue. It is good that these cars were exported to milder climates so that there are more survivors to be appreciated. Besides Australia they went to the Americas, New Zealand and South Africa, but there were reports from central Africa of insufficient ground clearance. Around 100 chassis were bodied by other coachbuilders including 26 drophead coupés with rear quarter windows by the Dutch company Pennock. On a longer chassis the factory built 122 limousines, many of which

The Station Coupé, with seat for rear passengers inside the cab, on display at Geneva in 1952. The Utility had a smaller cab and did not have ventilator windows in the doors, which were shorter.

were bought by Godfrey Davis for hire work, and two laundaulettes (with opening rear quarters), one for the British Governor of Aden, the other for the Sultan of Zanzibar. Hooper made one long-chassis drophead.

These cars were not designed for rallying or competition but, in addition to their Australian experiences, featured in several long journeys. Roger Barlow had set up International Motors in Los Angeles to import European cars. With his wife Louise they met up with George Kirby from the factory in New York Docks in December 1945, uncrated the two Hurricanes and drove the 3,500 miles back to sunny California via New Orleans and El Paso. It was so cold in Virginia and the Carolinas that radiators had to be drained each night, but the weather changed when they reached the Gulf and they were able to drive up through Texas and Arizona with hoods rolled back. Except for an initial problem in adjusting carburettors to the American petrol the cars were trouble free. In 1950 H.K. Jones shipped his Hurricane, which had already covered 30,000 miles, out to New Zealand and drove 5,000 miles on roads and tracks: "The car never caused a moment's anxiety except a certain amount of 'nerves' going through some of the fords and creeks." The cars were so completely reliable because every component was carefully designed by conscientious British engineers.

Production – 2 litre: *1946* 1,653; *1947* 2,245;
1948 1,687; *1949* 396. **2.3 litre:** *1949* 981; *1950* 2,175; *1951* 2,026; *1952* 1,267; *1953* 40

STATION COUPÉ AND UTILITY COUPÉ 1949-1952

It was in the Siddeley tradition to consider all additional outlets, especially where they could be satisfied via existing designs and production facilities. Thus, when the Australian distributors reported the demand for utility vehicles which combined passenger and goods accommodation, it was realized that the factory could make a simple body for the strong Thornett chassis. There were two models, the Station Coupé with two rows of seats and a modest load area, and the Utility Coupé with one bench seat and larger load area. Both were well made but furnished without frills for hard work. The majority went to Australia. Some are still there – even in use. Others followed the cars to Africa and the Americas.

In the November 1979 issue of *Thoroughbred & Classic Cars* there is a letter from a Mr Tolson whose father had owned a Utility Coupé for 14 years: "A good and practical workhorse which was a very neat handler on the dirt tracks which served for roads in our district. It was one of those cars where the balance and steering were so good that cornering was an almost subconscious and effortless affair. The gearing was so well matched to the torque of the very smooth engine that our favourite hills could be climbed at 50-55mph either full or empty". Mr Tolson then went on to list the problems. First, the seals soon burst in the shock absorbers, which ties in with Penn Bradley's comments; second, body bolts rattled loose and the aluminium bonnet cracked; and third, the old bugbear of not enough service agents. He concluded that the vehicle was "a near miss". It's probably fairer to refer back to the comments about the cars – that modern gas shock absorbers, which would have countered the first two problems, were not available. As to service, it would have been difficult to cover that vast area, and the factory policy of aiming for reliability (only really let down by the shock absorbers) was the pragmatic response to selling vehicles in small numbers.

Production (Not known by year): Station Coupé 1,022; Utility Coupé 717

SAPPHIRE 346 MKI & II SALOON, PICK-UP, LIMOUSINE 1952-1959

The big Sapphire, subjected to less corrosion, has come into its own in Australia. In the 1960s the MkVII Jaguar received more praise, but Sapphires are still going strong Down Under after three decades. The passing of the years has confirmed the merit of Armstrong-Siddeley engineering. Like their predecessors the cars have gained a reputation for reliability in difficult conditions. They are comfortable over long distances on poor roads and easy to service. Penn Bradley writes of examples that have been driven more than 500,000 miles.

At the end of 1954 Philip Turner of *The Motor* talked to managing director Tom Chapman about the genesis of the Sapphire. The aim had been to study the design of each component so as to achieve the lowest possible weight which would do the job of transporting up to six people in many different countries. This was the proper application of aircraft experience. Too many pre-war designs had been given extra mass to make sure, and the additional weight meant more expense and less performance. Thus the new frame was 44lb lighter and much stiffer than the previous Hurricane. It also foreshadowed design of the 1970s in having deformable sections front and rear which took the brunt of an accident without distortion to the main section. The simplest effective solutions were also sought. Coil spring technology had developed and they took up less room at the front than torsion bars. At the rear, conventional leaf springs had plenty of deflection and, at last, there were reasonable shock absorbers.

Preparing the Sapphire team for Monte Carlo 1955. This is Don Bennett's car. Tommy Sopwith is facing the camera.

The same philosophy applied to engine design. The twin overhead camshaft unit designed by W.O. Bentley and Donald Bastow during their consultancy after leaving Lagonda was discarded as too complicated for export markets. In its place there was a short-stroke pushrod 3,453cc six with much attention given to efficient valving and combustion chamber shape. It was a square configuration, with bore and stroke the same measurement, so that at 2,500ft per min. piston speed the car was travelling at 85mph in top gear. Here is a clue to longevity: the big Jaguar MkVII would only be travelling at 69mph at the same piston speed. The first Sapphire was on display at the 1952 Show, and a twin-carburettor option became available in June 1953 with a power boost from 125 to 150bhp. At first only pre-selector or manual gearboxes were available, but with the MkII in October 1954 there was a fully automatic option as fitted by Rolls-Royce. Acceleration 0-80mph took 24.9 seconds in a twin-carburettor manual car and 32.6 seconds in a single-carburettor automatic version, thus demonstrating the differences between specifications.

The Australians are adamant that the pre-selector is the best bet. It has the advantage of a snappy change without power loss as well as the centrifugal Newton traffic clutch which disengages the drive below 575rpm. Bodies were built by hand at the factory from pressed steel with a few pieces of structural wood in the roof area. The majority were six-light with 381 four-light saloons. Forty-nine MkI cars were assembled in Belgium.

Chapman told Turner of flogging an early development car for 75,000 miles non-stop and another early example was shipped out to Kenya and pounded up and down those rough roads.

Development continued as imperfections showed up in service. Components that other firms might have left well alone were modified: rear spring gaiters were deleted as they retained moisture, horns were moved inside the engine bay, according to Penn Bradley "to prevent water damage when fording creek crossings". As well as the auto option, the MkII had improved brakes with larger finned brake drums and a servo. In August 1955 power steering was offered with the degree of assistance under the driver's control. Electric windows also became available, so that most of the features sought today on the executive car were then on the Sapphire.

In 1955 there was also a long-chassis limousine which rode and handled as well as the saloon. Nearly 400 were made, including 15 for the Australian Government. As with the earlier Utilities, niche markets were investigated. Spartan pick-ups devoid of chromium were built for Middle East oil companies. The company was hoping for more orders than the 44 which were exported (one stayed in England), but Humber were pitching for the same sales with their pick-up based on the Super Snipe, and the offerings from Chevrolet, Dodge, Fargo and the like already had a good reputation. Other vehicles on both short and long chassis included station wagons, ambulances and hearses.

This time there were rally entries supported by the company. For the 1954 Monte Carlo Mike Couper, renowned for his previous Bentley and Rolls-Royce exploits, fitted a four-light saloon with all sorts of goodies including one of the earliest headlamp wipers and two foglamps on extendible stalks. After difficulties on the regularity circuit he only finished 82nd but won the Grand Prix for road safety equipment. The indefatigable Air Vice Marshall "Pathfinder" Bennett (record-breaking pilot, ex-MP, Fairthorpe creator) and his wife did much better but then the starter motor failed before the final test. In 1955 a full factory team was entered. Tom Wisdom was 21st after the road section and the acceleration and braking test so could have made the first ten with an epic performance on the mountain reliability test. But whereas, for example, Peter Harper hoisted the smaller Sunbeam from 27th to finish 9th, all Wisdom and co-driver Peter Wilson's experience couldn't push nearly two tons of loaded Armstrong-Siddeley any

Douglas Uren's privately entered Sapphire came to grief on the 1954 Monte Carlo Rally near Cologne, but was pulled back on the road and finished 141st.

faster up and down the cols of that 200-mile circuit. Wisdom was 39th and Bennett managed to get into 33rd place, having finished lower down after the road section. Couper was 51st and again won the Grand Prix. Douglas Uren's Sapphire was a private entry. They slid off the road on a treacherous surface near Cologne but the car was pulled back on the road and finished 141st.

Apart from the 400 or so which went to Australia, Sapphires found their way round the world. In March 1953 *The Motor* wrote that eight Sapphire 6-light saloons had left Coventry for delivery to the King of Siam. The car continued in production after 1956 and was followed by the further developed Star Sapphire.

Production – Saloon: *1952* 12; *1953* 1,750; *1954* 2,806 (estimated); *1955* 1,500 (estimated); *1956* 1,000 (estimated). **Pick-up:** *1956* 45. **Limousine:** 1956 381

SAPPHIRE 234 AND 236 1956-1958

There have been articles in recent years stating that poor sales of the small Sapphires contributed to the demise of Armstrong-Siddeley. If there is some truth in this, it is not the whole story. We have seen that the company was not organised for volume production and was not solely dependent on cars for profits. What does seem to have been true is that it was always an option for Hawker-Siddeley either to concentrate on aviation and wrap up the car side or, just possibly, to increase vehicle production. One can therefore suggest that, if there had been an enormous initial demand for the small Sapphires, and if there had not been demanding challenges on the aviation side, the decision might have favoured the cars.

Careful study of the layout and design details show how the 234 and 236 were far ahead of their time. It is instructive to make a point-by-point comparison with the 1985 Mercedes 190 2.3:

	1955 234	1985 190 2.3
Cylinders	4	4
Capacity	2290cc	2298cc
Gears	5 (incl. overdrive)	5
Weight	2968lb	2689lb
Wheelbase	111in	105in
Length	180in	175in
Height	62in	55in
Max. speed	98mph	122mph
Consumption	24mpg	30mpg
0-60mph	15 sec	10 sec

A 236 with Manumatic gearbox during a trial run by *Autocar* Editor, Maurice Smith (on left), before the 1955 Motor Show.

Great minds think alike? When Mercedes engineers drew up the dimensions of their new small executive saloon they confirmed that those Coventry engineers had been on the right track 25 years earlier. Study of the side profiles reveals further similarity: two deep windows, two wide-opening doors and, in each case, the rear seat well forward of the rear wheels. At the front, traditional grilles blend into a flowing shape. Certainly the 190 is lower, lighter, faster and more economical but the difference is not startling considering the development time that had elapsed. (And test figures do not tell all: The 234 class winner in the 1956 Mobilgas economy run for unmodified entries – no freewheeling, 20 laps at Goodwood averaging 51mph – recorded nearly 30mpg over 650 miles). Like Mercedes (and BMW) today, the small Sapphire concept offered engines with different characteristics. The 236's improved 2,309cc Hurricane-type six retained that silky smoothness but gave less performance than the athletic four of the 234, which was in effect two-thirds of the 346 engine. There was also a choice of transmissions: an ordinary 'box with or without overdrive, the clutchless Manumatic for the 236 and, to special order, the pre-selector.

The cars were still built on a chassis, a lighter version of the 346's, and suspension was a longer-travel version of the larger car's. The body broke new ground: to keep weight down the steel shell was partially clothed in aircraft high duty alloy known as Hiduminium. That shape was essentially functional – the high cabin to provide room and visibility for passengers and the low snout to cleave the air with minimal disturbance – but it seems that it did meet with resistance in the showroom. Some potential buyers never got round to trying the car on the road.

There's an intriguing historical snippet in *The Motor* of 12th October 1956: "The absence of that important word 'no' reversed the meaning of a sentence in the 234 Road Test. It should not have read 'in the transmission there are vibration periods', but rather 'there are NO vibration periods'! It is, in fact, smooth throughout the entire speed range." We shall never know how many were put off by this misprint. Penn Bradley writes warmly of the cars from Australian experience, where they take carefully tuned engines over the rev limits suggested in the 1956 Road Test: "The 234 is a real flyer. Cars with overdrive cruise at 100mph in an uncanny way. The body is almost turbulence free with this characteristic most evident at, say, 80mph where it wafts along in near total silence, and so good is the design that there are no structural problems even after extended outback use." Of the 236 he says: "The performance is not brisk but once speed is built up it becomes a sweet touring car with the engine just quietly humming away."

E. Walker demonstrating the cornering powers of his 234 at Prescott in the 1958 RAC Rally.

And of both models: "The 234 and the 236 endear themselves on rough unmade roads. They revel in coping with stones, potholes and corrugated gravel surfaces, the long suspension travel being ideal for such use." Bradley also reports that the Sydney distributors had 78 firm orders yet were not sent a single car.

There seems little doubt that, when the company car market developed, the 234 and 236 and their successors could have met the demand for executive cars and our company car parks might not now be so full of German vehicles. Bristol, the other partner before the aviation engine side became Rolls-Royce, did not proceed with its all-independent 3.6-litre 220 saloon. The Government ordered new aircraft tests after the Comet airliners fell out of the skies, and, to meet the cost, the Bristol directors curtailed other developments.

Let us take heart that there are at least Rovers in those car parks. British Aerospace would not have been in a position to take over Rover if former constituent companies like Hawker-Siddeley had not seized the aviation opportunities at the expense of the cars three decades earlier. With more secure prospects under BAe control, the Honda-Rover partnership prospered. Without that BAe and Honda input Rover would not have been such a desirable prospect for BMW. Both the original success of Armstrong-Siddeley cars and the subsequent decision to consign them (and the 220 Bristol) to obliv-

ion have been building blocks which have led to the current strength of Rover, even if BMW owned; and to the potency of BAe and Rolls-Royce in the aviation industry.

Production – 234: *1956-58* 803. **236** *1956-58* 603

ARMSTRONG-SIDDELEY ACHIEVEMENTS

1945
Journeys Hurricane: R. Barlow 3,500 miles New York to Los Angeles.

1950
Journeys Hurricane: H. Jones 5,000 miles in New Zealand.

1954
Monte Carlo Sapphire 346: W. Couper 82nd & RAC Trophy & Grand Prix de Sécurité Routière.

1955
Monte Carlo Sapphire 346: D. Bennett 33rd, T. Wisdom 39th, W. Couper 51st & Grand Prix de Sécurité Routière.
Journeys Sapphire 346: Wyborn & Riddill with caravan to New Zealand.

1956
Mobilgas Economy Run Sapphire 234: D. Elldred 1st in class.

AUSTIN

Leonard Lord (on left), Billy Rootes talking to Kay Petre (pre-war Brooklands driver) in centre and, beside Kay, E.L. Payton just before his retirement in 1945. "Would there have been a different story to tell if Payton had been able to retain the chairmanship?" Chassis is Austin Sixteen.

To my generation, growing up in the 1940s, Austin, like the Rock of Gibraltar, was an ever-enduring part of Britain. "Austin – you can depend on it", ran the slogan, and we believed that their strong, reliable products would be available for our children and grandchildren. The name continued under successive combines, BMC, BLMC, BL. Now, whilst the last designs with Austin input are still, as I write, being assembled, the marketing people reckon the Rover badge has more renown.

In and before our decade two men were primarily responsible for the development of Austin. If they had taken different decisions, would the company have been able to build on its reputation and become so pre-eminent that it would have been inconceivable to bury the name? Herbert Austin was 39 when he started his own company in what had pre-

viously been a printing works on the Longbridge site. He had already spent ten years in Australia, eventually joining Frederick Wolseley's sheep shearing machinery company. In 1893 he was offered the position of general manager when Wolseley decided to transfer production back to England. The sheep shearing machinery was followed by other products including parts for the then flourishing bicycle trade. In 1896 Austin built a tri-car. His later success with a four-wheeler in the 1900 1,000 mile trial led to Vickers interest and their take-over (see Wolseley). It was Austin's relationship with these new masters and their subsequent preference for Siddeley's ideas which led to his departure in 1905. For 15 years his Longbridge company prospered. Aircraft engines, ambulances, armoured cars, shells and, on the dark debit side, his only son Vernon's life (killed in action at La Bassée just east of Béthune in 1915) were contributed to the Great War. By 1918 Austin himself was Sir Herbert and a Member of Parliament, (not a sensible step, he later confessed) and employed nearly 20,000 people. But he was not infallible. The company approached the peace with the wrong designs and in 1921 the principal creditors, including the Midland Bank, called in the Receiver.

These creditors played their part in reorganisation. Carl Englebach (ex-Armstrong-Whitworth) was appointed production director. Ernest Payton became the financial guru. Sir Herbert, at the age of 55, had the vision to see the need for a proper small car to take over from the cyclecar and the motorcycle and sidecar. His colleagues did not agree. He therefore used his own resources and had the sense to employ a younger designer-draughtsman. Stanley Edge concocted the Austin Seven, the Receiver was discharged, and the triumvirate of Austin, Englebach and Payton steered the company through the rest of the 1920s and '30s. The products remained dependable but, with heavy separate chassis, leaf springs and big sidevalve engines, their performance was behind what was available in Europe. The six-cylinder Fiat was only just over two-thirds the weight of the Austin and, with an ohv engine three-fifths of the Longbridge unit's capacity, was 10mph faster and more economical.

By 1937 Sir Herbert was over 70, with Carl Englebach over sixty and his eyesight deteriorating. Sadly that German bullet having obliterated Vernon (though nepotism often isn't the answer), it became imperative to find a new leader. Leonard Lord was available, after falling out with William Morris, and signed on. He had proved his worth through his reorganisation at Cowley yet was still only 40. Whatever Lord Austin's (he had received a peerage in 1936) personal view of Lord's rather brash personality, he was one of the few men in England of that age and vigour with so much precisely relevant experience. When Austin died in 1941 Lord became joint managing director under chairman Payton.

After another enormous wartime contribution (amongst other products, nearly 3,000 aircraft were built at Crofton Hackett), the story of our postwar decade becomes the tale of Lord's prodigious and dedicated achievements, diminished by mistakes and an increasingly dictatorial attitude which led him to reject expert advice. There was no triumvirate; no Englebach and no Payton to curb excesses. Englebach had had to retire in 1938, by that time hardly able to see his way round the Works. Payton, a man of wide interests (Lloyds, JP, honorary Air Commodore and other directorships besides Austin), and knowledgeable in the ways of the world, was struck down by illness in November 1945 and died just three months later. In his autobiography Miles Thomas writes of a summons to Longbridge "in 1946" (it must have been 1945), and that over lunch Payton suggested that he should take over the business and marketing side of Austin leaving Lord to concentrate on production. Thomas remained loyal to Nuffield (a loyalty that proved misplaced – see Morris), but the incident confirms that Payton was already aware of Lord's deficiencies and did not see

C.R.J. Englebach, Works Director, who had to retire in 1938.

Alan Hess led a team of three Sixteens on a goodwill tour to the Geneva Show in the icy and snowy winter of 1947, visiting seven capitals in seven days.

him as the man to have unfettered control. Would Lord have been forced to reflect before taking unresearched decisions, and would there have been a different story to tell, if Payton had been able to retain the chairmanship for a few more years? He was 69 when he died.

EIGHT, TEN, TWELVE & SIXTEEN 1945-1948

In the last year before the war re-styled Austins were reaching the showrooms. The same old sturdy mechanical features hid behind a modern front with one-piece top-opening bonnet, a fashion taken from the new American offerings and christened the 'alligator' bonnet. On the smaller Eight and Ten there was a hint of integral construction, with the floors welded straight to the chassis, and these models were the basis of utility and tourer versions used by the armed services. The cars were re-announced as early as 1944, offering mediocre performance in line with their design origins. The Eight, Ten and Twelve were all fully stretched at 60mph and were only good enough because of the enormous pent-up demand for any form of transport. At least there was a hint of better things to come.

The first new offering had a more muscu-

lar overhead-valve 2,199cc engine in the Twelve chassis and body. *The Autocar* reported on this Sixteen saloon in 1946: "An extremely satisfactory unit as regards power, smoothness and quietness of operation. So effortless is this Austin that the driver, having observed the speedometer at 50 and not being conscious of having accelerated, may then observe with surprise that the needle has crept round to 60".

Not quite the words of a 1990s tester, but the point is made! It was the beginning of a new era of more athletic Austins under the Lord regime. The Sixteen was an interesting synthesis of old and new. Top speed was up to 75mph but the car still had the old style Girling brakes (leg muscles operating on rods but no messy fluid to leak), an opening windscreen, and comfortable supportive leather seats each with their own arm rests. Alan Hess, Austin's public relations officer, led a team of three Sixteens on a "good-will tour" to the Geneva Show in the icy and snowy winter of 1947. Despite treacherous surfaces they drove 3,000 miles from Oslo, visiting seven capitals in seven days. The trip is amusingly written up with all the traumas – ferries trapped by pack ice, roads blocked by fallen trees or floods, bridges out of action – by Hess in *Gullible's Travels* (published by Motor Racing Publications in 1948). It's a fascinating insight into postwar Europe. On the debit side Basil Eyston (brother of record-breaker George) wrote of the defects of the Sixteen station wagon which he drove 5,000 miles from Cape Town to Rhodesia (now Zimbabwe) in 1949: "The wooden body so much admired in England behaved like the wrong end of a vacuum cleaner. The wood expanded under the hot sun and the corrugations loosened the joints so that the inside of the car was covered with thick dust at the end of each day's run. There are trap doors for operation of the jacking system. Dust also poured through these openings however I tried to seal them."

The lower powered models also played their part, appreciated for the combination of simple suspension and simple side valve. In 1948 an unsigned *Autocar* correspondent from Cape Town wrote: "I bought my Twelve sixteen months ago and have driven it for over 20,000 miles over all kinds of South African roads. The Austin has proved to be superior to the Americans in regard to road holding on badly corrugated roads, sustained hard work without overheating and absence of driving fatigue." There was no mention of dust but then the Twelve did not have the built-in jacks of the Sixteen. A west country doctor commented: "It would be a great mistake to cease making the 8-10hp variety of car. The long, low new models are just useless to us, we must have ground clearance and short overhangs for driving in lanes and negotiating fords and ferries. When I came in from my round today I pushed three large buckets of mud out of the wings. With the new wings you could not get in to prod it out without taking each wheel off."

There were those who were not panting for the new designs.

Production – Eight: *1945* 12,000 (est); *1946* 20,000 (est); *1947* 22,550; *1948* 114. **Ten:** *1945* 15,000 (est); *1946* 18,000 (est); *1947* 20,620. **Twelve:** *1945* 750 (est); *1946* 2,000 (est); *1947* 3,937. Sixteen: *1945* 2,000 (est); *1946* 7,000 (est); *1947* 8,187; *1948* 14,590

A125 SHEERLINE AND A135 PRINCESS SALOONS & LIMOUSINES 1947-1956

Alan Hess's arrival at Geneva in the Austin 16 also drew attention to two enormous new saloons on the Austin stand. They were pre-production examples of the Sheerline and the Princess, the former more imposing than any Austin yet seen, with well-balanced razor-edged lines and those vast Lucas P100 headlights. In fact the wheelbase at 9ft 11¼in was over a foot shorter than the largest pre-war offering, the sidevalve 4016cc 28hp.

Leonard Lord wanted postwar models which reached towards the Bentley market. Barney Sharratt, who has delved into so much Austin history for his erudite magazine articles, comments that chief designer Jules Haefeli and body stylist Dick Burzi were already at work in 1942 in intervals from war work. The Sheerline styling was developed at Longbridge whilst the Princess was handed over to coachbuilders Vanden Plas, purchased by Austin in 1945. The massive separate chassis and Austin's first independent front suspension evolved under chief engineer H.N. Charles. W.V. Appleby was responsible for the rugged ohv six, a variant of the 1939 lorry engine itself based on the contemporary Bedford. Capacity at Geneva was 3,460cc, but it was soon increased to 3992cc.

It took two years of testing – across Europe and up and down the Alps – to achieve an acceptable standard of steering, suspension, brakes and engine reliability, the difficulty being that this result had to be achieved without using the highest quality bearings and other materials or the low price targets would have been scuppered. Tester George Coats reported ball-races in the hubs heating up so much that wheels would hardly turn, and George Eyston, on hand for some Alpine passes, complained that the steering was impossibly heavy. But the target was reached, and all that motor car was on sale at a basic price of £999, nearly £1,600 cheaper than the standard Bentley at £2,595, and thus avoiding double purchase tax. At the 1949 Show

there was a six-light limousine development on an 11ft chassis.

The Autocar and *The Motor* both used a Sheerline (the same car, HON156) for European trips in 1948. Sammy Davis did a 1,300-mile tour to Brussels, Spa and Rheims and commented: "Quite how the Austin company produce this machine for sale at under a thousand pounds remains something of a puzzle. As value for money it is second to none. The body is really comfortable and remained so even when we had three people in the front as well as three in the back. The car did not roll when cornering fast. The suspension absorbed road shocks admirably but the rear dampers were on the weak side. Some people think the top-gear ratio is low. I do not agree. There is excellent acceleration on top and one-gear performance over most runs". Lawrence Pomeroy, driving to Geneva, disagreed: "The good top-gear acceleration results in a somewhat high piston speed. In consequence cruising speed is 10mph slower than one would wish, which adds materially to the length of time on a longish journey. It is also open to doubt whether even the best of modern braking systems is quite up to stopping a two-ton motor car with full load.

The first Princess on the short wheelbase before changes to the rear windows and the wing line.

Some form of servo assistance might lessen fatigue on this score". Note also that in the 1952 Monte Carlo Rally a Mr Paulsen managed to get this big saloon into the first hundred finishers.

Sheerlines were despatched to world markets. Australia took 700, but efforts to sell in America were not successful. They did not measure up in direct competition with the home product and some cars had to be shipped back across the Atlantic. The Princess's coachbuilt body had an ash frame and aluminium panels built up on the Sheerline steel floor and dash structure. It was a little heavier and considerably more expensive (especially when double purchase tax was in force) but, as *The Autocar* commented: "Part of the charm is, of course, the excellent finish and appointments. The Princess has that quiet air of quality which is expensive to produce but infinitely satisfying to the owner."

Another difference up to 1950 was that the Princess's engine developed more power with three carburettors and the gearing was higher than the cheaper car, with the following results:

	Sheerline	Princess
Speed at 1,000rpm in top	18.4mph	20mph
Speed at 2,500ft/per min. piston speed	63mph	69mph
Maximum speed	81mph	89mph

However, Austin listened to critics and in 1951 the Sheerline was fitted with the higher axle and gear ratio. The Princess was developed in MkII and MkIII versions with changes to the windows, grille and wing line. A touring limousine included a division. For 1952 there was a full limousine on the long chassis which soon took over from the Sheerline limousine. *The Motor* wrote enthusiastically: "Driven gently this car seems to 'steam roller' most bumps out of existence in a very pleasing fashion which no small car seems able to emulate. Sounds have all been so effectively subdued that a passenger is hardly aware of whether he is travelling at 40 or 80mph". All those long-wheelbase Mercs and American limos on the streets today, and the UK was producing the goods years before! A few laundaulettes and other special orders were completed and chassis were supplied for ambulances and hearses.

A40 Dorset, A40 Devon and Sheerline at Montlhéry test session in November 1947. A Sixteen is in the background.

Production: *1947* 5; *1948* 564; *1949* 2,827; *1950* 2,715; *1951* 2,547; *1952* 1,390; *1953-56* 2,000 (est)

A40 DEVON, DORSET, SOMERSET AND SPORTS 1947-1954

Leonard Lord's response to the UK government's exhortation to export and earn dollars was to give priority to the North American market. Lord took a Sheerline, a Princess and the new small A40 across the Atlantic early in 1947. Whilst he was obviously disappointed by the lack of enthusiasm for the larger cars, there was satisfaction in the dealer orders for the A40. They preferred the four-door Devon to the two-door Dorset.

Drawing on experience with the 16 and the Sheerline, Haefeli, Charles and their team developed a new ohv 1200cc unit and independent front suspension. They reasoned that there would be enough problems without trying to develop integral construction in the time available. A separate chassis would also be a good base for future van and pick-up variants. Compared with modern design the A40 was low geared – only 13.6mph in top at 1,000rpm and 58mph at 2,500ft per min. piston speed – but in the words of *The Motor*, penned early in 1948: "It is an exceptionally willing engine which combines good low-speed pulling powers with an ability to rev. To be more explicit it will pull smoothly down to 10mph in top

gear and will provide a true maximum speed of 67mph at 5,000rpm which it will exceed given favourable conditions."

In other words the car did not feel low geared and could be driven almost flat out without problems. There were no UK rivals at that time, and it is not difficult to sympathise with Lord's haste to get cars on sale, even when this led to hundreds of thousands of pounds spent on warranty claims and by rectification gangs working on the early production cars. Chassis and shock absorbers fractured on some European surfaces. There were rattles and even failures in steering and suspension. By today's standards there was nothing like enough product development, but Lord did not want to miss that market – and who can say that he didn't get away with it, at least in the shorter term?

Of the 30,000 A40s produced in the first year 1,,000 were shipped to America. Taking March 1948 as an example, and with acknowledgement to Colin Peek's researches, of 1,200 UK vehicles sent across the Atlantic that month more than 1,000 were Austins. But Lord's long-term appraisal of the market was flawed. At the end of 1949 an American engineer, J.P. Probst, wrote in *The*

10,000 miles in 10,000 minutes in an A40 at Montlhéry in 1950. Alan Hess is at the wheel.

Motor: "The fact that a substantial number of British cars have sold in the US these last two years is predominantly due to the shortage of new low-priced US cars. All through '47 and '48 the 9-18 months waiting period for a new car could be avoided by buying 'second-hand' at 25-50% above the factory list price. Thus Austin A40s at £375 sold well because Fords, Chevrolets and Plymouths cost around £550 on the black market. Those who wanted a car urgently, and did not want to pay the black market price, reckoned an A40 would suffice. Now 'second-hand' US cars are below list price and a British import would need to sell at £250 to maintain the differential."

As US producers satisfied home demand, there was no way in which a British product could succeed by competing head on for the custom of the average motorist, especially when those already sold had not been flawless. In time, unfilled market slots would be sought, but the A40 Devon wasn't a Jaguar or MG, nor did it have the unique qualities of a Volkswagen. Lord slashed the price below the cost of production. Low fuel consumption was underlined in advertising campaigns and in 1950, after the Long Island Record run, Hess recorded 42mpg on a 514 mile New York to Toronto drive. Sales still dropped. Most transatlantic families preferred an old Chevrolet or Plymouth if in the market for a second car, and it was to be some years before economy became a bonus in the showroom. Back in Europe the same year the A40 was publicised by a successful 10,000 miles in 10,000 minutes run at Montlhéry.

One can now see the defects of Lord's hit-and-miss approach. He might have done better to complete the product development (and not risk forfeiting some of Herbert Austin's legacy of dependability) and then concentrate on other markets, but the two-year US bonanza would have been missed. The cars were better received in Africa, Australia and Canada. Many were built up from components having been shipped CKD, as it was called, i.e. "completely knocked down". The Australians built up their own variants like the two-door Ruskin tourer. Basil Eyston reported: "One saw the A40 everywhere in South Africa and Rhodesia and I never came across one in trouble or with a dissatisfied owner."

James Watt (see Healey) was commissioned to drive a two-door Dorset 15,000 miles through Africa. His only problems were a jammed starter and a punctured petrol pipe. Gordon Wilkins wrote of opening up the Canadian market when recording an A40 drive from British Columbia over the Rockies to Alberta with J.F. Bramley (M.D. of the Austin export corporation). Numerous modifications had been dictated by local conditions: speedometer cables and locks had frozen, engine life had suffered from inadequate filtering, but the company engineers had persevered and a successful one-make exhibition was held in Vancouver in 1951. In Europe Bunty and Averil Scott-Moncrieff also used a Dorset christened "Little New Look" for Eastern journeys: "After Neunkirchen the road is dead-straight. Here we held the speedometer just under the 75 mark for miles on end without overheating, diminished oil pressure or other signs of distress."

Over 150,000 A40s had been exported by the end of 1950. 1951 was an interim year with a new column change. For 1952 the Devon was replaced by the Somerset, still with a chassis but also with a wider body, larger rear doors and a higher axle ratio. More important, in the words of the initial *Autocar* description, "The chassis had proved itself to be thoroughly robust in many countries where roads are rudimentary, but modifications adding nearly 50% to overall

James Watt's A40 Dorset crossing the Rovumu River in Central Africa in 1948. Note the water bottles on either side of the radiator grille.

A40 Somerset Equator-Arctic Expedition. Ken Wharton (with camera) and Ron Jeavons on a ferry crossing the Black River in Sudan in 1953.

stiffness have resulted from lessons learnt."

That this was evidently so was convincingly demonstrated during Hess's Somerset escapade with Ron Jeavons and Ken Wharton in March 1953: "We were sailing along at something over 50mph when suddenly we seemed to have struck a brick wall. The car first plunged down, and then the front shot up into the air at a crazy angle, and finally came down wham on its four wheels enveloped in a cloud of dust. We got out to find that we had driven into a deep gully and

that it was only due to our speed that we had actually leapt up on to the other side."

The ever-inventive Hess had worked out that there was just one fortnight in the year when snow should have melted sufficiently to reach the Arctic circle and it was also still possible to drive north from the Equator before the rains started. Despite that gully incident (one buckled wheel had to be changed), and despite near human collapse due to running out of water when the official escort vehicle broke down in the Nubian Desert (rescue came from a railway maintenance gang on its twice-yearly inspection!) the A40 was driven from Entebbe to Jokkmokk in the north of Sweden in 11 days without any suspension repairs or replacements. The Somerset was the first model from the new assembly plant built on the site of the wartime Crofton Hackett airfield. Suspensions, engine plus gearbox, and bodies were fed through three separate tunnels to join the 750-foot assembly line. The Japanese delegation which visited Crofton Hackett were so impressed that they contracted to build the Somerset in Tokyo. Thus they learnt about volume production. There was also a practical Carbodies drophead which benefited from that strong chassis.

The other A40 was the soft-top "Sports",

Ralph Sleigh, George Coates, Ron Jeavons and Alan Hess with A40 Sports after their Round-the-World trip in 1951.

1954 Monte Carlo Rally. Sleeman's A40 Sports at the Luxembourg control surrounded by European rivals – three Simca Arondes and a Peugeot 203.

with aluminium body designed by Eric Neale (see also Singer) and built by Jensen. This was the car which Hess, Coates, Jeavons and Sleigh took round the world in 21 days in June 1951, lifted over the oceans and parts of the Middle and Far East by a Douglas Skymaster. The team were criticised at the time for not driving through Iran and the Malay peninsula or going near Australia. Of course the critics had a point, but the fact remains that 9,263 miles were driven without any mechanical problems and on the same set of tyres and sparking plugs. As *The Autocar* wrote, "All four drivers were proud of their vehicle. It had done its stuff just as they expected. One puncture in India (a nail from a bullock cart) had been mended to keep the same set of tyres. There was no sign of boiling or overheating".

It was further proof that the Longbridge engineers had achieved a sturdy design, but had the marketing people thought out the potential? After 3,500 miles use throughout Europe Pomeroy commented: "a very flexible, easy-to-drive and comfortable touring type, but with its low gearing and insensitive steering not a sports car".

As Singer also found there was never going to be a stampede of buyers for a small-engined four-seater which had neither the appeal of a powerful two-seater nor the roominess and charisma of the old-style tourer. Around 4,000 were sold. In 1954 (after production had ceased) Sleeman and Holmes achieved 43rd place in the Monte Carlo Rally despite losing the use of third gear.

Production – Devon/Dorset: *1947* 29,000; *1948* 64,270; *1949* 75,397; *1950* 78,551; *1951* 29,437. **Somerset:** *1951* 38,131; *1952* 58,912; *1953* 81,117; *1954* 2,020. **Sports:** *1950* 500; *1951* 2,610; *1952* 849.

A70 HAMPSHIRE AND HEREFORD 1948-1954

Alan Clark, whose recent writings after his ministerial career have gained him a wider readership, recorded his experiences in *The*

Motor after a visit to America in 1950. After describing American teenagers' addiction to "playing chicken", he continued, "It is with considerable trepidation that your correspondent approaches this highly controversial topic. But, in his opinion, the right cars for the American market, if one must try and sell ordinary cars there, are not the A40 and the Minx but the A70 and the Hawk. These cars may be medium sized in the UK but in America they are small and their baby brothers seem real midgets. They must have snappy performance – why not the 88bhp [A90] engine in the A70?"

Did Leonard Lord made another misjudgement? Or was Colin Peek nearer the mark in his *Classic Cars* article when he wrote of rumours of a deal between Austin and General Motors whereby GM agreed not to make a fuss provided only A40s and the A90 were imported? Barney Sharratt suggests that the A70 was the cause of the final break between Lord and chief designer Jules Haefeli. The designer could not accept that a satisfactory vehicle would result from fitting a Sixteen engine to a longer wheelbase (by 3½in) A40 chassis.

However, the development engineers did their work and by the time the new Hampshire was on sale before the 1948 show it had acceptable running gear for a more powerful, wider and higher vehicle. This Hampshire was almost unique in its time. The Standard Vanguard was the only other £500 offering with nearly 70bhp and it only had three gears. The Vauxhall Velox developed 54bhp and the Ford Zephyr was still two years away. *The Autocar* was lavish in praise: "This compact saloon possesses a performance which sends it leaping up to 70mph with an ultimate maximum of over 80. One can easily visualise this sturdy feeling, smooth-running high performer covering 60 miles in the hour on a continental run or an inter-city trip in the Dominions and being little affected by surface deteriorations, for the suspension is effective in its adaptability to bad surfaces."

Historians label the A70 with sloppy handling but contemporary reports suggest that

In the first post-war Monte Carlo Rally in 1949 Hess (on right) partnered the Monegasque racing driver Louis Chiron (centre) and George Coates.

Jopling and Sleigh reached Cape Town in an A70 Hampshire at the end of 1949, having covered 10,300 miles in 24 days.

The strength of 1950s Austins was demonstrated by French stuntman Gil Delamere, who chose an A70 Hereford to show off the safety of Britax seatbelts. Here he is launching into a roll at Harringay Stadium.

The Autocar's judgement was sound. The suspension was set up for overseas mile-eating, not the winding British road. Peter Jopling and Ralph Sleigh in a Hampshire reached Cape Town in 24 days at the end of 1949, averaging 430 miles a day for the whole 10,300 miles. On the better roads south of Nairobi they stepped up the pace and did one 1,000-mile stretch in 19 hours. Earlier in the year Hess had done the first postwar Monte Carlo Rally with Moné-gasque racing driving Louis Chiron and George Coates. It did not go unremarked that the A70 was placed 5th at the finish. That would have done Longbridge a power of good but the officials, relearning their skills, had made a mistake! My last reference comes from an article written by an Australian family in 1952. After 35,000 miles their A70 "was a very fine car; fast, comfortable and easy to work on. Cornering had improved wonderfully after the front wheel alignment had been set up correctly". Three front shock absorbers had been replaced. Perhaps the soft-riding Hampshires had problems of wheel alignment and deficient shock absorbers? Certainly in later life Hampshires, Herefords, Somersets and Devons could often be seen with front ends wildly bouncing up and down as they trundled along.

The Hereford took over after two years with a 3-inch longer wheelbase and a Somerset-style, but 6 inches wider, body. The result was more knee-room between the seats, and rear doors as much as 8 inches wider. The lot of the passengers had been improved, with no loss in performance, but the Sixteen and Hampshire's four folding arm rests had been deleted, which may account for some of the adverse comments about body roll. Impressions are less likely to be favourable if sliding around the seat.

The Hereford had been subjected to extensive testing in Central Africa. The suspension, as on its predecessor, was soft to absorb the worst of the rougher surfaces. Important also was the development work on equipment like Smith's new heater and demister

for countries like Canada where motorists liked the model. Doctor Archibald wrote from Nova Scotia that he had recently purchased his second Hereford: "They are superior to the Hampshire in roadability and economy. My present monthly mileage averages 1,900-2,000 and I get a consumption figure of 26-27mpg. There was one long trip in the last car, 700 miles in 16½ hours. Although I drove steadily at 65-70mph fatigue was surprisingly slight. I particularly appreciated the quick steering and excellent brakes".

Sound though it was, comparison with UK rivals shows how the A70 failed to become the medium-sized winner which Longbridge needed:

Basic Price	Production		
	1951	1952	1953
A70 Hereford (£537-£627)	14,998	18,251	6,008
Ford Zephyr (£475-£524)	3,463	23,894	44,090
Standard Vanguard (£515-£550)	38,186	23,818	16,579

There were small sales of dropheads and estate cars, and around 20,000 A70 pick-ups were sold between 1948 and 1954.

Production – Hampshire: *1948* 4,000; *1949* 18,219; *1950* 16,359. **Hereford:** *1950* 4,900; *1951* 15,585; *1952* 16,470; *1953* 12,008; *1954* 5,745.

A90 ATLANTIC 1949-1952

If the jury remained undecided after the introduction of the A40 and A70, they might have returned a guilty verdict after Lord's next American adventure. Alan Clark continued in his article, "Your correspondent is by no means convinced that the family field is a worthwhile market, whereas he feels that America has a permanent market for specialist cars. Drive anywhere, survey the scene: rows and rows of elephants, all excellent in their way but all fundamentally the same".

And J.P. Probst wrote in the same vein, "In direct competition for sales to average buyers, British industry stands no chance on the US market. If, however, Britain makes a conscious and thorough attack on those portions of the market ignored by the American manufacturer, it is a strong possibility that a permanent place awaits their cars".

Lord was on the right track in trying to create a special car for America, but instead of surveying the market he fell into the trap that awaits unrestrained leaders. He still thought he knew best what American buyers wanted and the faithful Burzi was commissioned to interpret the boss's own sketches. The order went out for a bigger and more powerful A70 engine in a modified chassis to be clothed with this showy, bechromed convertible body. The Atlantic was shipped across its namesake ocean in 1949, but those buyers did not queue up in the showrooms. Why should they when an 140bhp eight-cylinder home-produced convertible could be purchased for the same price as the 88bhp four cylinder A90.

Alan Hess discovered that American records for ordinary production cars had not been tackled since Studebaker's efforts in 1928. In April 1949 an A90 and drivers Buckley, Goodacre and Hess circulated the Indianapolis speedway for seven days. They

Alan Hess setting off for a further session in the A90 Atlantic during the Indianapolis record run in April 1949.

were just fast enough at 70.5mph, compared with the Studebaker President's 68.6 twenty years earlier, to mount a massive advertising campaign underlining that four cylinders were up to the job. At the time not too much was made of the mechanics' heroic efforts coping with engine and suspension maladies. The price of the car was reduced but still buyers did not come forward.

Lord had got it wrong. Whilst Americans flocked to buy the nippy little MG and the elegant six-cylinder Jaguar, only 350 pulled out their cheque books for what was to them an inferior clone of their own products. If the

The Tower hotels of Sestrières in 1951. De Domio's UK registered Atlantic drophead was no match for the Italians in their Lancias and Fiats.

target customers demurred, there were others who quite liked the car, particularly in the hardtop form introduced at the 1949 Show. This sports saloon was praised for good visibility and ventilation (the back window could be wound down), but testers in both weekly magazines would have preferred the higher gearing of the convertible. At 2,500ft per min. piston speed the saloon was travelling at just 64mph and the convertible at 71mph.

The Autocar was pleased with the Atlantic it used to follow the 1951 Monte Carlo Rally, but most journalists who drove the car pointed to a suspension weakness: "No actual trouble was experienced although the front suspension dampers lost most of their effectiveness", (*The Autocar*), and "A greater degree of damping would represent a distinct improvement" (*The Motor*).

It was the same old Austin bugbear. If the Longbridge engineers had been able to achieve more effective suspension in the 1950s before Mercedes and Peugeot got into their postwar stride, there might have been a different story to tell. Issigonis was to work wonders at the end of the decade but that was ten years too late.

Despite these limitations Trigano and Mimard's Atlantic was one of only sixteen other cars that joined Sydney Allard in reaching Valence without loss of marks on that snowy 1952 Rally. They were in 11th place at the finish. If the Atlantic was a relative failure, at least the engine went on to greater things as power unit for the Healey Hundred which became the first Austin-Healey.

Production: *1949* 1,425; *1950* 2,614; *1951* 2,599; *1952* 1,245.

A30 1952-1956

One can only admire Leonard Lord for the personal energy he gave to Austin and then to BMC. But was the enormous effort that the engineers put into the mid-range Austins misdirected? Would they have done better to concentrate on one or two designs? There is no controversy over the new small car. The proposed Austin-Morris merger had been on and off in 1949 and 1950, so thoughts of developing a joint success from the Morris Minor were postponed. Lord then gave the go-ahead for Austin's own project.

Many of those who inspected the A30 on its stand at the 1951 Show were disappointed by the conservative appearance. They did not realize that the shape had evolved after years spent investigating alternatives, some of whose features were still beneath the skin of the car they were examining. In 1948 Lord had purchased Ian Duncan's (see Fedden) Dragonfly prototype, an advanced concept with unitary construction, transverse two-cylinder "motorcycle" engine, front-wheel drive and Alex Moulton's rubber suspension. He had also enticed Duncan to work at Longbridge. The Dragonfly was the basis of early efforts which led on to experiments with two- and three-cylinder air- and water-cooled power units. Gradually these features, like FWD and the Moulton suspension, were rejected, to reappear in the Mini at the end of the 1950s.

But the Austin engineers working with Duncan did achieve a strong, light, unitary body and chassis structure. It was not discarded when the decision was taken to stick with a conventional 800cc 'four', rear wheel drive and suspension similar to the A40's. Bob Koto came from the American Loewy organisation and achieved a body style with some of the flow of the 1960s DAF 55 and VW 1500, but with unique semi-enclosed rear wheels. This was still too futuristic for management, and it was Dick Burzi who took the basic Duncan-Koto package and gave it the mini-Somerset look. The earlier years of work were not wasted. The strength of the structure (proved by the survival of so many) came from careful design of scuttle, floor, side members and rear seat pan. Four people could squeeze into the four-door package helped by ingenious initial details like the deletion of interior handles (later altered in response to customer disapproval).

A long way from home. Millard and Jackson, from Eire, in 803cc A30 between Barrême and Castellane en route to Monte Carlo in 1954.

Comparison with the A40 and A70 show what was achieved:

	Width	Wheelbase	Height	Weight
A30	4ft 7in	6ft 7½in	4ft 10in	13½cwt
A40	5ft 3in	7ft 8½in	5ft 4in	19½cwt
A70	5ft 9½in	8ft 3in	5ft 5½in	26cwt

It was no mean feat to build a proper car which was nearly half the weight of the A70.

The A30 was produced in two and four-door versions plus "countryman" estate cars, vans and a few pick-ups. Both magazines recorded fuel consumption above 40mpg and emphasized that the car gave its passengers much more than marginal motoring. It was not an obvious competition machine, but A30s were 1st and 2nd in the small car class of the 1953 Redex Round Australia Trial, and Millard and Jackson finished ahead of 73 other competitors in the 1954 Monte Carlo. The Brookes team, father and son, won the 1956 Tulip Rally when the handicap system favoured smaller-capacity engines. At the 1956 Show the replacement A35 was introduced with a larger, more durable engine and higher back axle ratio. Accompanied by an A50 and other BMC models it successfully completed an endurance run of 25,000 miles at 60mph on the Autobahn between Stuttgart and Munich.

Production: *1952* 4,791; *1953* 29,177; *1954* 59,910; *1955* 68,558; *1956* 62,564.

A40, A50, A90, A105
1954-1959

Despite the lack of agreement in the two previous years, Austin and Morris did still come together as one company, the British Motor Corporation, controlled by Leonard Lord, in 1952. These four vehicles produced by the new Corporation wore the last body style to be sold only as an Austin, and the A40 and A50 were the first to use the rationalised BMC ohv "B" Series engines also used in contemporary Morris cars. Another strong unitary structure followed on from the A30.

The shorter wheelbase (8ft 3in) Cambridge was announced at the beginning of October 1954 (the year Lord became Sir Leonard). It was available as the 1200cc A40 and 1489cc A50. All components were developed conventional designs and at last the shock absorbers were tougher. In 1956 overdrive was available for the larger A50.

The Cambridge was well liked. A.E. Mainwaring wrote from Cape Town of his "decent-sized, sensibly sprung and high set, huge booted A50. I have just driven from Windhoek, 1,023 miles, heavily loaded through miles of deep sand, through rivers up over the radiator grille, on mile after weary mile of atrocious corrugations. When I took her in for servicing – just routine oil change, greasing and a good clean."

A90 ROC 616, which, in 3-carburettor form, Ken Wharton nearly drove to victory at Silverstone in May, seen earlier in 1956 approaching Monte Carlo. Wharton left rear, Gordon Shanley on right.

The A90 which Richard Pape drove 17,500 miles from the North Cape to Cape Town in 1955.

The Cambridge was competent, reliable and easy to drive but, despite being the third 1¼ to 1½ litre Austin design since the war, it still seemed to lack the flair of a creation like the 203, which Peugeot had introduced in 1948 and steadily developed as their sole product (till the 403 in 1955) without major design changes. During the 203's twelve-year production run from 1948 to 1960, Austin, Morris and BMC designed and made five different cars in the Peugeot's capacity class. A detailed comparison between the A50 and the 203 also gives clues as to how Peugeot have achieved their present position:

	Austin A50	Peugeot 203
Weight	20¼cwt	18cwt
Wheelbase	8ft 3in	8ft 6in
Engine capacity	1,489cc	1,290cc
Bore × stroke	73×89mm	75×73mm
Output	50bhp	42bhp
Top gear speed per 1,000rpm	15mph	16.6mph
Turning circle	36ft	29½ft
Steering	cam	rack & pinion
Rear springs	leaf	coil

The last Austins of our decade did have flair. For a wider, longer wheelbase (8ft 8in) structure using the same doors, Morris engines built the new ohv 'C' Series 2,639cc six. With weight kept down to 25½cwt, and 85bhp, the 1955 A90 Westminster was one of the first of the modestly priced distance swallowers. It was available with the American Borg-Warner overdrive. Demonstrated at Montlhéry with other BMC cars, and in torrential rain, John Gott achieved 102 miles in one hour. Buyers were told: "No-one need fear driving the length of the Autobahn from, say, Cologne to Frankfurt with their right foot flat on the floor all the way". Cruising at 85mph in an Austin without worrying about an engine blow-up was a new concept, but there was more to come. At Silverstone in early May 1956 Ken Wharton so nearly won the production car race: "Bueb and Wharton were wheel-to-wheel throughout this most frenzied and thrilling battle, Wharton holding full throttle from Club Corner to Copse where he often crept ahead on the inside".

After sixty miles on the track the triple-carburettor A90 was just one second behind Bueb's 3.4-litre MkVII Jaguar. Two weeks later Austin announced the twin-carburettor 102bhp A105, with lowered suspension and

The winning team in the 1956 RAC Rally. Left to right: Douglas and Joan Johns (modified A90), S.E. Croft-Pearson, Gerry Burgess (stock A90), Marcus Chambers (with cap and coat), Ken Best, Peter Garnier, Jack Sears (modified A50).

Eileen Cullen and A50 in Paris en route to Monte Carlo in 1955. She was placed last, at 273rd.

Endurance test of A30 and A50 on German autobahn, 1956. 25,000 miles at 60mph.

comprehensive equipment. In overdrive the gearing gave 27mph at 1,000rpm and, if the driver could have got it there, 115mph at 2,500ft per min. piston speed! Contrast this with the 1946 Hawk (see Humber) where road speed at the same piston speed was 57mph! Such was the enormous performance advance in one decade – and in the deluxe versions the front seats again had four arm rests.

These big Austins were entered in European rallies but never gained the winner's laurels. It was bad luck that in 1957, when the A105 was highly competitive in its class, the Monte Carlo Rally was cancelled because of Suez. The A90 was the car which Richard Pape drove 17,500 miles from the North Cape in Norway to Cape Town in 1955. Starting on July 28th Pape just survived a Sahara rock encounter which tore out a front coil spring.

Walking to find help he collapsed in the pitiless summer heat, was rescued by Shaamba Arabs and then managed to drive on to Adrar with palm tree wedges replacing the metal spring. It was the rainy season in Central Africa. Near Fort Lamy, "Lake Chad had been pouring out millions of gallons of water", and the flooded highway was closed. Pape turned back to Kano and then south over the Mandara mountains in what were then the French Cameroons.

After Albertville, a Belgian, "not expecting any other traffic", and driving fast in the centre of the road over a blind rise, hit them head on. Unlike its attacker, the Austin was still drivable and local mechanics hammered, bashed and welded the metal straight. Pape reached Cape Town on October 22nd, having amply demonstrated the exceptional strength of that era of Longbridge design. Neither the robust and simple six nor other mechanical components faltered on the journey, a fitting note on which to conclude this Austin chapter.

Production – A40: *1954* 4,000 (est); *1955* 25,469. **A50:** *1954* 16,081; *1955* 60,816. **A90 & A105:** *1954* 6,096; *1955* 21,894.

AUSTIN ACHIEVEMENTS

1947
Goodwill Tour 16: Oslo to Geneva D. Buckley, G. Coates, A. Hess, S. Davis, S. Yeal.

1948
Lisbon A40: A. Hess 12th, 3rd in class; L. Goncalves 4th in class.
15,000 Miles in Africa A40: J. Watt.

1949
Monte Carlo A70: L. Chiron 23rd.
Lisbon A90: L. Goncalves 2nd in class.
Los Angeles to New York A40: 3,062 miles in 57½hrs F. Hocevar.
Indianapolis A90: 11,875 miles at 70.6mph A. Hess, C Goodacre, D. Buckley.
Britain to Cape A70: 24 days to Cape Town R. Sleigh, P. Jopling.

1950
Monte Carlo A70: C. Glenie 48th.
New York to Toronto A40: 514 miles at 42mpg A. Hess.
Montlhery A40: 10,000 miles in 10,000 mins A. Hess, R. Jeavons.
Westhampton, Long Island A40: 1,000 miles at 65mph A. Hess, Goldie-Gardner.

1951
Luanda A70: 1st and 3rd.
Cape Town-Johannesburg-Cape Town A40: 1,650 miles in 28½hrs G. Anderson, J. Radcliffe.
Round the World A40: 9,260 miles in 21 days A. Hess, G. Coates, R. Jeavons, R. Sleigh.

1952
Monte Carlo A90: A. Trigano 11th. A40: D. Taylor 63rd. Sheerline: K. Paulsen 98th.
Tulip A40: J. Kokkes 14th, 2nd in class.
RAC A70: R. Prout 6th in closed car class.

1953
Monte Carlo A90: G.. Shanley 86th.
RAC A90: R. Syms 34th & 2nd in class.
Redex Round Australia A30: E. Brotherton 1st in class, J. Ellis 2nd in class. A40: D. McKay 2nd in class.
Equator to Arctic Circle A40: A. Hess, R. Jeavons, K. Wharton.

1954
Monte Carlo A40: Sports: J. Sleeman 43rd, A70: J. McLaughlin 80th, A30 J. Millard 256th.

1955
Monte Carlo A50: A. Olsson 29th, A90: Mrs Wisdom 68th.
North Cape-South Cape A90: 17,500 miles R. Pape.
Liège-Rome-Liège A50: J. Gott, A90: G. Burgess 31st Team Prize with Stross's Jaguar.
RAC A90: F. Tyldesley 3rd in class.
Scottish A90: R. Woolaway 1st in class, Mrs J. Johns Ladies' Prize.
Mobilgas Economy Runs South Africa A30: 1st, A50: 2nd in class.
Montlhery A90: 102 miles in 1 hour J. Gott.

1956
Monte Carlo A90: J. Gott 55th, K. Wharton 56th
RAC D. Johns 6th, Johns, Burgess & Sears Team Award. A40 Sports: Miss A. Palfrey Ladies' Award.
Tulip A30: R. Brookes 1st, A90: J. Sears 2nd in class.
Geneva A50: J. Sears 19th 1st in class.
Viking A105: J. Sears 36th.
Ampol Round Australia A90: P. Anthill 8th.
Silverstone A90: K. Wharton 2nd.
Mobilgas Economy UK A90: H. Kendrick 1st.
Mobilgas Economy South Africa A50: 1st, A90: 2nd.
Stuttgart-Munich Autobahn A35 & A50: 25,000 miles at 60mph.

DAIMLER

An English patriot may find this section the saddest in the book. Whereas Daimler-Benz (Mercedes-Benz) in Germany continues to flourish, the English Daimler company is no more and the name but a badge on the cars built by Jaguar, itself now part of Ford. Yet both companies were set up towards the end of the nineteenth century to exploit the work of Gottlieb Daimler. Gottlieb did not make a complete vehicle, that was the work of Karl Benz. His achievement, with the help of William Maybach, was to radically improve the ignition of Gustav Otto's stationary engine so that it could achieve the higher speeds required for vehicle use. In 1886 Gottlieb ordered a typical horse-drawn vehicle from a carriage builder in Cannstatt, cut off the shafts, fitted steering gear and then installed his higher speed engine. Frederick Simms bought the British Empire rights for this engine and then sold out to Harry Lawson in 1896.

By 1900 the two companies were embarked on their different journeys. After Gottlieb's death that year Mercedes' advance was spearheaded by his son Paul and Maybach. Coventry Daimler came to be led by Percy Martin and Ernest Instone, later by L.H. Pomeroy, father of the journalist quoted in these pages. Advanced and innovative engineering included sleeve valves, V12s and the fluid flywheel transmission. Neither company maintained a solitary existence. In 1926 Mercedes merged with Benz. Coventry Daimler did less well. In 1910 it was taken over by the old-established armaments and engineering company BSA (Birmingham Small Arms) whose origins went back to 1700. Henceforward major financial decisions had to be referred to a higher board (vitally significant in 1960) for whom making motor cars was not the primary concern. But in February 1946 at the 50th Anniversary lunch at the Savoy thoughts were of proud achievement. Lord Brabazon spoke of the company as "a national institution, its history national history in which we all felt national pride". During the war they had built 50,000 Bristol aero engines and around 10,000 armoured and scout cars which were prized for their reliability (and they had 70% of the Radford factory bombed out of existence by Gottlieb's native country for their efforts!). They had purchased the Barker and Hooper body-building companies. They were suppliers to Royalty and providers of official cars, and there were plans for ambulances, buses and more armoured cars.

Yet with all this promise and effort it didn't work out. It has been fashionable to blame chairman Bernard Docker and to deplore the lavish expenditure on the Earl's Court Show cars (the so-called Docker Specials), but we shall never know whether they repelled more people than they attracted and at least they demonstrated that the Daimler Company did not only build limousines. Docker's management skills have also been criticised, but he was only one of an able team. C.M. Simpson and his engineering colleagues, Ron Dawtry, Sydney Shellard, D. Tate and later Edward Turner, and successive managing directors, George Hally till September 1948 and then James Leek, seem to have been heading in sensible directions. The Sprite (see Lanchester) showed that they had come to terms with unitary construction and a modern automatic. The creators of the all-independent

Chief Engineer C. M. Simpson, leader of the dedicated Daimler engineering team.

Five Straight Eight Daimlers ordered for the Royal Tour of South Africa in 1947.

Dingo and Ferret armoured vehicles could certainly have developed similar car suspension, and power steering was on the stocks for the later Majestic Major.

The problems were so much wider than the Docker attitude and behaviour. Management allowed themselves to be overwhelmed by the burden of war damage. Time was lost in temporarily organising the Brown's Lane Shadow factory at Allesley. There were delays and considerable expenditure in rebuilding the Radford plant. At that anniversary lunch George Hally told guests that £523,000 was to be spent on new plant and equipment. There was a further setback when the competent James Leek had to retire at the beginning of 1953 because he was "making only slow recovery after an operation".

These circumstances led to Bernard Docker taking over as managing director. Whilst his old-world approach was useful and acceptable as chairman, he was not the man to take on both positions when the urgent priority was to make up time. If only the Sprite had been rolling off the production lines in 1955, and good sales achieved, before Docker was ousted! The new management of Jack Sangster and Edward Turner would have found it more difficult to chop what could have been the brightest hope. Without a volume seller it must have been all too easy for the BSA board to say "yes" when Jaguar appeared as buyers in 1960 and became the beneficiaries of the expenditure at Radford. Would a Sprite-like car have been more appropriate for the 1970s, '80s and '90s than the XJ6? If Daimler had made it through the 60s and reached the era of the company car would they have survived?

1st June 1956: John Sangster, chairman of BSA, takes over following the dismissal of Bernard Docker.

DE27, DH27, DE36
SIX & STRAIGHT EIGHT 1946-1953

Whilst, as we shall see, there were difficulties in launching the later postwar designs, these large cars were a success. Announced in

March 1946, the six-cylinder, 11ft 6in wheelbase DE27 had a 4,095cc engine and was joined by the 12ft 3in wheelbase DE36 with revised 5,460cc straight eight. The design merits study as proof of C.M. Simpson and his team's commitment to engineering excellence. The coil spring front suspension was located both by a longitudinal arm running back to the chassis side member and a transverse link to the centre of the front chassis crossmember. At the back it wasn't enough just to provide leaf springs. There were also rods to provide better location and a torsion bar cross-coupling the shock absorbers. Long hours of dedicated work and testing resulted in servo-assisted brakes which did not fade and effectively and smoothly stopped a heavy machine. The 1947 road test commented: "To say that this limousine behaves like a sports car so far as high speed steering and cornering is concerned might seem absurd but such is indeed the case. It was possible to drive two elderly non-motorists for 200 miles at speeds ranging from 50 top 70mph and at no time were they made velocity conscious." This praise was the direct consequence of the meticulous design. If further confirmation of ability is sought, Tom Wisdom and Lord Selsdon were in the first 50 in the 1952 Monte Carlo Rally.

The cars took British Royalty on their foreign tours and were supplied to Kings, Queens, Presidents and Embassies in other countries: a fluid flywheel was still a good bet for ceremonial work. Fifty extra long (12ft 6in wheelbase) six-cylinder DH27s were supplied to Daimler Hire, and 500 DE ambulances were built. The luxurious bodies are often referred to collectively as Docker Specials. In fact there were show specials as early as 1948 (a year before the Dockers were married) with the "Green Goddess" roadster designed for an "owner-driver who indulges in continental touring". This was no immobile effigy. Those who drove it marvelled at the road behaviour: "Steering characteristics give no clue to the weight. Even on narrow winding roads the car seems to take itself round corners without roll or

effort." And it earned its keep by drawing the crowds to the Daimler stand at the 1950 New York Show.

In 1949 Freestone & Webb completed a grey four-door sports saloon for Ivan Hendricks, a patriotic Englishman resident in Jamaica, who had worked on a machine tool in the Daimler factories during the war. The cabinet work was in Yellow Sanders, a Jamaican wood resembling satin walnut. At Earl's Court the company had a further example of this design in café-au-lait with maroon wings. Lancefield showed an invalid car and Hooper a grey and black Sedanca. 1950 was a leaner year with just Hooper fielding another (cream and black) sedanca though complete with an indication of what was to come – cocktail cabinet and ladies' companion drawer.

Then in 1951 came the first of the true Docker Specials, a black Hooper limousine with gold instead of chromium plate (including the bumpers!) and sides embellished with gold stars. Upholstery was handwoven gold silk. This "Golden Daimler" was followed in 1952 by "Blue Clover", a two-door fixed-head coupé with four-leafed clover motifs and blue-grey lizard skin in place of traditional woodwork. So far all these specials, the Dockers and their predecessors, had been built on DE chassis. More were to follow on the Regency and DK400.

Production – Six cylinder: *1946* ?; *1947* 43; *1948* 54; *1949* 71; *1950* 42 (est); *1951* 60 (est) *1952* ?. **Straight eight:** *1946* ?; *1947* 54; *1948* 41; *1949* 28; *1950* 32; *1951* 11; *1952* 14; *1953* 11.

2½-LITRE 18, CONSORT, SPECIAL SPORTS & EMPRESS 1946-1953

Side-stepping the Radford problems and determined to have a car on sale, M.D. George Hally announced before the end of 1945 that a developed version of the pre-war 2½ litre would soon be in production at Brown's Lane. The original specification – six-cylinder 70bhp engine, fluid flywheel,

The 2½-litre "Empress" saloon which was on the Hooper stand at Earl's Court in 1949 – a large and luxurious body propelled by only 80bhp.

separate chassis, independent front suspension, underslung worm drive (allowing a low propellor shaft and flat floor), rod operated brakes – had benefited from the lessons of military experience. It wasn't an advanced concept like the Jowett Javelin but became well liked as one of the better examples of conventional quality engineering and, for once, Jaguar hadn't got all the answers. Between 1946 and 1949 3,013 2½-litre Daimlers were sold and only 2,525 2½-litre Jaguars.

The Motor's testers praised the suspension: "Road irregularities of horrifying aspect can be ignored... When a car is sprung for comfort, some roll on corners is expected, but the Daimler has to be cornered at speeds which would do credit to a sports car before tyre scream is induced." There was also criticism: "Surprising is the absence of any means of securing draught-free and rain-free ventilation", and "brake pedal effort required altogether too high."

The cars were exported to America, Australia and South Africa, and did duty as Embassy and Imperial hacks. They were praised for their reliability, but did not escape contemporary design faults. In 1947, R.A.Stavert drove a 2½ litre 1,600 miles from Bombay to Rawalpindi and reported in *The Autocar*: "Engine oil consumption 4 pints. No other oil or water loss. It would be unfair to single out a fine specimen of engineering for criticism which really should apply to British cars at large. British manufacturers seem quite unable to understand that nothing less than hermetic sealing of floor boards, toe boards, etc., will deal with the nuisance of dust." He then wrote of the ventilation: "Neither do manufacturers appear to appreciate that it is possible for it to be most unpleasantly hot when rain is coming down in torrents. Main windows cannot then be opened, and the scuttle ventilator is only a help if measures are taken to exclude insects. Readers would be doing a real service to the motor industry if they could get serious attention focused on the question of ventilation for the export market."

A revised model, to be known as the Consort, was introduced for the 1949 Show. Pivoted quarter-windows, which would swing round to act as air scoops, were fitted to the front doors. There was also the new Smiths fan-driven heating and ventilation system drawing in air through "a rearward-facing fixed vent protected by a close mesh screen". Someone seems to have been listening at Brown's Lane, but how many repeat orders were lost because of the earlier deficiencies? The Consort was also better in other respects. The Girling system of hydraulic front and mechanical rear brakes meant less brake pedal effort and a higher top gear increased the cruising speed. *The Motor* was again complimentary: "In few cars has the journey been done more quickly and in none with such lack of fatigue", and this theme was taken up by Joe Lowrey from the same magazine after he had used a Consort to report the 1951 Alpine Rally: "Arrival at a destination untired was above all else, the thing which made the Daimler a success for a seemingly inappropriate job. Never having to slow down very much for corners or for rough going, we gradually realised we were reaching each point of destination ahead of time and with the minimum of fuss."

The rally entries of the later 1950s were not just an isolated development. The Daimler engineers had been working to improve the appeal of their smaller models since 1946. In 1951 the Monte Carlo Concours de Confort judges favoured W.M. Couper's Bentley for the third year in succession, with the Adams brothers' black Consort a few points behind. Daimler just missed valuable publicity. In February 1953 the company had their sally at the 66⅔% purchase tax, reducing the Consort price to a figure equal to 33⅓% tax.

A four-seater drophead coupé body was offered until 1949 and at the 1948 Show there was a new coupé with 85bhp twin-carburettor engine christened, inaccurately, "Special Sports". This was in fact a splendid touring car for the few who could afford to pay over £2,000 for a two-seater with a sideways facing third seat which could be fitted either side or taken out for extra luggage. The special feature was the high overdrive top gear, which gave 22mph per 1,000rpm, and 78mph (compared with the DB18's 63mph)

at 2,500ft per min. piston speed. With the smooth six-cylinder engine the result was relaxed, economical cruising at today's motorway speeds, while gentle driving would return nearly 30mpg. The magazines did not stint their praise: "All the most modern refinements of suspension, transmission and the like, yet retains the individual charm of the handsome, easy running touring cars of a past age... The whole essence of the car is that no single shortcoming mars the overall standard of excellence".

Yes, Daimler were then ahead of Daimler Benz. With power steering and 40 years' engineering development today's successor might have become a formidable competitor to the current £50,000 3-litre SL Mercedes. Much of that development has been to combat adverse and heavy traffic conditions. The 0-60mph acceleration times of the two models are 23 seconds for the Daimler and 8.6 for the Mercedes, but if you happened to have a newish SL and a low-mileage Daimler together on an empty, well-surfaced motorway under a cloudless sky, which car would have the most appeal when cruising at the legal limit? Hooper built four-door "Empress" sports saloons on this twin-carburettor chassis but they were rather large and luxurious bodies to be propelled by 85bhp.

Production: *1946* 400 (est); *1947* 691; *1948* 869; *1949* 1,053; *1950* 1,447; *1951* 2,203; *1952* 1,558; *1953* ?. (Approximately 600 of the above were Special Sports.)

CONQUEST, CENTURY, DROPHEAD COUPÉ, ROADSTER, SPORTS DROPHEAD COUPÉ 1953-1958

Price for Daimler was not the problem that it was with the other marques. In a series of announcements in the months before the 1956 Show Daimler's new Management underlined their intentions. The Sprite (see Lanchester) was to be discontinued, the Daimler would be established as "a most competitive unit in the field of high quality motor-cars" and the total price of the MkII

Sir Bernard and Lady Docker seeing off the first of the new Daimler Conquests.

Conquest was to be further reduced (after an earlier reduction the previous May) by £254 to £1,295, over £100 cheaper than the 2.4-litre Jaguar MkI.

The Conquest and Century were sound, well-developed cars with substantial improvements over the already respected Consort. Chief Engineer Simpson's team had worked over the earlier engines, paring a full hundredweight from the weight and producing a shorter-stroke unit with piston speed down from 3,050 to 2,320ft per min. at maximum bhp. The increased power hadn't spoilt the torque and flexibility, and even the 100bhp twin-carburettor unit was still creamy smooth. The laminated torsion bars which replaced the earlier coil spring front suspension, together with the solidity of the still separate chassis, provided ride, road-holding and steering balance which were well up to the standards of the time, probably better than the MkI Jaguar, but not in the same league as Daimler-Benz with their four

independently suspended wheels. The cars had the Pressed Steel bodyshell introduced for the Leda in 1952. The useful "Bijur" chassis lubrication system continued, automatically actuated by the changing temperature of the exhaust.

Whey then were the Conquest and Century not the foundation of a series of smaller-than-Jaguar cars still competing with BMW and Mercedes today? There seem to be two reasons (plus the factor common to much of this book, namely that it was still some years before the company car took a large part of new vehicle sales):

THE FLUID FLYWHEEL TRANSMISSION

The ability to preselect a gear by an effortless one notch movement on the steering column quadrant, and then change gear at any time thereafter by one press on the pedal which took the place of a normal clutch, was full of potential if you understood the system. Cruising, for instance, in top on a pre-motorway main road, you could pre-select for third

ABOVE Gordon Shanley hurling the Conquest round the Monaco circuit in 1954 and hoping to retain or improve on his third place (one point behind Chiron's winning Lancia) after the road rally. Just after this picture was taken the gearbox broke. LEFT 1955 was Nancy Mitchell's Daimler year. She is seen here winning the 5-lap Ladies' Handicap at Goodwood with a Conquest.

and then press for an instantaneous change to overtake. Thanks to the slip in the fluid fly-wheel, you could hold the car on the brake in traffic after engaging gear and drive it like an automatic. With the Conquest's engine torque you could trickle through a town in top (even start off from rest), and slow speed manoeuvres were aided by a hand-throttle. The problem was that many potential buyers did not understand. As *The Autocar*'s

Michael Brown wrote in one of his eulogies after a transcontinental journey: "If I were a Daimler salesman I would be generous with my demonstration runs, allowing prospective customers several hundred miles to succumb to the ease of control."

Too often the reaction was "Daimler equals fluid flywheel equals the older person who has lost his driving skills – fine for a chauffeur or ceremonial work, but not for

T.H. Wisdom and A. Jeffries at Sarrebourg en route to Monte Carlo and 76th place in 1954.

me. It wasn't sufficiently realised that a skilled driver might get more out of a car with this transmission. It also has to be said that there were those who did not like the sharp separate pedal movement after years of synchronising clutch and gear lever. The management were obviously aware of the predicament – witness their Lanchester efforts – and, when the fate of the Sprite had been decided, a fully automatic Century with Borg-Warner transmission was announced.

THE DAIMLER IMAGE

It wasn't just the fluid flywheel. In those pre-company car days, those who wanted a tough and reliable car to get them about their business hestiated before choosing a Daimler. There were still class and wealth overtones, not helped by Lady Docker's efforts or the marque's associations with royalty. Whereas today a Mercedes spells success, a Daimler could then suggest pretension.

The management tried to change the image, supporting entries for the Alpine and Monte Carlo rallies and the Silverstone production car races. A Conquest came very near to a good placing in the 1954 Monte. After the road section and before the final speed test Shanley and Dalkin were as high as third behind Chiron's Lancia and Adams'

Jaguar. Chiron was finally declared winner but not before there had been protests about the Aurelia coupé's eligibility which many thought were valid. That final test was weighted towards smaller cars – so much so that despite second fastest time the Jaguar was down to sixth place. Shanley had to battle against that same weighting. He threw the Daimler round the Grand Prix Circuit, the gearbox complained and the car came to a halt. He was demoted ninety-three places. There were still five Conquests in the first hundred.

In July the three Alpine cars were to Century specification though the latter was not announced till March 1955. Whilst they did not feature in the class results against more powerful sports cars (Aston Martin, Salmson and Sunbeam Alpine), it was a thorough test with lessons learnt. Corbishley was out first when a gearbox oil seal leaked, Hardman then lost a front wheel on the Falzarego and Bolton, still on time, had to be rescued from near disaster on the Cayolle when the edge of the road collapsed whilst he was creeping past a bus. How they had tried to change that image! *The Motor* reported: "Two Daimlers were repeatedly battered against the scenery without breaking completely."

At Silverstone, still in 1954, famous drivers

belted the cars round the track. Wharton led the whole field from the start, was third at the end of the first lap and then "hit a spinning Lancia a resounding whack". Reg Parnell finished fourth having beaten one of the MkVII Jaguars. 1955 was Nancy Mitchell's Daimler year. Seventeenth at Monte Carlo, she entered but was not placed in the RAC and Tulip rallies, and then won the 5-lap Ladies' Handicap at the Goodwood Whitsun weekend meeting.

There were other Conquest variants. Before the 1953 Show a two-seater roadster with a lightweight aluminium body on the saloon chassis had been designed and built in six weeks. It wasn't a big seller. The majority in that market preferred the cheaper offerings without fluid flywheel, but the car did have the merit of relative economy and 81mph at 2,500ft per min. piston speed. The drophead coupé with the twin-carburettor engine was shown at Paris in 1953 but was not introduced to the British market till June 1954. Finally, for the 1955 Show the roadster and the drophead were replaced by the sports drophead with wind-up windows, larger doors and a more substantial hood.

Sadly all these endeavours – the competition entries, the open versions, the price reductions and, in 1956, fully automatic

The two-seater roadster prototype on the saloon chassis designed and built in six weeks before the 1953 Show.

transmission – did not lead to increased sales. The Conquest ceased production in 1958 and, together with the decision on the Lanchester Sprite, this meant that Daimler no longer had a smaller car on sale.

Production – DS251 Saloon: *1953* 1,990; *1954* 2,604; *1955* 1,869; *1956* 1,367. **DJ254 Roadster:** *1953* 5; *1954* 60. **Roadster Fixedhead:** *1954* 3 (est). **DJ252 Drophead:** *1954-55* 234. **Sports Drophead:** *1955-56* 54.

REGENCY I, CONVERTIBLE COUPÉ, EMPRESS, REGENCY II, SPORTSMAN, 104 & SPECIALS 1951-1956

The Regency story was a telling example of Daimler's problems in the 1950s. It was announced in October 1951 as "The answer to overseas demands for a six-seater with good ground clearance", and as "designed for maximum production". The specification was developed from the Consort's, with the 3-litre engine well forward and a 9ft 6in wheelbase. The body, continuing the Lanchester Fourteen theme, was another forerunner of the Conquest. Unfortunately the car fell foul

"Golden Zebra", the last Docker Special, at Earls Court in 1955. The seats of this exotic Hooper offering on the DK400 chassis were covered in zebra skin.

of the rebuilding programme and, despite full-page advertisements ("Distinction, sir, is not won by self-praise. It's not what we say. It's what you find out for yourself" and "It's undoubtedly a Daimler") only around 30 cars were put together in the first two years. Hardly "maximum production"! Time and money were expended on derivatives which did not become part of the range. These included the 1952 LHD 3-litre Barker convertible and further Empress saloons. Following the announcement in February 1953 that Regency production was to be postponed, there were no examples on the Daimler stand in October, though the name was kept alive with that year's Hooper "Docker Special" on a Regency chassis. This was a fixed-head coupé in green with red crocodile skin covering the dashboard and silver accessories. It became known as "Silver Flash".

By 1954 Conquests and Lanchester Ledas were coming off the production lines and those busy engineers had reorganised the Regency, moving the headlights outboard, raising the wing line and extending the luggage boot. The Regency II was now to be available with both 3½-litre and 4.6-litre engines and a four-light Sportsman saloon. With the 4.6-litre specification (and on the 3½-litre Sportsman) an overdrive top gear (3.03:1 in place of 4.3:1) meant lower revs at cruising speeds. *The Motor*'s testers again approved of Daimler roadholding: "The Regency is, in fact, a car with handling characteristics which will be enjoyed by all critical motorists. There is almost neutral steer on dry roads and a very quick response to the steering wheel".

The company now had a good large saloon, but there was more to come. Still trying to overcome the image problem, they increased the power output of the 3½ litre by 20bhp and raised the standard top gear to a ratio nearer the overdrive models. The importance long given to 100mph was always irrational when the figure had no significance in kilometres per hour, yet when the revised Regency achieved this figure (102.5mph in *The Motor*'s test) the car was renamed the One-o-Four for 1955. Both frame and body mountings were modified to provide a stiffer structure and servo-assisted brakes were standard. There was also a "Ladies' model" with appropriate fittings. For 1956 the top gear ratio was up again and *The Autocar* wrote: "As to road behaviour there was an indefinable something about this newer car which suggested that a little more development work had come to fruition. Those of us who had driven the earlier car found greater pleasure in handling this one". Fully automatic transmission was available in December.

Does Daimler deserve praise for perseverance, or condemnation for taking so long? Sales improved but were still minimal compared with Armstrong-Siddeley or Jaguar. At least all those developments paved the way for the Majestic and Majestic Major which were widely acclaimed. We shall never know what would have happened if the Jaguar offer had not been accepted.

Production – 3½ litre: *1951* 5; *1952* 16; 1953 (est); *1954* ?; *1955* 350; *1956* 221. **4.6 litre:** *1955* 21; *1956* 39.

DK400, REGINA, CARBODIES, HOOPER & SPECIALS 1954-1960

With the launch of the MkII Regency the chassis was extended to a 10ft 10in wheelbase to provide replacements for the previous straight-eight limousines and a platform for more exotic bodies. The first Hooper "Docker Special" on the DK400 chassis was in royal blue decked out with silver stars along the side panels. The car became known as "Stardust", with silver grey silk brocatelle and blue crocodile skin upholstery, and lighter aluminium cabinet work covered in the same materials. There were technical advances, with double glazing (38 years before Mercedes), effective roof insulation, and sophisticated heating and ventilation. Stardust was backed up at the 1954 Show by a slab-sided Regina limousine which was good value for money, some £2,000 cheaper

than the Hooper effort.

For 1955 the Regina name was dropped. The utilitarian eight-seater (with three separate seats in the middle row) built by Carbodies had sculpted wings in place of the slab sides. It was known just as the DK400. The exotic offering on the DK400 chassis was an ivory and gold plated two-door coupé, with three separate front and two folding rear seats upholstered in zebra skin. Christened "Golden Zebra", this was the last Docker Special. By 1956 the Docker era was over. Carbodies continued with a revised eight-seater now with a straight wing line. Hooper had a simpler fixed-head coupé on a 3½-litre 104 chassis. Over the years there has been criticism of these cars but let's not forget the painstaking work of those who built them, and that, at the time, many took heart from seeing what could be built in England.

Production: *1954* 3 (est); *1955* 18; *1956* 22.

DAIMLER ACHIEVEMENTS

1948
Journeys 2½ litre: R. Stavert Bombay-Rawalpindi.

1951
Monte Carlo 2½ litre Consort: A. Adams 1st in class, Concours de Confort.
Alpine 2½ litre Consort: J. Lowrey, Press car.

1952
Monte Carlo Straight Eight: T. Wisdom 47th, 2nd in class, Concours de Confort.

1954
Monte Carlo Conquest: R. Worledge 46th, C. Corbishley 64th, P. Bolton 75th, T. Wisdom 76th, G. Shanley 96th.
Silverstone R. Parnell 4th, 1st in class; G. Abecassis 6th, 2nd in class.

1955
Monte Carlo Century: Miss N. Mitchell 17th, 3rd Coupe des Dames; K. Wharton 22nd, 2nd Prix de Confort; C. Daetwyler 61st.
Sestriere Century: K. Wharton 7th, 2nd in class.
Goodwood Century: Miss N. Mitchell 1st in Ladies Handicap.
Australian Mobilgas Economy Conquest: V. Brown 2nd in class.

1956
Monte Carlo Century: C Key 227th.

FEDDEN

The one and only Fedden sleeve-valve radial prototype photographed in Cheltenham, winter 1945 before its fateful Stoke Orchard somersault. Rear-wheel angle hints at "tuck-in" problem. Hillman Minx behind.

Roy Fedden, that great engineer and leader of the team responsible for the sleeve-valve radial British engines which powered so many of Britain's fighters and bombers, was one of the architects of victory in 1945. He was also a motor industry pioneer. Before the First World War (when still in his 20s) he had built up his first team, which designed the successful Straker-Squire. In 1919 his C.A.R. Utility car with 1200cc overhead-valve three-cylinder air-cooled radial engine was on the road. B.H. Davies drove the prototype from Clifton to London in under four hours and, writing in *The Autocar*, was mightily impressed: "In a thirty minute Piccadilly traffic jam on the day of President Poincaré's visit no over-heating developed though practically every water-cooled engine in the block developed steam."

The C.A.R. succumbed to the financial dif-ficulties of the Cosmos parent which had taken over Straker-Squire. Bristol Aircraft, who then took over, were not at that stage in the car business. Developments of the design were discussed in magazine articles during the '30s and early war years. Further encour-aged by his aircraft engine experience, Fedden wrote that the radial fitted to a car was the way to produce more power per pound weight than the conventional engine. There was no need for the length of crank-shaft and crankcase required by in-line or even V8 configurations.

After his dismissal by the Bristol directors in October 1942, and whilst still working full-time as adviser to the Aircraft Minister, Sir Roy's thoughts (he had been knighted in January 1942) were again turning to motor cars. He began to set his sights on producing a superior world car, no less, for sale in home and export markets. The aim was a six-seater (as described in other chapters, the desired objective of those times) "with the performance of a pre-war V8 and fuel consumption better than 30mpg". The key had to be weight reduction using the radial engine and other radical innovations. By 1943 Roy Fedden Limited was in embryo. Many of those who gathered at the new Cheltenham headquarters during 1944 were to make significant contributions to other companies. They included Ian Duncan (see Austin), assistant to Fedden at Bristol and after, who was prime mover, and Alex Moulton (see Alvis), and later at BMC, who was in at the beginning but then returned to Cambridge. Peter Ware, also ex-assistant, stayed the course (and in the '60s became engineering director at Rootes), and Gordon Wilkins (see Jowett) was responsible for body styling.

This galaxy of talent set themselves to interpret the Fedden ideas. In his pre-war articles Sir Roy had also written of unsatisfactory British chassis frames and the team now achieved a light part-aluminium structure. Four-wheel independent suspension used the Lockheed Thornhill hydro-pneumatic strut (see also Singer), though Spencer Moulton rubber discs were a possible alternative. The power unit was another three-cylinder air-cooled radial, this time with sleeve valves, mounted above the rear wheels and driving through a torque converter. After cramming what now would be years of development work into months, all components were functioning by the end of 1945. But, when assembled, they were incompatible. Engine weight and height had increased during development. The independent rear suspension struts were too soft in their rebound movement and could allow the wheels to tuck in. Although, to quote from Bill Gunston's Fedden biography, "the big sleeve-valve cylinders pulled surprisingly smoothly", and "the Thornhill struts gave a wonderfully comfortable ride", it soon became obvious that the car had cornering instability. The engineers experimented with different camber angles and other adjustments as the prototype piled up the miles over the Cotswold roads. Then came the fateful February day in 1946 when the car somersaulted after a series of tests on the runways of the Stoke Orchard airfield.

That brilliant team had been too radical. They had needed a more conservative element to persuade Fedden that so much innovation could not be put into practise so quickly. The commercially successful innovative postwar designs were the product of years of development and massive funding. In fact the crash was not the end of Roy Fedden Limited. Another more conventional car design was proposed, but then the developing aero engine side was in trouble when a major order was cancelled, and the company was forced into liquidation in June 1947.

Production: 1

HEALEY

What is the definition of a good car? Is it the cost-effective product whose sales bring profit, jobs and dividends? Or is it the machine which satisfies and delights owner and driver? Even if the sums are correct the second definition can lead only to the first when the car buying public is peopled by the discerning with sufficient money. It is salutary to note that both the companies whose cars Donald Healey improved before the war, Riley and Triumph, were in liquidation by the end of the '30s. Healey had been only one member of a team which had taken the wrong decisions, but in the book put together by Peter Garnier he admits that he was not a good accountant and that his enthusiasm after the war could also have led to liquidation if he had not been helped by Nash at a critical time.

Healey may not have scored high marks in the test of the balance sheet, but the world of motoring would be much poorer without

Donald Healey with Westland-bodied roadster at Warwick.

those practical engineers who took the opportunity of the postwar seller's market to create better driving machines. Healey's rôle was to educate as well as produce. He encouraged discernment so that more prospective customers sought better handling and performance when affluence returned and many had that extra purchasing power from company money. Volume manufacturers had to respond, and those who did get their sums right were able to make a profit from a more satisfactory machine.

Like Sydney Allard, Healey developed the product by his own physical effort in the driving seat and under the bonnet. John Dugdale, writing in *The Autocar* in May 1948, gives a vivid picture of his visit to "the five wartime blister huts" in Warwick. Healey, then aged 50, and not long back from a 5,000-mile drive across America ("If we want to sell to America, we don't send the sales manager because we don't have one, I just send myself"), had just returned that morning from taking a car to the French agent and was to drive a car to the Belgian agent the next day. It was a different approach to that of the large manufacturers: Leonard Lord drove a Bentley whilst managing Austin! Healey's advantage over Allard was a long life span. He had 57 years after his 1931 Monte Carlo victory in the Invicta (whereas Allard lived for only 14 years after 1952) and, when he started on his own after the war, his task was made easier by the string of contacts from his rally successes, his pre-war work and wartime duty at Rootes.

Ben Bowden did the first body, aiming as he wrote in a 1948 response to criticism, "for the minimum weight and of such a size that it would only just accommodate four people in comfort". Sammy Sampietro did the suspension and he and Bowden (they had both been at Rootes) tackled the chassis. The pre-war contacts were a boon. Victor Riley "found" a spare engine, gearbox and rear axle. Jack Tatton, Riley supplies chief, helped with the Ministry permit for purchasing steel. Wally Allen, who had been a Triumph director, provided working space in his cement mixer factory. James Watt was another ex-Triumph pillar of strength. He joined Healey after "demob" from the RAF and put in some of his own money. One of his exploits was to drive a bodyless chassis to Turin to be fitted with Bertone coachwork. The proprietor of the Hotel de la Poste at Avallon personally welcomed "this gallant Englishman who had

James Watt, who was with Donald Healey from 1945 to 1947 and later worked for Austin and Bristol.

arrived in half a motor car."

The Riley-engined cars could never have been the basis of a long-term project. The engine, good as it was, would not remain in production for ever and was heavy and expensive. The answer, as for Allard, was America. So Healey "sent himself" across the Atlantic again in December 1949, hoping to purchase Cadillac V8 engines. During the sea crossing he met up with George Mason of Nash who said, in effect, "Those Cadillacs are in short supply, what about using our six-cylinder?" The result was that Healey's £50,000 overdraft was paid off by Nash in return for some free cars, and profits from the rest of the 500 Nash-Healeys were sufficient to fund the next development, the Healey Hundred, which in turn led to the long line of Austin-Healeys.

RILEY-ENGINED HEALEYS 1946-1953

James Watt explained the genesis of the car to Bill Boddy and Cecil Clutton when they travelled to Warwick for *Motor Sport* soon after the saloon had been timed at 104.64mph on the Milan-Como *autostrada*. The aim had been to keep weight down to one ton with a 100bhp engine. in fact the saloon weighed 22½cwt and modifications to the engine, carburettors, exhaust, etc., brought power to 104bhp. The 160lb chassis was made as stiff as possible so that the soft coil springs with 6in movement in the Sampietro trailing link front suspension could do their work. At the back there were also coil springs, with the axle kept in order by a Panhard rod and two other stays. Clutton commented, after driving a roadster, that it had all the necessary qualities – stiff chassis, low unsprung weight, and a low centre of gravity – to provide good roadholding allied with the comfort of those soft springs. He also remarked on the steering. The geometry of the linkage was carefully calculated so that the wheels maintained the correct Ackerman angles, despite that softness, and the steering box was mounted on the frame with reinforcing webs so that there was no wayward

Donald Healey and Geoff Price on their way to 4th place in the Touring category in the 1949 Mille Miglia.

Robin Richards and Rodney Lord in a Healey Silverstone at Pescara in the 1950 Mille Miglia. They hit a fence near Vicenza when another competitor skidded and blocked the road just ahead of them.

movement. The result was accurate control without kickback at the steering wheel.

The shape of the bodies evolved after tests in the Armstrong-Whitworth wind tunnel and they were built by two companies who had worked for the wartime aircraft industry. Aeroparts at Hereford, part of local Rootes distributor the Westland Motor Company, did the roadster. Elliot, whose previous trade had been shop and exhibition fittings, made the saloon in Reading. Healey's 1948 publicity drive saw him proclaiming the car almost as an extension of his own cheerful personality. In February he was aboard the first *Queen Elizabeth*, with a new Westland "taken great car of by Cunard in the spacious garage". Geoffrey joined him in New York and they set off across the Allegheny Mountains "which reminded him of a very severe portion of the Monte Carlo Rally". Next it was Toledo, Detroit, Chicago, all the time demonstrating to the cognoscenti of the American auto world, and then Dallas, where "The firm which specialised in British goods had a magnificent showroom filled with MGs, Bentleys and Rolls and had imported 8,000 James motorcycles in 1947." They travelled on down to the Mexican border and back North-West 1,000 miles through the Grand Canyon and across the desert to California and Los Angeles. Healey was the best sort of ambassador for Britain and it wasn't all demonstration. "Hardly a day passed without my writing to Sampietro, Roger Menadue, Geoffrey Price and the rest suggesting modifications which I never dreamt were necessary before making this journey", Healey wrote in his account of the trip, which concluded: "America wants British products, but let us be sure that the stuff we send is our best so that there will still be a demand when the seller's market folds up".

Back in Warwick, Healey and Geoffrey prepared another Westland, GWD 43, for the Mille Miglia at the beginning of May, coming second in the unlimited sports class after "the biggest dog they had ever seen leapt at them from a hedge", an encounter which did neither the dog nor the front of the Westland much good. That same GWD 43 was *The Autocar*'s road test car in June and then in July Healey drove it to a class win in the Alpine Rally. A jade green Elliott, OVE 722, was collected by Count Lurani and Serafini from Menadue in London and driven to Sicily to come 2nd in the touring category round that 680-mile circuit which included the old Targa Florio roads. Lurani then, with Sandri (as Serafini was ill), won the touring category in the Mille Miglia. It was another car which worked for its living, helped to heal Anglo-Italian relations after, in Lurani's words, "that tragic war" and showed up a weakness in that Panhard torque rod location. On both circuits Lurani showed his skill by driving hundreds of miles without the rear

axle control exerted by the rod.

Fortune did not smile in 1949. Healey and Wisdom started from Florence in the Monte Carlo Rally and, in ice and fog, "came upon a tangle of wreckage at the entrance to a village. Four or five lorries had piled up across the road. Another, swung by its trailer, smashed broadside into the tangle and burst into flames. In the lurid glare of the glaze, which shone a few yards through the fog, they tried to get through, but there was no room and no detour." Then in the Alpine he and Appleyard were all set for a penalty free run and a Coupe des Alpes when they were held up at a level crossing and lost two vital minutes.

The Sportsmobile was a roomy, slab-sided drophead, the Silverstone a stark two-seater with which many drivers began their track careers in club races. Ian Duncan built the Duncan saloon and Drone two-seater in Norfolk after leaving Fedden. Bertone, Competition Cars, Fox & Nicholl, H.W. Motors, Leacroft, Pourtout and Van den Plas (in Belgium) also built bodies on this chassis. At the 1950 Show the Elliot and Westland were replaced by the Tickford saloon and Abbot drophead.

Production: Annual production figures are not available. These are estimated figures for different body types: Westland 64; Elliott 100; Silverstone 105; Sportsmobile 23; Duncan 20; Abbott 77; Tickford 220.

NASH-ENGINED HEALEYS 1951-1953

After meeting George Mason of Nash, Healey again had the resources for his favourite activity of developing a car through races and rallies. He realised from the start that his ideal would be thwarted by the weight of the six-cylinder Nash but he also knew that the unit was one of the toughest around, so its forte would be long-distance events. Warwick used all their preparation skills, Healey recruited good drivers and the result was an impressive string of places at Le Mans. By 1953, up against the much more powerful C-Type Jaguars and Cunninghams the Healey could not be considered a contender, but *The Autocar* noted that Johnson's car spent only nine minutes at the pits, less time than any other entrant. In the Mille Miglia either Healey or Johnson got a car to the finish three years in succession. In true Healey fashion there was no fleet of works cars. The 6th-place 1951 Le Mans car crashed after a burst tyre in the 1952 Mille Miglia, was then re-bodied and came 3rd at Le Mans two months later.

The original bodies had been made by Panelcraft in Birmingham, but then in 1952 the Healey, together with Nash's standard saloon, was restyled by Pinin Farina. The result was handsome and expensive, but it continued to sell until the merger with Hudson in 1954, by which time American affluence was beginning to wane. There may not have been much profit for Mason by the time the Warwick-assembled cars were shipped to the USA for sale, but all these efforts did not go unnoticed in America. In 1953 the "Le Mans dual jet-fire" with twin carburettors and an extra 20bhp, was announced as an engine option on all Nash cars.

Production: *1951* 182; *1952* 318; *1953* 74.

Wisdom at Arnage in the Nash-Healey during the 1952 Le Mans. Co-driven by Johnson it finished 3rd and was the first British car home.

Nash-Healey open sports six-cylinder 3-seater.

The Alvis-engined car, and below viewed from the rear.

ALVIS-ENGINED HEALEYS 1952-1953

The Nash-Healey was never available on the UK home market, all the production being for America. Commentators have written that the Alvis-Healey's main merit was its scarcity value, but this doesn't do justice to the hybrid which came about because Healey wanted to have one product which didn't need "for export only" stuck on the windscreen.

First there was the Healey chassis in its Silverstone form, modified with trailing links instead of the Panhard rod set-up for the rear suspension, and still with that precise steering and good roadholding. Then there was the smooth six-cylinder Alvis engine, with its good torque and long life potential, together with a four-speed gearbox instead of the Nash's three speeds and overdrive. The gear ratios gave 85mph in top gear at 2,500ft per min. piston speed compared with the Jaguar XK120's 79mph. *The Autocar*'s testers liked the Alvis-Healey's dual character: either leisurely progress in top gear, or a swift change down to the high third and thoroughbred response. An owner was purchasing good design details which reflected Healey's experience and there was a comfortable body with effective hood and wind-up windows.

Production: 25

ABOVE The first Healey 100 at Warwick before it was agreed that Austin should take over production and before the Austin badge was fitted.
RIGHT Leonard Lord and Donald Healey standing by an Austin-Healey 100-6 at 1956 Earls Court. Sir Anthony Eden, then Prime Minister, who had opened the Show, is sitting in the car.

AUSTIN-HEALEY 100 1953-1956

By the end of 1951 Healey accepted that the Nash could only be a repeat of the Riley experience: too heavy, too expensive, insufficient profit, and no long-term future. The Americans still wanted British sports cars. The Jupiter and the Lea-Francis were too expensive to fill the gap between the MGTD and the XK120. The need was to find cheaper components and build them into a cheaper simpler structure, even if it meant forgetting the delights of the Silverstone chassis.

The answer was supplied by Leonard Lord, who had planned to make large quantities of a 2,660cc ohv four-cylinder engine for the A90 Atlantic. But the Americas (as we saw) did not want the Atlantic! Instead Lord let Healey have engine, transmission and suspension parts at a much lower price than the Riley components. The first car was constructed in Healey's own garage so as not to upset Nash people visiting the Warwick factory. The legacy from the Silverstone was

the proof that independent front suspension needed a really stiff chassis and this was concocted by Geoffrey Healey and Barrie Bilbie. The body shape was created by Gerry Coker with input from the boss. Tickford produced a prototype body and this was built onto a sample frame from John Thompson's. This was the car that was taken to the 1952 Motor Show and exhibited as the Healey 100, with the Austin engine producing 90bhp. Leonard Lord so liked it that he agreed that Austin should take over production – 200 a week rather than Warwick's potential of 20 – and thus the Austin-Healey was born.

Twenty-five cars were hand-built at Warwick. Healey then repeated the 1948 Westland exercise, this time taking six vehicles with him to America at the end of February. Healey knew how to reach the American public. The cars were exhibited at the World's Fair in Miami, demonstrated before the Sebring twelve hours race in March and exhibited again at the New York Motor Sports Show in April, all the time with full press coverage. Healey and Lord had a sales success! Series production started in May 1953 with Jensen producing the body, whilst Warwick was kept busy concentrating on special versions. First there was the lighter 100S with power up to 132bhp. This was the bumperless oval-grilled car, usually resplendent in duotone blue and white, the American racing colours. Warwick also modified over 1,000 Longbridge cars to produce 110bhp and christened the model 100M. Healey seldom missed a trick! Once again he was able to give time to development and publicity through competition and record-breaking, and think about the next move – which led to the Sprite. At the 1956 Show the 100/4 was replaced by the 100/6 with the six-cylinder A90 C-type engine. This in turn was followed by the 3000 which remained in production till 1968.

Production – 100 BN1: *1953-55* 10,688. **100 BN2:** *1956* 3,924. **100S:** *1955* 50.

HEALEY ACHIEVEMENTS

1947
Records Elliott saloon: D. Healey, Jabbeke 110.8mph.

1948
Alpine Westland Roadster: D. Healey 1st in class.
Mille Miglia Westland Roadster: D. Healey 9th, 2nd in class. Elliot saloon: G. Lurani 1st touring category.
Records Elliot saloon: T. Wisdom, Montlhéry 102 miles in one hour from standing start.
Tour of Sicily Elliot saloon: G. Lurani 1st in class, 2nd Touring Category.

1949
Alpine Silverstone: D. Healey 1st in class, E. Wadsworth 2nd in class.
Monte Carlo Elliot saloon: W. Fowler 36th, D. Healey (see text).
Mille Miglia Westland Roadster: T. Wisdom (& G. Healey) 1st Touring Category. Elliot saloon: D. Healey 4th Touring Category.

1950
Le Mans Nash-Healey: A. Rolt 4th. Elliot saloon: N. Mann 19th.
Mille Miglia Nash-Healey: D. Healey 177th & 9th in class.

1951
Alpine Silverstone: E. Wadsworth 1st in class, Alpine Cup.
Le Mans Nash-Healey coupé: A. Rolt 6th.
Mille Miglia Nash-Healey: D. Healey 30th & 4th in class.
Liège-Rome-Liège Silverstone: P. Riley 1st in class.

1952
Alpine Silverstone: A. Tasker.
Le Mans Nash-Healey: L. Johnson 3rd.
Mille Miglia Nash-Healey: L. Johnson 7th.
Records Austin-Healey 100: Jabbeke: 111.7mph.
Paris-St. Raphael *Rallye Feminia* Silverstone: Betty Haig 1st in class.

1953
Monte Carlo Tickford saloon: A. Meredith-Owens 94th.
Le Mans Nash-Healey: L. Johnson 11th. Austin-Healey 100M: M. Gatsonides 12th, M. Becquart 14th.
Records Austin-Healey 100: D. Healey, Bonneville 142.6mph (advertised as world's fastest production car under 3,000cc).

1954
Alpine Austin-Healey 100: R. Flower 4th in class, Stross 5th in class.
Mille Miglia Austin-Healey: L. Macklin 5th in class.
Records Austin-Healey 100S: D. Healey Bonneville 192.6mph.

1955
Mille Miglia Austin-Healey 100S: G. Abbecassis 11th & 5th in class, L. Macklin 8th in class.

1956
Mille Miglia Austin-Healey 100S: T. Wisdom 2nd in class.

HILLMAN

The products of Peugeot, the world's second oldest car manufacturer, roll off the production lines at Ryton-on-Dunsmore. yet 40 years ago this same factory was the headquarters of the organisation built up by Billy Rootes through years of unremitting effort. The outpouring of energy had been prodigious. He helped to get Coventry back on its feet after devastating air raids. As chairman of the Dollar Exports Council, he spearheaded the postwar export drive to the USA. There had been steady growth in the companies where he had taken the helm, faithfully supported by brother Reginald. It had all begun when Billy left the Royal Naval Air Service after the First World War and set out to sell other manufacturers' products – Austin, Clyno, Hillman, Humber and Singer. He soon reckoned that he had a better idea of what customers wanted. Attempts to take over Clyno and Standard were rebuffed but Hillman and Humber were beset by problems. Financed by Prudential, Rootes had control of both companies by the early '30s. The Hillman-Coatalen Company (its original name) was but a small part of William Hillman's engineering enterprise and by the later 1920s was bereft of both its founders. William Hillman was dead and Coatalen had gone to Sunbeam.

Once it is realised that Billy's attitude was the opposite of the likes of W.O. Bentley or Hugh Rose, the story falls into place. He knew that the multitude of his middle-class customers (who between them were going to have more money available than all the millionaires in the land) weren't interested in the niceties of valve operation. They wanted reliability and low running costs, both just as easily provided by simple side valves. Such engines may not have been efficient. Not to worry, if more power was required, make them bigger! Billy also realised that if he could achieve pretty bodies, well furnished with all the fashionable details, the customer

The war-time shadow factory taken over by Rootes after the war. It is now used by Peugeot. The author worked here in the 1950s.

would be attracted to the showrooms.

"Minx" was an inspired given name; vivacious, memorable. It is curious how those three letters M, I, N, seem to have appealed to car buyers. Minor, Mini and Minx: They were all winners. Billy's car was introduced in 1932 with an 1,185cc sidevalve engine, leaf springs and cable-operated Bendix brakes. By 1940, just before civilian production ceased, essentially the same features were worked into a new chassis-less unitary bodyshell. The manufacturing organisation built up by a super-salesman then became one of the major contributors to eventual victory. Besides making saloons and tourers for the military, and over half the total war output of armoured cars, Rootes produced one in seven of all British bomber aircraft, 50,000 aircraft engines and multitudes of bombs, ammunition boxes and the like.

Wartime profits built up the financial base and in 1945 Rootes were able to lease the large Ryton shadow factory. A decade of success followed. Whilst not an innovative designer who would press for radical ideas, Bernard Winter was a competent engineering director who understood Billy's aims and thinking. He was supported by A.G. Booth, in charge of passenger car engineering, and Ted White who was to become chief stylist.

Drophead version of
Phase I post-war Minx
in the Mojave Desert in
1946, and pictured
below in *The Autocar*.

Why then can't we buy Hillmans today? It seems that men like Billy Rootes could do everything except provide for their own mortality. He became Lord Rootes in 1959 and departed this world, having neatly completed his biblical span, in 1964. The remaining family struggled on against problems which crowded in from all sides. New designs did not repeat the success of the Minx and competed with each other. There were expensive tussles with the unions and struggles with the Government over factory location. Billy's flair was no more. He had not left behind a cadre of professional managers experienced in making decisions who would systematically thrash out the necessary answers to ensure his empire's continuing future. Those professionals came into the company when Chrysler and then Peugeot took over. By then there was no Rootes involvement.

HILLMAN MINX PHASE I & II
1946-1948

The simple and unsophisticated Minx became a favourite of prewar transcontinental motorists and Rootes encouraged travellers to use the cars. There are articles in *The Autocar* and *The Motor* by colonial engineers and colonial policemen describing their journeys home on leave and always praising the faithful Hillman. Before the days of regular air services it could be as quick to drive, and

certainly more interesting than yet another sea journey. Precision handling wasn't the prime concern if you were travelling on muddy or rutted tracks for hours on end.

It was a brave move to replace a satisfactory and well-tried chassis plus separate body with a one-piece structure, but that was the way the Americans were developing and it was realised that there could be considerable cost and weight savings. Most of the early unitary Minxes were used by the three Armed Services so that by 1946 purchasers had another well-proved design which, until attacked by rust, was as strong as the old chassis. Mrs Geoffrey Smith – wife of *The Autocar*'s Editor – wrote of their first postwar return to Europe. They had decided to take her Minx because the £10 car allowance was the same for any size of car, and the cross-channel fare was scaled according to wheelbase. She captures the

character of the model whilst also commenting on the devastation and food shortages in France: "314 miles, our grand little Minx had run like a dream all day… alternatively using second and third gears we quietly topped the summit at 6,919ft in a faultless ascent… the Hillman's blameless record, 790 miles at 33mpg", but there was one contrary note: "Fast empty roads brought a sigh from the driver for more power".

The Phase II was announced in December 1947 "with synchromatic finger-tip gear change and a wealth of new features". What had actually happened was that the American Loewy organisation was now assisting Rootes and together they had come up with a new corporate style. Hillmans and Humbers were to reflect the American image and, as US drivers had taken to column gear changes to provide more leg-room for a third passenger on their big bench seats, it was deemed advisable to follow suit. This development made sense on the big Humbers but had little point on the small Minx. The testers went to some lengths to explain how this new lever could make it easier to wear greatcoats and spread out rugs in winter (such was the expectation from the car heater) and to

Minx Phase II, announced in December 1947 and fashioned by the American Loewy organisation.

reach the driving seat from either side of the car, but the siren call of fashion was the real reason for the more complicated linkage. Top-gear mph was only 57 at 2,500ft per min. piston speed, but, as R. Gordon-Barrett found driving his Phase II drophead 4,000 miles across Canada in 1950, the appeal of the car was its ability to slog on for hours on end at 20mph over indifferent roads. In such conditions the ability to cruise at high speeds was of no concern. The Phase II also benefited from the new Lockheed hydraulic brakes.

Production: *1946* not known; *1947* 23,867; *1948* 26,985.

MINX PHASE III-VIII 1949-1956 & HUSKY 1955-1956

Whilst Phase Is and IIs, and many pre-war versions too, were slogging on all over the world, the Loewy studios were helping the home team to create a smaller scale version of the "American" car. It was another typical Rootesmobile. The attractive shape drew

Sheila Van Damm early
in her rally career with
Nancy Mitchell and
Phase IV Minx entry
for the 1951 Monte
Carlo Rally.

George Hinchcliffe and
John Bulman crossing a
river in the Congo en
route to Cape Town in
1952 with a Phase IV
Minx.

customers to the showrooms. There the
salesmen, drilled in positive selling on
courses at Ryton, would orchestrate the new
features, and customers would write out their
cheques. Most of the new owners were not
bothered that the engine was much the same
as in 1932. They liked the feeling of spa-
ciousness in a small car and the column gear
change now made more sense with a roomy
bench front seat. On the road the driver
appreciated the light steering and the
comfort of the new independent front suspension which "certainly takes the sting out
of a definitely bad surface". The testers did go
on to say that "the suspension permits more
lateral movement than is liked at the highest

ABOVE John Dugdale and John Campbell drove a Phase IV Minx from Buenos Aires to La Paz and back. They are seen here with the San Francisco church in La Paz. BELOW Phase III Minxes at Cardiff Docks in 1950 for shipping to Vancouver on MV Silver Briar.

speeds", but that wasn't meant to be the car's forte. In fact the engine was a better bet than that other renegade sidevalve in the Morris Oxford. The 1,185cc Minx engine averaged 35mpg, the 1,476cc Oxford only 29mpg. Both accelerated their vehicles to 50mph in 24 seconds.

In December 1949 the Minx engine was enlarged to 1,265cc for the Phase IV. There was increased torque throughout the speed range but no increase in fuel consumption. The testers emphasized the smoothness of the power unit and "the fact that jerkiness and snatch do not come in at even below 10mph on top gear". It was all these characteristics and the fact that you could thrash the car, in any of the gears, for hours on end – it didn't boil, it didn't show distress – which made the car, like its predecessors, so popular for tougher motoring.

John Dugdale wrote of his 3,570-mile drive with John Campbell from Buenos Aires to La Paz and back in *The Autocar*, February 1950: "It was a long and rather dismal struggle that damp morning at well over 14,000 feet. The road became steeper still. At the crests of the hills, as if the road builders had finally got out of breath, it ceased to twist and often went straight up gradients of 1 in 6 or worse. It was like a nightmare reliability trial with every corner and gradient having to be rushed flat out but without full power being available [owing to the altitude]". Dugdale and Camp-

Peter Harper with battered Phase IV Minx at Monte Carlo in 1951 on his way to 43rd place with R. H. Austin.

Disabled Neville Cohen with Danny Weiner talking to London Lord Mayor Ackroyd after Cohen's drive from Johannesburg in his Phase VI Minx.

1952 Phase V drophead at Bourton-on-the-Water.

bell had embarked on this journey to see if the car would still function without jet changes or other modifications. It did! "One takes the Minx on such a trip with confidence. It is an outstandingly successful design and it is typical of the initiative of the Rootes companies in the Americas that such experiments are encouraged".

George Hinchcliffe and John Bulman chose a Minx for their London to Cape Town record at the end of 1951: "In the Sahara there were times when the extreme heat and mile after mile of low-gear work made the overworked engine cry out for respite, yet nothing broke". Making up time once in South Africa they were still able to cruise the

Two Huskies at the Nairobi start of the 1956 Coronation Safari Rally. They were not placed. DKW came 1st and 2nd, Fiat 1100 3rd and 4th.

Minx flat-out for ten hours (using the bench seat to change drivers without stopping) and reached Cape Town in just under 22 days – over two days quicker than Jopling and Sleigh's 1949 record in the A70. Neville Cohen's three-year-old Minx Phase VI did not let him down when he fulfilled his childhood ambition of driving from Johannesburg to London. Four years earlier Neville had been in the passenger seat of a car which had overturned. The after-effects of that crash had left him paralysed from the waist down.

The Minx was sold worldwide, shipped either complete or in component form for local assembly. In 1953 an agreement was signed with Isuzu. The Phase VI and its successors were built up at Omori near Tokyo from a mixture of parts created locally after metric conversion of the English drawings and some components freighted out from Coventry. In that first postwar decade Japanese households still didn't have much spare cash so most of these Minxes were sold as taxis. At home two coupés, the Californian fixed head and the drophead, and the estate car, had joined the range.

By the early '50s European mass producers were showing what could be achieved by fitting more athletic overhead-valve engines. New designs like the Fiat 1100 and the related Simca Aronde cruised at higher speeds with lower engine revs. After making over half a million sidevalves, Rootes produced their own square (i.e. bore and stroke to the same measurement) 1390cc overhead valve unit. It was fitted as the last major modification to the 1948 car, the Phase VIII announced in October 1954, and transformed its performance. At 2,500ft per min. piston speed top gear road speed was 77mph compared with 56mph for the sidevalve engine. A new anti-roll bar tightened the front suspension to cope with higher speeds but the result was not so absorbent of rougher surfaces. The Phase VIIIA of September 1955 was christened the "Gay Look" Minx with, inappropriately in these times, entreaties to "go gay with Hillman"! Innovative use of colour included bright yellow and a choice of twenty-five different single or two-tone paintwork schemes.

Slogging days were not quite over because, in addition to a sidevalve special saloon, Rootes had thought up a utilitarian economy estate with the 1265cc sidevalve and a shorter wheelbase. There were no frills and an economy price, at £398 (without P.T.) the same as the 803cc Austin A30 Countryman and cheaper than the Morris Minor Traveller or Standard Ten Estate. Fuel consumption was 35mpg overall and as much as 40mpg with gentler driving. The buying public warmed to the Husky and it remained a favourite in successive forms for nearly a decade. It had some of the appeal of the later Renault 4, but lacked the design flair which took the Renault into the million sales league.

Production: *1949* 41,348; *1950* 50,789; *1951* 40,250; *1952* 43,074; *1953* 58,193; *1954* 68,614; *1955* 89,223; *1956* 29,000 (est).

MINX SERIES I 1956-1957

The next Minx, the same basic shape a the 1955 Rapier (see Sunbeam), and designed from the start around the 1390cc ohv engine with more Loewy styling input, arrived in 1956. At Isuzu, engineers were working towards total production from locally sourced raw materials and components. The Series I became the first completely Japanese Hillman, a local difference being that quick-drying cellulose had to replace synthetics because of the dust from unsurfaced roads in the Tokyo atmosphere. Kenneth Middleton, then resident British engineer at the Omori factory, records that his Rootes colleagues had been "mightily impressed" by the quality of components sent back to Coventry. He was given the "final accolade of acknowledgement that the Japanese Minx was better than the homespun model".

At home and in other export markets, the "Series" Minxes were appreciated as stylish, dependable cars. In the words of *The Autocar*, "they provided the compromise between many a motorist's desires and his pocket". The problem lay elsewhere, namely that the volume sales of the next decade came from cars with smaller engines, BMC's 1100, Fiat's 1100, Ford's Anglia, Renault's Dauphine, whilst the Minx was enlarged to 1592 and later 1725cc. Rootes then fell into a trap of their own making by producing the

bigger Super Minx, alongside the standard Minx and introducing a smaller car, the Imp, with too small an engine. The irony is that in the early '60s they left this huge gap between 875 and 1592cc at a time when cars of the original Minx's size, 1185cc, were leaders in the sales charts.

Production: *1956* 30,453.

HILLMAN ACHIEVEMENTS
(All Minx except where Husky shown.)

1948
JCC Eastbourne D. Russell 1st in class in three tests Standard Award. Mrs Wisdom 1st in class Concours d'Elegance.
Monte Carlo M. Gatsonides 19th, 2nd in class. M. Anderson 1st in class, Concours de Confort.
3,000 miles across America Roger Barlow.

1950
Monte Carlo P. Harper 15th, Kouwerberg 37th, M. Anderson 39th, 1st in class, Concours de Confort.
MCC 1000 Mile R. Walshaw 5th, D. Absalom 16th, P. Fotheringham-Parker 18th.
Buenos Aires to La Paz *(South America)* John Dugdale.

1951
Monte Carlo P. Harper 43rd, M. Anderson 1st in class, M. Shears 2nd in class, Concours de Confort.
Tulip P. Harper 10th, 4th in class.
RAC R. Walshaw 6th in class, J. Kemsley 10th in class, Miss S. VanDamm 14th in class.

1952
Monte Carlo P. Harper 35th, M. Anderson 1st in class, J. Kemsley 2nd in class, Concours de Confort.
MCC Daily Express National P. Cooper 1st in class.
Mexico-Puebla R. Corona 2nd.
London to Cape Town G. Hinchcliffe, 10,500 miles in 21 days 19¾hrs (record).

1953
Circuit of Ireland J. Dowling, C. Maunsell, B. McCaldin, Team Prize.

1955
MCC National J. Robinson 3rd.

1956
Victorian Alpine Rally *(Australia)* H. Firth 1st.
London-New Zealand A. Field (Husky).
4,000 miles Nigeria-London P. Duncan.
11,000 miles New York-Buenos Aires P. Saccaggio (Husky).
Johannesburg-London N. Cohen, in wheelchair.

HUMBER

Billy Rootes' ascent to the take-over position has been described (under Hillman). Humber had been a more substantial company than Hillman's motor subsidiary. It expanded from cycle to car production before 1900. The success of the Humberette light car led to the building of the Coventry factory, in 1908, in the re-named Humber Road, which became Rootes' centre of operations before Ryton-on-Dunsmore. After the First World War and Thomas Humber's death, a full range of solid ponderous vehicles were produced, with Colonel John Cole

as Managing Director. The name became sufficiently well regarded for Rootes to use it for their larger and more expensive cars. Billy used the Hillman formula (don't bother with a complicated engine when a larger, simple unit will do) but never achieved the success of the Minx. The Peugeot organisation has not used the name.

HAWK I & II, SNIPE & SUPER SNIPE I, PULLMAN I 1946-1948

The pre-war Humbers earned their reputation as rugged, inexpensive cars. For 1936 the front suspension had been uprated with the familiar edict, i.e. Keep the cost down! Barney Roos had come over from America and adapted the independent transverse leaf layout which he had first used for the 1935 Studebaker. This was not as well located as more sophisticated transverse concoctions on cars like the French Delahaye, but at least the bumps were absorbed. By 1940 the 4-litre sidevalve had found a new rôle as officer transport. There were two Montgomery tourers. "Old Faithful" traversed the battle-

Barendregt (on left) and Gatsonides (on right) holding the cup after their second place in the Super Snipe, only just behind the Hotchkiss, in the Monte Carlo Rally of 1950.

Maurice Gatsonides on the Mont des Mules during the Regularity Test in 1950. The letter 'B' marks the start of the second timed two-mile section.

Dutch Tulip entrant demonstrating the limitations of Barney Roos' simple front suspension at Zandvoort in 1954, and underlining Gatsonides' Monte Carlo achievement.

grounds of North Africa and Italy. In "Victory" the two cap-badged Field-Marshal was driven 60,000 miles to victory in Europe, but not before the car had fallen over the side of the floating Mulberry Harbour into 40 feet of water off the Normandy beaches. Salvaged by the Royal Engineers it was dried out and still in use at the surrender on Lüneberg Heath in May 1945! Simplicity and strength have their value.

After the war the 4-litre car was on sale again as the Super Snipe, together with the 2,731cc Snipe (for only two years), and a four-cylinder version, the Hawk, based on the pre-war Hillman 14. The testers wrote of "the fine power" of the Super Snipe: "It approaches nearly to being a top-gear car, a naturally effortless cruising speed is between 60 and 70mph. Having started smoothly from rest on second gear, the driver can pass straight into top; the surge of power from depressing the throttle at low speeds is extremely good."

The Hawk, with half the engine size in the same body, was a different proposition:

whereas the Super Snipe driver could "sprint" to 60mph in 24 seconds, the Hawk owner had to press the accelerator for the best part of a minute to reach the same speed. Today the Hawk would seem desperately slow with its maximum of 65mph and only 57mph at 2,500ft per min. piston speed. The three models served as effective official and police transport into the '50s. They may not appeal to devotees of advanced engineering but only Rootes could have produced so much car for the money. In August 1946 the Super Snipe was on sale at under £900 including purchase tax when a 3½-litre Jaguar cost £1,100 and a 4¼-litre Bentley £2,997.

Production – Hawk: *1947* 1,616; *1948* 2,900 (est). **Snipe:** *1947* 225. **Super Snipe & Pullman:** *1946* not known; *1947* 2,227; *1948* 2,050 (est).

HAWK MkIII-IV 1949-1956

The three Mk IV (2,267cc) Humber Hawks, driven by P. Braid, K. Carter and R. Carter, which won both the best radio-equipped team and the best rally-type coachwork awards at Monte Carlo in 1951.

The next Hawk MkIII, announced in October 1948, was the model which might have repeated the success of the Minx. It had an attractive shape, still with Loewy input. There was a strong separate chassis and Minx-type coil spring front suspension, but, true to form, not worrying as much about the mechanics as the showroom appeal, the car was fitted with the old sidevalve engine. This was acceptable in the Minx because of all its other valued features at a low price. It was O.K. in the Super Snipe because the 4-litre unit had abundant power and few rivals, but the 1944cc sidevalve Hawk, priced at £625 (£799 with P.T.), was selling against cheaper Austin A70s, Morris Sixes, Standard Vanguards, Vauxhalls, Wolseleys and, from 1950, Fords; all of them with some type of overhead valve layout. The practical consequence in the Hawk was that even 60mph cruising was above that 2,500ft per min. piston speed. Pressing on towards the 71mph top speed was accompanied by engine roar and vibra-tion. Even the friendly Motor wrote that "the interior noise level was not as low as on some contemporary cars". The Hawk was geared at 16.3mph in top gear at 1,000rpm compared with the Morris Six's 19mph and the Vauxhall Velox's 18.2mph. For 1951 the MkIV was fitted with an enlarged but still sidevalve 2,267cc engine and the gearing was a little higher.

An annual average of around 8,000 cars were sold between 1951 and 1953. The puzzling part of the story is that the ohv version of the engine already fitted to the Sunbeam Talbot would have been available. If that unit had also gone into the Hawk in 1951, would the car have taken sales from Austin (then around 17,000 with the A70) and from Ford and Vauxhall (then above 20,000 and increasing)? Higher volume could have brought the price down. Would an ohv version have become better established in Africa and Australia? The rest of the car did have some of the features which those markets required and was available before the postwar success stories from Holden, Mercedes and Peugeot. The MkV for 1953 had a bolder front and small but useful modifications which underlined the continuous if conservative development effort. The rear window was larger, the chassis strengthened and heavier duty shock absorbers fitted. In other words the car was all the better for world use but still the ohv engine was delayed.

Eventually, in June 1954, came the ohv MkVI. Top speed was up in the 80s, and an overdrive option gave nearly 22mph at 1,000rpm, a vast increase on the original 16.3mph. The Hawk would now cruise happily at 70mph and still return 27mpg. Brakes and suspension were further developed, the rear wings made more shapely, and a limousine version was available. At the 1955 Show there was an attractive estate car version, a Volvo before its time.

Why didn't Billy press for an ohv Hawk before 1954? With a second volume seller to back up the Minx in the '50s, the Group might have been in a better financial position to face the problems of the '60s. Was it general fatigue after years of flat-out work, or was it the still permeating influence of America, where side valves had been common when the Hawk was introduced? Was it also the consequence of employing an engineering director who was reluctant to stand up to the family?

Production: *1949* 4,153; *1950* 985(?); *1951* 7,647; *1952* 6,370; *1953* 10,101; *1954* 9,438; *1955* 12,849; *1956* 6,749.

SUPER SNIPE II & III 1948-1952 IMPERIAL & PULLMAN II & III 1948-1953

It was decided not to introduce a radical new Super Snipe derivative at the same time as the MkIII Hawk and based on that car's less

roomy bodyshell. The earlier style still had sales appeal and presence, and the faults had been hammered out in those millions of miles of war service over desert tracks and devastated European roads. Discussing the MkII, introduced in September 1948, Christopher Jennings, then Editor of *The Motor*, wrote: "I sometimes wonder if the Humber Co. quite realises the enormous amount of goodwill those war-time saloons built up among a generation, even persuading American officers that for fast high-speed transportation over every sort of bad surface there was nothing at that time produced in the USA which was quite so satisfactory in an all-round manner". And a German prisoner of war, quoted in an *Autocar* letter, "For the last two years he had been driving Snipes and Pullmans for which he had great admiration. They were far superior to anything he had driven in the German Army."

Instead of being redesigned, the MkI chassis was modified by moving the front wheels forward 3½ inches and by welding outrigger brackets to the side-members. Thus it was possible to mount a 4-inch wider body using the same doors and other panels.

Idiosyncratic the Humber may have been but the Austin Sheerline was the only European alternative which came near to offering so much – and it was more expensive. With further front suspension development, a variable ratio steering box, rear anti-roll bar and an equal proportion of weight on front and back wheels (in the '30s there was a rear weight bias, now its the other way), the handling was an agreeable surprise. The big side-valve produced enough power and fuel costs were not a disaster if you could put it on the business. The car would readily pull horse-boxes and trailers and was much more comfortable than the early Land Rovers or ex-WD Jeeps. It was not uncommon to see a row of Super Snipes at agricultural shows. Some of the more affluent farmers might have purchased one as a result of meeting Billy, who loved a day out to see his prize cattle in the ring. Tickford built around a hundred dropheads between 1949 and 1950.

John Boyd Carpenter, Minister of Transport, plus ministerial Humber Pullman at the first vehicle testing station, Hendon in 1955.

On the morning of 1st February 1950, those rally enthusiasts who had access to a copy of *The Motor* (published two days before *The Autocar* and both still in short supply) read that Maurice Gatsonides driving a Super Snipe was one of just five entrants who had reached Monte Carlo without loss of marks, despite heavy snow and blocked roads on the way south from Nevers. There was still the Speed and Regulatory Test on the ten-mile circuit running up the hairpins of the Mont des Mules to La Turbie. The aim was to go as fast as possible but also to cover two two-mile sections at the same speed on successive runs. Three small Simcas were in the running but the real contest lay between the 33cwt 100bhp Humber and Marcel Becquart's 28cwt 125bhp Hotchkiss. Those who were watching that Friday wrote of the Humber "swirling the corners without wheel-spin, rock steady round the hairpins, at an astonishing speed for so large and luxurious a machine". Gatsonides so nearly achieved a sensational victory for British industry. His two times on the measured sections were more nearly equal, but Becquart was able to use the greater power of the Hotchkiss to just

achieve a sufficiently faster time to compensate. One mark separated the two with the Humber three marks ahead of the third place Simca. (Sydney Allard would probably have beaten them both if his car's ignition lead had not jumped off.)

August 1950 produced an even better MkIII and a touring limousine version with division. Springing was still further developed and, in the words of the 1951 *Motor* test, "Revision of the suspension has certainly obtained the objective of eliminating leaf friction and any consequent jerkiness, it being possible for a passenger to write legibly whilst the car is in motion." At the same time a Panhard rod was added to the anti-roll bar fitted to the rear axle to maintain stability with the softer ride.

The MkII Pullman had been introduced before the Snipe in May 1948 on a 13½-inch longer wheelbase, which provided sufficient room for three rows of seats. This was a true limousine with fixed division behind the front seat to isolate the driver. It became the staple of central and local government and the more up-market hire firms. In September 1949 the Pullman was joined by the similar Imperial with no division, and in 1950 both models received the Panhard rod and front suspension modifications (adjusted to the higher weight) like the MkIII Snipe. The rear suspension was not softened on the larger cars. Those testers were impressed: "The quietness of the passenger compartment is at all times truly delightful… complete exclusion of both wind noise and sounds of passage over rough surfaces as well as silencing of engine and transmission".

They also stressed the value for money, and, if there wasn't much profit, the prestige made the effort worthwhile for Rootes. It must have been pleasing to Billy and other members of the family to find rows of Pullmans on duty when attending official functions at home and overseas.

Production: *1948* 608 (est); *1949* 5,000 (est); *1950* 5,000 (est); *1951* 4,553; *1952* 3,829; *1953* 255.

SUPER SNIPE IV 1952-1956
IMPERIAL & PULLMAN IV 1953-1954

Retrospective opinion has not been kind to the last Super Snipe introduced in October 1952, but by what standard has the car been judged? Different sources record different production figures but they all confirm that the MkIV far outsold other British 3½- to 4-litre cars with the exception of Jaguar and Armstrong-Siddeley. In the period 1952-1955 the figures for the A135 Austin Princess, the remaining A125 Sheerlines (production was ending), the R-type Bentley and the various larger Daimlers were all below 3,000.

There was obviously still a market for a larger car than the Hawk and the previous Super Snipe had built up a powerful reputation on which to trade. To design from scratch would have eaten into capital resources so Rootes, as before, did what they could with existing components. The basic Hawk chassis was strengthened and extended at both ends to support the larger and heavier engine and the cavernous new luggage compartment, but was only reinforced in the centre section. So the car was conceived with a major shortcoming. Use of the Hawk centre section dictated a Hawk-size cabin and there was no more passenger room than in the smaller car. Although the seats and engine were further forward, so that the weight distribution became 53/47 biased to the front (which some preferred), the measurement from dashboard to the backrest of the rear seat was 4in less and the rear seat width 2in less than the previous MkIII Super Snipe. The 4,139cc ohv six was already used in Commer trucks and designed for a hard long life. Some customers, particularly in countries where fuel was cheap,

Rootes family at Scottish Motor Show. From the left: Brian, Tim, Desmond, Geoffrey, Reginald and Billy.

Moss and Cutts (front), Johnson and Humphrey (back), with the Super Snipe Mk IV at Villar Formoso on the Portugese border 3 days and 18 hours after leaving Oslo in 1952.

bought the car because of these engine features. There was, for instance, an additional groove in the pistons so that at high mileages an extra oil-control ring could be fitted instead of reboring. Others baulked at the higher initial and petrol cost when there was no gain in accommodation – and in any event the Hawk was by then so much improved.

D.E. Copping wrote from Perth, Western Australia: "After owning reliable and comfortable American cars for years I took delivery of a Hawk in England four years ago (he was writing in 1954; that would have been the 1,944cc sidevalve). It has given wonderful service as a family car for urban use and occasional long country runs. The need for a new car arose and I awaited with interest the arrival of the new Super Snipe. It had the power, it had the weight; it had everything except the seating space which was needed. This beautiful machine had the same seating capacity as the Hawk! That just does not make sense in this country where British manufacturers have still not produced the car that many require: It has to be large, powerful, reliable, easily serviced and able to carry six adults comfortably over long distance on roads ranging from first class asphalt to badly corrugated bush tracks".

Did Rootes miss another opportunity? It wouldn't have been easy to extend the centre of the chassis in the way that seven-seater limousines have been concocted from modern monocoque structures like Carltons and Granadas, but ingenious "cutting and shutting" of the Pressed Steel shell by the Thrupp & Maberley subsidiary might have pushed the rear seat and the rear window back without spoiling the lines.

There is also evidence that the cars were not trouble-free. In the only recorded private journey (written up by Frances Howell in *The Motor*) the Snipe had to be taken to the Zurich agents with an engine knock. They found a faulty piston. En route to Afghanistan in 1955 we had contact with oil company managers in the Middle East.

S. Hall and I. Luke with Mk IV Super Snipe at the end of the 1953 6,500 mile Round-Australia trial. They were not placed but another Super Snipe nearly won and these cars were 1st and 3rd in the large car class.

George Murray Frame made a massive effort in the speed test on the Monaco circuit to retain his 9th place in 1954, but the Super Snipe's 4-litre engine was too great a handicap in a formula which related engine size to performance.

When I spoke of working for Rootes I was told of how they had lost patience with niggling faults in patriotically ordered MkIVs and gratefully returned to Chevrolets. Yet individual cars showed the model's potential. In December 1952 the Hinchcliffe team (co-drivers were R. Walshaw and C. Longman) got to Cape Town in a record-breaking 13½ days, 8½ days quicker than their earlier Minx journey. After just 24 hours rest they set off homewards again and were reported ahead of the outgoing schedule when they split the sump on a Sahara rock. (There and back in 27 days would have been only 3 days longer than the A70's one-way record in 1950!)

The same month saw Norman Garrad's own publicity effort for the car. There weren't enough MkIVs built for an entry in the 1953 Monte. They thought of and rejected an attempt at London to Moscow and finally decided on 15 countries in 5 days with Moss, Johnson, Cutts and Humphrey in the crew. At the Oslo start the temperature was 18 degrees below freezing. Down through Copenhagen, Hamburg and Maastricht there was thick slippery ice and heavy snow. They were over the Julier Pass before the snow ploughs which meant forcing through drifts, chains on and in bottom gear. By the start of the Autostrada at Bergamo they were behind

time and soon had the Super Snipe cruising at over 90mph. As they caught up they realised the alternative 4-day schedule might still be attainable. For the last three hours, past Valladolid and through Salamanca, Johnson averaged 64mph (and just avoided meandering donkeys which came out from behind some rocks to cross the road in front of the Humber batting along at an indicated 95). They crossed the Portugese border having driven 3,352 miles in 3 days 18 hours. It was all good material for the copy-writers but why didn't they include Andorra and cut out the diversion to Yugoslavia?

Subsequent Monte efforts did not produce a good European placing (though Murray-Frame was 9th at the end of the road section in 1954), but the car's inherent strength was demonstrated by those tough Australian drivers in the Redex reliability trials. Robinson so nearly won the 1953 6,500-mile trial just one point behind the leading Peugeot 203. In the longer 9,600-mile 1954 trial Sulman finished 5th, and 2nd in the big car class to winner Jack Murray's Ford V8. MkIVs travelled the world. There were many Super Snipes amongst the 57 Rootes cars supplied for the 1954 Royal Tour including seven specially converted cabriolets which were sent to Aden, Australia and Ceylon. Sixty-three saloons were delivered to the Chinese government in 1956.

Meanwhile development at the factory was not neglected. By 1956 engine power had been increased to 130bhp. Automatic and overdrive were both available. The magazines had differing opinions after both testing the same car. *The Autocar* wrote that "the car did not produce any physical driving fatigue even after very long periods at the wheel". It handled well and they liked the steering. *The Motor* commented on the low-geared steering: "For easy parking with a heavy car it is inevitable that the steering will be rather indirect, but this effect is magnified by a springiness in the linkage. Despite this there is still a strong reaction at the wheel on a bad surface, whilst the car is rather slow to answer its helm". Both magazines experienced brake fade after repeated crash stops. The need for power steering and disc brakes for larger cars was now strongly evident.

From May 1953 the long chassis Imperial and Pullman version of the previous MkIII, already described, also had this "truck" engine, so it was possible to buy an ohv 6-8 seater. The trouble was it wasn't quite what D.E. Copping and his compatriots had in mind. They didn't want to charge over the Australian landscape in a vehicle that was 15 inches longer than the Super Snipe, had the rear seats on top of the rear axle and a turning circle of 48 feet (compared with the smaller car's 40 feet). Would Rootes have done better if they had based an ohv MkIV Snipe on that longer version of the older chassis, using the extra length to bring the rear seats and the luggage forward? They could then have cut down the rear overhang and worked to reduce the turning circle.

Production (combined): *1952* 178; *1953* 3,184; *1954* 2,776; *1955* 2,508; *1956* 1,481.

Pick-up version of Mk IV Super Snipe built for Middle East oil companies and others.

HUMBER ACHIEVEMENTS

1949
London-Gibralter & return Super Snipe Drophead: I. Boswell.

1950
Monte Carlo Super Snipe: M. Gatsonides 2nd.

1951
Monte Carlo Hawk: R. Carter, K. Carter, R. Braid, Best Team rally-type coachwork & Best radio-equipped team: Concours de Confort. Super Snipe: Captain R. Minchin 56th (Metropolitan Police).
London-New Zealand Hawk: Miss J. Whitehorn.

1952
Monte Carlo Super Snipe: M. Gatsonides 42nd.
RAC Super Snipe: W. McKenzie 7th in class, J. Tew 9th in class.
London-Cape Town Super Snipe: G. Hinchcliffe, 13½ days (Record).
Oslo-Lisbon Super Snipe: S. Moss, 15 countries in 4 days.

1953
Round Australia Super Snipe: Robinson 2nd, 1st in class; Masling 3rd in class.
Safari Hawk: E. Temple Boreham 4th.

1954
Monte Carlo Super Snipe: G. Murray-Frame 26th, J. Skeggs 88th (Metropolitan Police).
Round Australia Super Snipe: Sulman 5th, Lane 17th.

1955
Monte Carlo Hawk: J. Skeggs 163rd (Metropolitan Police).
Round Australia Super Snipe: W. Rudder 3rd in class.
Australian Mobilgas Economy Hawk: A. Peck 2nd, 1st in class.

1956
Monte Carlo Super Snipe: H. Shillabeer 160th (Metropolitan Police).
Convoy to Corinthia Miss F. Howell.

INVICTA

What was it that drove British engineers and entrepreneurs to create individual designs which could then only be put on sale at a high price? I grew up in a home where my father had the same objective in the aircraft industry. Simply put, British engineers who served their apprenticeship in the '20s were taught to look for the best engineering solutions. The analogy of the playing field suggested that, if a team strove to excel, they would be rewarded by success. Thus, if a machine which had been created had the best possible features, it was assumed that it would be purchased. Competitors were not seen as a threat. It was thought that the market was limitless and that it would benefit the customer to have maximum choice. It was the likes of Billy Rootes who took a fundamentally different approach. They studied the market, not engineering ideals – what would customers want? What could they afford?

The postwar Invicta team had particular reasons for their individual approach. At a London lunch to christen the new car on 12th November 1946, chairman F.H. Mabley revealed that the original intention had been to build a steam-powered vehicle: "Only after this had been investigated to the full was it decided to aim for steam-type performance with a petrol engine. Therefore it was a logical development which led to two-pedal control, both clutch and gears being regulated automatically". William Watson, who had previously worked on the design of Noel Macklin's pre-war Invicta at Cobham, had left Lagonda and joined the new Invicta Car Development Co. Ltd based at Virginia Water. Four years of unrelenting effort and hard work only led to a short run of "Black Princes". On 23rd January 1950 Mr Justice Wynn-Parry in the Chancery Court heard the petition from JHM Components Ltd, and ordered the compulsory winding up of the company. He rejected Invicta's counter-petition to keep going by a "scheme of arrange-ment" and agreed reduction of capital. Historians have suggested that £100,000 was lost and it is tempting to comment with hindsight that it might have been better for Britain if Watson had remained with Lagonda and the money had been invested in that company.

For the record Noel Macklin was never involved in this postwar company, but his ideas and talents are remembered. He died, aged 57, just two days before the Black Prince's christening, worn out by his heroic efforts first advocating and then overseeing the production of wartime motor torpedo boats. Churchill recommended his knight-hood in 1944. Sammy Davis wrote in *The Autocar*: "There was literally no difficulty which Macklin would agree was a difficulty, while disagreement, though at times intense, left no ill-feeling."

BLACK PRINCE 1946-1950

Like the Lagonda, the Black Prince had a cruciform frame, inboard rear brakes, and four-wheel independent suspension; but components and design details were different. As well as the cruciform, the frame had side members along whose outer face ran the four torsion bars to adjustable attachment points in the centre of the car. The suspension links and other parts were so arranged that both front and rear wheels remained vertical over disturbances. A serrated collar at the outboard end of the steering arm fitted over a spline on the suspension assembly. This spline allowed the wheels to move up and down whilst the position of the steering arm remained constant, and steering precision was thus enhanced. On the early chassis the mechanism was rack and pinion but on the display chassis shown at Geneva in 1948 Bishop cam steering had been substituted.

The 2,998cc six-cylinder twin overhead camshaft power unit came from Henry

The Invicta at Virginia Water in 1946. This is the Wentworth saloon body built by Charlesworth.

Meadows, supplier to the pre-war Invicta. This engine certainly looked the part, with each polished valve cover secured by 28 chromed nuts, 12 sparking plugs (two per cylinder) and three SU carburettors (five if you count the two starting carburettors); but its output was only 120bhp and it had to cope with the inevitable power losses of the Brockhouse "turbo-transmitter". In this new type of automatic transmission the ratio between engine input and propellor shaft was varied by the interaction of impeller, turbines and reaction rotor. The engine and impeller turned at high speed when the car started, or was on a severe gradient, then gradually the turbines speeded up. When all components were turning at the same speed it was the equivalent of top gear. The clutch was electrically operated via a solenoid and there was a separate gear train for reverse. It was yet another praiseworthy British endeavour but soon overshadowed by American efforts. The Brockhouse needed more development. Sometimes the driver would find himself stuck in reverse and there was no form of kick-down or "hold" to cope with growing traffic volumes.

Inevitably all this complication meant a price way up near Bentley money. Those early purchasers deserved a medal for their support of innovation. The Wentworth saloon was built by Charlesworth before the financial problems which led to the Lea-Francis takeover. Airflow Streamlines built the Byfleet drophead and Jensen also built some bodies. In *The Motor* (11th May 1949) there is a picture of another drophead by Ronald Kent Coachbuilders shown just before shipment to South Africa, and in recent years this car has been restored in Australia. Noel Tuckey writing in Classic & Sportscar magazine tells of others in India, Holland, Norway and California plus three still in the UK. Because so few were built there was little recorded owner experience, but there was one letter in *The Motor* signed by "Facile Princeps" from Guisborough, Yorkshire: "Having just collected my Invicta from London, I consider that the two-pedal control is, without doubt, the greatest contribution to safe motoring since the introduction of four-wheel brakes. I have been driving since 1922 but have never experienced anything comparable to the joy of handling this car". The picture with the letter showed that this was a two-door Jensen drophead. Watson's solo effort pleased at least one owner, though for how long is not known! If the rich had been unfettered and the transmission more fully developed, more niche sales might have been achieved. The cars were not entered in rallies.

Production: Approx. 15.

JOWETT

The Jowett story is an example of the second category of companies outlined in the first chapter. When the founder departed, there was no one single personality with both the vision and the invincible controlling position to push and pull the enterprise through the next stage of development to a stable future. Charles Calcott-Reilly, who took over as managing director in 1939 when William Jowett left (brother Benjamin had retired in 1936, the year after Jowett became a public company), was so nearly that man. He had the vision, as we shall see when describing the Javelin, and he successfully managed the wartime production of engines and munitions, with Harry Woodhead as chairman from 1942. He also saw that bodies would have to be made by an outside firm and from pressed steel, which would involve heavy tooling costs. Negotiations were completed with Briggs Bodies, who wanted work for their wartime Doncaster plant, and an allocation of steel was eventually agreed. But Calcott-Reilly did not have an invincible power base. He remained an employee when Charles Clore bought William and Benjamin's shares and control of the company in 1947. He was still an employee when he fell out with these new masters and was forced to depart at the end of 1948.

Then Frank Salter, who had devised the ingenious assembly procedure whereby the body from Briggs was turned upside-down for the fitment of mechanical parts, was also sacked because there were too many delays. (At least he was brought back as technical director by Jopling in 1952.) The following year Calcott-Reilly's protegé, designer Gerald Palmer, accepted the offer of a senior design post back with Morris. Whilst Harry Woodhead, a loyal Jowett servant who had started as company secretary in 1919 and who was in John Baldwin's words "a big shrewd man, slow-moving and speaking, the prototype of all Yorkshiremen", remained as a competent administrator, the men who had so carefully plotted the company's postwar course, and had a personal commitment to its success were no longer on the scene. Lazards then purchased Clore's shares and George Wansbrough, an energetic, well-known establishment figure and motor car enthusiast (he later helped finance the Gordon-Keeble) became chairman. Wansbrough made use of his contacts in the City and industry to further Jowett's interests, and had approved the Jupiter project when he became the subject of adverse press comment over other share dealings. This upset the Jowett Board. Though nominally their chief he was so only by appointment, and was dismissed.

I have written of Leonard Lord's failings but Jowett badly needed a character with both his determination and his position of strength within the company. There are enough problems with dictatorships but they can be preferable to this sort of ever-changing control. In 1950 Lazards appointed Arthur Jopling as managing director and he was to stay to the end, with Harry Woodhead as chairman until he reached retiring age in 1952.

Jopling was an experienced accountant and, as Lazards' man, his priority had to be safeguarding their investment. At the end of 1952, with over 1,000 Javelins and bodies stockpiled at the factory, he remained true to his profession and took the cautious decision which ultimately did safeguard that investment but also made it more difficult for the company to continue. He cancelled 500 of the Javelin bodies still on order from Briggs and suspended the further order for 5,000 bodies for the replacement to the Bradford (see next section) designated the CD. He wanted, or was told by Lazards, to sell off those Javelins and repay the company's debts to Briggs and others before agreeing to further production.

C. Calcott-Reilly, Managing Director, outside the London showrooms in Albemarle Street with an early Javelin in 1947.

In early March 1953 Briggs asked again about CD production, for which they had by then completed the tooling. Jopling, still the figure-conscious accountant, replied that he must wait till the account was cleared, hopefully by May. This was achieved with a cheque for £70,000 sent to Briggs on 22nd May. It was too late. When Jopling visited Briggs (now under Ford control), he was told that it would be uneconomic to make more Javelin bodies and that a much larger order was needed before they could embark on CD production. All too soon the stockpile of Javelin bodies, which had seemed such a burden the year before, was used up. The car, now much improved through the efforts of Donald Bastow (appointed chief engineer the previous August) and the rest of the engineering and development team, remained in demand.

The R4 Jupiter (see next section) also languished when Roy Lunn was headhunted by Ford. If those extra 500 Javelin bodies had not been cancelled it might, with something to build meanwhile, have been worth making the larger commitment to the CD. Or was this the outcome that Lazards hoped for? They were spared from further financial commitment.

In March 1954 the Oak Mills Plant was sold to the British Wool Board and in October the Idle factory was taken over complete with employees and machine tools by the International Harvester Company for the manufacture of a light tractor. Contemporary reports stated that no one lost money and bills were paid. Arthur Jopling did his job. A new company, Jowett Engineering, then provided parts and service for another ten years. At least International Harvester was an appropriate successor. Their robust 1906 "high wheelers" had been specifically designed like the Jowett to give reliable service in harsh rural conditions, and also had a flat-twin engine.

BRADFORD CA, CB, CC & CD 1946-1953

Before the first world war the Jowett brothers had created a tough, reliable sidevalve flat twin in their Bradford workshop. Until 1939 this engine powered a series of cars and vans with simple Jowett-built bodies, and delighted owners by its abilities on Yorkshire gradients. From 1937 a sidevalve flat-four was also available.

By 1944 it was becoming clear that the Javelin would take time to develop, and as already described, the cry was for immediate exports. It was decided to reintroduce the twin as a commercial vehicle available with van and platform bodies to be built by Briggs, the van with a simple ash frame, aluminium panels and a fabric roof. It was christened the Bradford. This book is about cars but the van was the success story that made Javelin production possible. Bradfords were widely exported, and were assembled from CKD packs in Australia and New Zealand. In time a utility (i.e. estate car) version with rear seats and side windows became available. Over the years the Bradford was revised with more engine power and improvements to the cooling and electrical systems, but by the '50s it was becoming dated.

In 1952 the prototype of the Bradford's successor, the CD, was on the road. The chassis was designed by Roy Lunn, helped by Phil Stephenson, with Javelin-style torsion bar front suspension and leaf rear springs. Plans were made for a full range of vehicles. Vans, pick-ups and economy saloons were to have an overhead inlet valve development of the flat twin, saloons and estate cars the flat-four Javelin engine. Briggs pressed on with the tooling, ten pre-production vehicles were ordered, and it was hoped that production would start early in 1954. But then, as described, Jopling hesitated. In his determination to avoid financial disaster, the chance of a promising future was lost.

Production: *1946* 4,280; *1948* 8,920; *1949* 6,095; *1950* 3,558; *1951* 3,576; *1952* 4,444; *1953* 139.

JAVELIN 1947-1953

The Javelin was Calcott-Reilly's vision. Was it possible to combine good roadholding and a comfortable ride in an economical six-seater which cost less than £500? In the middle of the war, in 1942, he advertised for a new designer. It was Gerald Palmer, then at Morris and who had worked with Issigonis on flat-four engines, who was eventually persuaded to accept the challenge and sketch out a completely new layout. Palmer had

Tulip Rally 1953. Count Van Zuylen Van Nyevelt (1st in Jowett Javelin) congratulated by 2nd-placed J.W.E. (Bill) Banks (in Bristol).

been in Africa before the war and well understood the need for toughness, good ground clearance and plenty of room without bulk. All this was brilliantly achieved with rear seat well forward of the rear wheels yet there was still 5ft 6in from screen to rear backrest on a wheelbase of 8ft 6in (the same measurement on the 9ft 9in wheelbase Humber Super Snipe was only 5ft 3in!). Ground clearance was nearly 8in. The suspension was outstanding. Palmer chose to use torsion bars front and rear mounted across the car and carefully attached to the strong box section components of the frame. There are no references to problems with this suspension. Effective torsion bars did not overload the new-style telescopic shock absorbers. Initial tests in *The Motor* reported: "The Jowett was outstandingly comfortable on rough roads at all speeds and rode even bad pavé with complete absence of shock and pitch. Performance on corners falls below the standard of a modern sports car but is considerably superior to a normal family saloon." Steering followed earlier Jowett practise, with a pinion meshing with an internally-toothed drum-like gear, i.e. the equivalent of a semi-circular rack with most of a rack's precision but using less space.

Few other designers have been in Palmer's position. Even Issigonis had an existing proven power unit and gearbox available for the Morris Minor after his proposed flat four was dropped. Jowett had used a 1,166cc side-valve of this configuration before the war, but more power was needed. Palmer kept the basic layout but enlarged the engine to 1,500cc and redesigned it with overhead valves. He did not get it right. As an older and wiser Palmer admitted in a 1990 inter-view, "I'm not proud of that engine. Had I known that the horsepower tax was to be replaced by a flat rate tax, I would have designed a shot-stroke, larger bore unit which would have been much more compact

Miss F. Grounds poses on bonnet of Javelin in Paris during 1952 Monte Carlo Rally.

and lighter with better combustion and a larger power output." Again engineering ideals had been affected by Westminster decisions.

The engine was satisfactory on test but as mileages built up on customers' cars, often hard driven as the design encouraged, defects became evident. Oil temperature was too high, water flow was poor, and both bear-ings and head gaskets failed. Joseph Lowrey of *The Motor* took his own Javelin to Barcelona via Andorra in 1950. Every spares kit for continental touring issued by Jowett included a full set of bearing shells and, sure enough, those for the big ends had to be fitted halfway through the trip. Paul Clark and Edmund Nankivell's comprehensive Jowett history tells how the engineering and development department headed by Charles Grandfield and Horace Grimley (with input from Roy Lunn, who had taken Gerald Palmer's place) struggled to sort out these problems, but it all took time.

Nor was it only the engine. The Javelin used the pre-war gearbox. Until 1951 these were built by Meadows and had a tendency to jump out of third. There were further prob-lems with the later Jowett-built 'boxes, some sticking in and jumping out of gear, others even seizing. Clark and Nankivell's book records that 10% failed on test and that even early in 1952 the service department reported that 150 home market owners were waiting for new gearboxes. Most of the prob-lems were solved when new tools were pur-chased, but again it was too late. Further-more, the car was never on sale for as little as Calcott-Reilly's planned £500.

Many of the competition entries started with low-mileage engines and often the cars were specially prepared at the factory – on occasions too carefully! After the 1953 Tulip Rally Becquart's Javelin was disqualified from a leading position because of non-stan-dard details, though in fact this gave victory to Nijevelt in another Javelin. The earlier successes at Monte Carlo and in other rallies encouraged buyers from all over the world who appreciated the combination of roadholding and comfort. But they were not so happy when, after a period of use, they were left with a car in the garage awaiting a new engine or gearbox. John Baldwin, who became responsible for the London offices and publicity, tells of "taking the latest press car, more or less handbuilt so far as bearings, selected gearbox and latest radiator" to Switzerland in 1949. After sorting out dealer problems, he visited a Swiss professor who lived part way up the Forclaz Pass, one of the steepest in Europe, and whose Javelin was not coping. After pacifying the Professor by promising to send new parts to the latest modified specification Baldwin commented that the Javelin needed "an oil cooler, bigger bearings, a bigger sump, a bigger radiator, a bigger fan, and probably a bigger engine to drive it"! Harry Ainsworth, who acted as consultant to Jowett after retirement from Hotchkiss in 1950 and had experience of the flat-four Grégoire, is reported as saying that "all flat engines were restricted in sump size and that 'dry sump' lubrication and oil coolers were necessary but expensive answers".

In fact by the end of 1952 the car was "right" having benefited both from Donald Bastow's immense experience (he had worked with Henry Royce and W.O. Bentley) and Charles Grandfield's work for the Series III engine (see Jupiter). In November three saloons had averaged 60mph for 30,000 miles on a circuit laid out on the airfield which now contains the MIRA test track. All Javelins then had an oil cooler, but it had not been found necessary to pipe oil separately to each bearings as in a "dry sump". *The Motor* tested a Javelin in April 1953: "The purpose of the extended trip abroad was to check the claim that every substantial weakness has been eliminated. The whole 27-mile length of the Ghent-Ostend motor road was covered without the speed falling below 75mph, the engine idling normally with correct oil pressure after a final mile at full throttle and over 80. Having completed the 2,500 mile journey without doing anything save pour in petrol and a little

oil we are pleased to record that those claims for true reliability show every sign of being justified."

Alas! This was published just months before Arthur Jopling failed to negotiate a further supply of Javelin bodies. At least the continuing modifications, particularly to crankshafts suggested by Bastow and others, were available on service replacement parts for owners like W. Lewis who remained faithful to their Javelins after production ceased. He wrote from High Wycombe: "Suppose Jowett owners put £10 in the kitty for the use of the firm. Would it suffice for production to continue? I will be pleased to contribute and expect to save money on second-hand value if ever I have to part with my Javelin. The people who produced this car deserve such a gesture."

Production: *1947* 30; *1948* 1,525; *1949* 5,406; *1950* 5,313; *1951* 5,658; *1952* 3,675; *1953* 2,021.

JUPITER MKI, MKIA, R1 & R4 1950-1954

The continuing cry for exports (and the fact that success meant more steel) led Jowett to investigate a sports car using Javelin mechanical components. Leslie Johnson had purchased what remained of E.R.A. Ltd from Humphrey Cook and hoped to build up an independent design and research organisation. Pre-war Auto-Union designer Eberan von Eberhorst was unemployed in Italy. Lawrence Pomeroy, with his many contacts, and Anthony Hume (driver of the class-winning Javelin at Spa) were instrumental in bringing Johnson and Eberhorst together at Dunstable, E.R.A.'s new headquarters, and a new, light, tubular chassis was on display at the 1949 Show. There were artist's impressions of the new E.R.A.-Javelin coupé but it was never produced. Wilfred Sainsbury, Lazards' representative on the Jowett board after Wansbrough's departure, would not agree to Johnson's plan to build the new coupé on a royalty basis and the deal was off.

A Jupiter poses on Waterloo bridge in front of a City skyline devoid of skyscrapers.

The new sports car, christened Jupiter, was to be built by Jowett themselves. Roy Lunn, helped by Charles Grandfield's development team, cobbled together a revised design which was heavier and many thought less attractive than the E.R.A. offering. It was saved by the Javelin-style roadholding. Despite Reg Korner's touring rather than sports body style, the decision was taken to race the car and hopefully in the process sort out remaining engine weaknesses. A standard but lightened Jupiter was entered for the 1950 Le Mans and Wisdom and Wise managed to win the 1½-litre class. A blown cylinder head gasket on the way back to Bradford was an indication of problems to come. Three months later Tom Wisdom was out of the Tourist Trophy with the crankshaft broken, wrongly reported in *The Autocar* as another head gasket.

For Le Mans in 1951 there was the first of the new R1s with slim body, cycle-type wings and bug headlights attached to the bonnet sides, and two standard but lightened cars. Engines had been improved with better lubri-

cation and stronger crankshafts. The R1 did blow a gasket after a cylinder head stud lifted and Hadley's standard car was stopped when a valve retaining collar broke, but Becquart and Wilkins again won their class with the other standard car. The bug-eyed R1 then went to America and redeemed itself in the hands of George Weaver by winning the Queen Catharine Cup race for 1½-litre cars at the Watkins Glen Sports Car Meeting in September. It was only 73 miles but "the Jupiter pulled so far away from the field (MGs, HRGs, Fiats, Crosleys and specials) that Weaver could not see who was following".

For the 1952 Le Mans there were three of the next generation R1s, identified by the new headlight mounting between the wing and the body. Becquart and Wilkins achieved the hat-trick for Jowett, winning the 1½-litre class for the third time, but only just. The crankshaft broke on the other R1s, but Becquart's French blue machine had been given a new engine after practice troubles. Phil Green had the task of driving the survivor back to England, a change from taking development Javelins over his Yorkshire test circuit. He remembers being told to exercise restraint, no easy task when the blue car's

racer appearance encouraged challenges from other sporting drivers. Idle was reached without mishap but, when the engine was taken down and the crack detector applied, hairline cracks were evident all over the crank.

Jupiters coped well with less strenuous rally conditions. In 1951, Becquart's Farina-bodied car was 5th and 2nd in class to a Simca. In 1953 the rear fan mounting broke and the radiator was holed on the regularity circuit when Becquart was in a leading position with the same car.

These experiences were put to good use back at the factory, and appropriate modifications were incorporated in the Series III engine available in the Jupiter 1A in 1952. Revised oilways fed into a larger capacity oil

TOP LEFT Unidentified Alpine Rally Jupiter, possibly John Gott in 1952. TOP RIGHT Alf Thomas driving the all-steel prototype R4 Jupiter on Beggars' Roost during the MCC Land's End Trial, Easter 1955. ABOVE R1 Jupiter, as raced at Le Mans, in front of a surfeit of completed Javelins. Bradford vans and "Spion Kop" behind.

pump, better cylinder head seals eased pressure on gaskets made from a new compound, a stiffer crankcase supported a redesigned stiffer crankshaft and Vandervell's new three-layer bearings (indium on copper-lead on steel) were incorporated.

The 1A also had an opening luggage boot and larger hood. It can be distinguished by the deletion of the moulding on the rear wing. *The Autocar*'s testers were pleased with this version in January 1953: "It is a safe car on snow and ice, amusing for the driver who appreciates the finer points of handling. The steering has been greatly improved, more sensitive and more accurate, and gives the driver the feel of the road without more than minor tremors on rough surfaces. Fast cornering is a pleasure and stability good in side winds."

This second edition was a competent machine, but it was a complicated design which would have had to be sold at a higher price than the market would accept to produce profits for the company. The Jupiter chassis was a better proposition when sold to the specialist coachbuilders. Bodies were built by Beutler, Farina, Ghia and Worblaufen, and in England by Abbott, Armstrong, Coachcraft, Farr and Richard Mead.

At the end of 1952 Donald Bastow and Roy Lunn started on Jowett's last project, a simpler Jupiter, the R4, to be built by Jowett themselves, if possible using the new developments in fibreglass. The car was based on a shortened CD chassis with the latest Series III engine. Phil Stephenson did the styling and one all-metal body was built. The Dibenzoyl peroxide hardener which we purchase today with fibreglass kits had not been developed and it took an age to cure the new plastic panels. Phil Green recalls taking an extra boot lid to display alongside the exhibition part-fibreglass R4 at Earl's Court in 1953. When he returned to the stand on Monday he found that it still had not cooked properly and the paint was peeling. A more positive memory was of the reaction to demonstration rides in the metal R4, which after completion in July (seven months' work!) had been thoroughly tested by Roy Lunn on a proving run to Italy. Phil reckons that thousands could have been sold at the suggested list price (with purchase tax) of £773. But the R4 was never available for sale. Before it was ready for production Lunn had departed and negotiations with International Harvester were under way.

Production (no separate year totals) – MkI: 736. **MkIA:** 95. **R1:** 4. **R4:** 3. **Chassis:** 68.

JOWETT ACHIEVEMENTS

1948
Eastbourne Javelin: S. Lawry 1st class award.

1949
Monte Carlo Javelin: T. Wise 14th, 1st in class; R. Smith 22nd, 3rd in class.
Eastbourne Javelin: C. Turner 1st in class.
Lisbon Javelin: T. Wise 2nd in class.
Spa 24 Hours Javelin: T. Wisdom 1st in class.

1950
Monte Carlo Javelin: T. Wise 44th.
MCC 1000 Miles Javelin: E. Farrington 15th, S. Wilton 20th.
Le Mans Jupiter (standard but lightened body): T. Wisdom 16th, 1st in class.

1951
Monte Carlo Jupiter: R. Ellison 6th, 1st in class. Javelin: L. Odell 26th, Ellison, Wilkins, Odell, Team Prize.
RAC Javelin: J. Van der Mark 2nd in class, S. Ginn 4th in class, Dr. J. Spare 5th in class. Jupiter: M. Becquart 4th in class, A. Imhof 5th in class.
Lisbon Jupiter: Nogueira 1st.
Tulip Jupiter: W. Robinson 16th.
Alpine Javelin: Dr. T. Smallhorn 5th in class.
Le Mans Jupiter (standard but lightened body): M. Becquart 23rd, 1st in class.
Watkins Glen *Queen Catherine's Cup* Jupiter R.1: G. Weaver 1st.
TT Jupiter: L. Hadley 1st in class, T. Wise 2nd in class.

1952
Monte Carlo Jupiter Farina: M. Becquart 5th, 2nd in class; J. Latune 58th. Javelin: G. Norlander 16th, A. Foster 37th.
RAC Javelin: M. Becquart 1st closed cars. Jupiter Special body: E. Booth 15th open cars.
Lisbon Javelin: Mrs N. Mitchell, Coupe des Dames.
Economy Run Javelin: G. Wilkins 1st 67.8mpg.
Le Mans Jupiter R.1.: M. Becquart 13th, 1st in class.

1953
Monte Carlo Jupiter F. Grounds 36th, J. Latune 46th, M. Becquart 98th. Javelin: A. Foster 95th, H. Brooke 96th.
RAC Javelin: E. Elliot 19th, 1st in class.
MCC Daily Express Jupiter: A. Gordon 8th, 3rd in class.
Tulip Javelin: Graf Van Zuylen-Van Nijevelt 1st, 1st in class; J. Scheffer 8th, 2nd in class; O. Homan 25th, 3rd in class. Nijevelt, Scheffer, Homan, Team Prize.
Economy Run Javelin: J. Lowrey 1st 65.9mpg.
MCC Exeter Trial Bradford: F. Dennis 3rd class Award.
Redex Round-Australia Javelin: D. Gorringe 45th.

1954
RAC Javelin: F. Dundas 37th, 1st in class.
Tulip Javelin: G. Willing 3rd in class.

LAGONDA

The Lagonda name is another which is not in oblivion. It has been used by successive owners of Aston Martin and may be used by Ford, but the company did not achieve its admirable post-1945 objectives, and its story is a telling example of the misapplication of resources in the postwar decade. Advanced thinking was coming from experienced engineers working for the smaller firms buoyed up in the short term by war profits but without the funds for unrelenting development and quantity production. Meanwhile larger firms were taking safer paths which would serve them well in a seller's market but leave them less well prepared to take on the world in the second postwar decade.

Founder Wilbur Gunn started work in 1900, adopting "Lagonda" from La Ohonda Creek near his home town, Springfield, Ohio. Gunn was followed by Colin Parbury and then Brigadier-General Metcalfe. After the popular monocled General's death (and money problems), a young solicitor backed by City friends bought the company in 1935, outbidding Rolls-Royce and Alvis. That solicitor was Alan Good and he brought the talent to the Staines factory. Richard Watney, who had been at Rootes, joined as managing director. He had driven the second-place Speed Six Bentley with Frank Clement at Le Mans in 1930 and was thus able to approach W.O. Bentley, who agreed to leave Rolls-Royce. W.O. in turn got hold of Stewart Tresilian, who had been with him at Rolls, and Charles Sewell who had been with the original Bentley Company and then gone to Napier. Percy Kemish, a former Bentley mechanic, came from Squire; and Frank Feeley, who had joined Lagonda at the age of sixteen, returned as body designer. Together they created the short-stroke V12, ignoring the restrictive horsepower tax in favour of a more efficient engine. With Charles Brackenbury and Mortimer Morris-Goodall, Alan Good took a luxurious V12 drophead from Tallinn to achieve 39th place at Monte Carlo in the 1939 Rally. They had been delayed by a faulty condenser but went on to achieve good times in both the acceleration and braking test and the Eze hill-climb, and then won the Concours de Confort for convertible bodies. Later in the year Brackenbury and Dobson and the Lords Selsdon and Waleran were 3rd and 4th at Le Mans in V12s fitted with light two-seater bodies.

Lagonda was riding high by the outbreak of war, and made their full contribution from 1939 to 1945. It now seems a less praiseworthy achievement, but they designed one of the first transportable flamethrowers and went on to develop the Wasp and Crocodile models which did their bit for destruction! On their own production line they also assembled 6-pounder anti-tank gun carriages. Meanwhile, in any spare time, Watney and W.O., assisted by William Watson before he returned to Invicta (Tresilian had left for other work) planned a postwar range which would be suitable for world markets. Together with Watson's solo effort at Invicta, the Black Prince, they were the only UK manufacturers who saw the need for four-wheel independent suspension and did something about it. After the war Donald Bastow left Rolls-Royce to join Lagonda, and became W.O.'s assistant. (One of his tasks, after Royce's death, was the evolution of independent front suspension for the pre-war Wraith and Phantom III).

The new chassis with coil springs and rack and pinion steering at the front and torsion bars at the back could, with development, have become as good as or better than anything Mercedes was to offer before the '60s. There were to be three models with four-, six- and eight-cylinder derivatives of the same basic design. The LB six-cylinder prototype saloon styled by Feeley was on the road by the end of 1945 and an application for steel was despatched to the Ministry of Supply.

LPF 775, the second of the two saloons which David Brown and party took to Europe in 1948. It was then used by the organisation for transporting VIPs, etc.

Watney and W.O. were confident they would soon be setting up production lines with body panels from Briggs at Dagenham, but then came the response from the Ministry. Lagonda would only be allocated steel for 100 bodies and such a short run made no sense to Briggs. This denial of longer-term supplies put off the few other body-builders who were not contracted to or controlled by rival manufacturers. The next blow came from the Law Courts in 1946 when Rolls-Royce won an action proving their ownership of the Bentley name. The LB6 could not be called a Lagonda-Bentley. Alan Good and his financier colleagues had had enough, their legal costs alone £10,000. Good resigned in March 1947 and six months later Petter, one of his other industrial interests, bought the Staines factory.

The prototypes and work in hand were put up for sale. Rootes thought about it (that engine might have made a good Super Snipe) and so did Jaguar. Eventually the remains of Lagonda were purchased by David Brown, housed in some of the aircraft hangers at Hanworth, and then amalgamated with Aston Martin nearby at Feltham. Brown realised that the smooth overhead camshaft six would make a superb power unit for the Aston. In the '50s W.O., although retired from the industry after consultancy work (still assisted by Bastow) for Armstrong-Siddeley, was to see the third of the engines which he had masterminded prove itself at Le Mans. To have succeeded with Lagonda he would have needed not only that steel but also investors prepared to pour in money for development between 1945 and 1947 and then wait several years for a return.

2½-LITRE LB6 1948-1953

From the start W.O. Bentley's objective had been to achieve a five-seater vehicle which was comfortable on good and bad road surfaces. There were other advantages in his

The early 2½-litre drophead which Sammy Davis took to Le Mans in 1949. "The car so obviously had a future."

design. Because the rear wheels went up and down independently the differential did not have to move, so the floor could be made lower. Brakes were inboard so that the wheels did not carry the weight of brake drums. The consequent suppleness in the suspension was practical provided the car had a really stiff frame – and W.O.'s was one of the best, the ends of the narrow X cruciform giving strength where the suspension did its work. Details had to be carefully developed and the prototypes' suspension was found to be too soft, the rear wheels insufficiently restrained for acceptable cornering and roadholding.

David Brown did not want to ditch the Lagonda and in June 1948 accompanied LPG 777 and LPF 775 (both saloons on which there had already been some suspension improvements) for the first stage of two months' extensive continental testing. With Percy Kemish, Rodney Walkerley (of *The Motor*) then took LPG 777 from Brussels to

Milan to meet up with colleague Laurence Pomeroy: "It was obvious that the Lagonda was a very unusual vehicle, the machinery was so uncannily quiet and Percy took it up to high rpm in the gears... we were over the summit, the car toying with slopes and hairpins... the cruising speed was a steady 80mph and five times the speedometer registered 96mph on full throttle."

It was a measure of the concern to perfect the design that during the next two weeks under Pomeroy and Kemish's care, LPG was driven by many of the leading Italian designers and engineers. There are pictures taken with Anderloni and Ponzoni of Carrozzeria Touring, Lurani (then Italian sports car champion) and Rapi of Isotta inspecting the Lagonda and its engine. They all commented on the car's potential.

Back in England development continued

The car which became the 3 litre, but then still fitted with the 2½-litre engine, at the Paris Show, October 1953.

and Brown set about organising production, his only stipulation being that a conventional David Brown gearbox be substituted for Bentley's preferred French Cotal box as fitted to LPG 777. (The English never took to the Cotal with its electromagnetically operated change, clutchless on the move.) As head of a large industrial complex Brown was in a good position to obtain steel. Engines and gearboxes were made at Meltham near Huddersfield and sent down to Feltham, where the bodies were coachbuilt by hand on a traditional wood frame. The trouble was that it was an expensive operation added to an already expensive chassis, and by the time the production cars were freely available there was that Jaguar MkVII again at half the price. As with Lea-Francis the purchase tax juggling didn't help.

Journalists were full of praise in the fol-lowing years. Sammy Davis, still then Sports Editor of *The Autocar*, had taken another earlier car, a drophead, to Le Mans in August 1949: "One of the curious things was that the three rear passengers had an even more comfortable ride than the two in front. The car so obviously had a future."

Then, in October, the latest saloon was tested: "Since the prototypes appeared the rear suspension has undergone considerable development and improvement. The use of a harder rubber in the suspension pivots has helped in obtaining really good handling. Drivers and passengers unversed in suspension practice would probably not realise there was anything unconventional. What they do appreciate is the quite exceptional riding comfort and the fact that the car can be taken round bends fast with a complete feeling of security. Part of the test was in torrential rain which demonstrated the remarkable grip of the road at speeds into the eighties on wet surfaces."

In January 1950 Pomeroy summed up in *The Motor* after more than a thousand miles in a drophead: "I have no hesitation in saying that this is the most stable and comfortable car in which I have ridden. It has the softness of suspension and ability to swallow up road irregularities which are characteristic of the good USA car, together with a really small roll angle, accurate control on corners and positive steering". Bentley's objectives had been achieved. If only the car had been in this form three years earlier and a way had been found to produce cheaper bodywork, the LB6 might have been sold in much larger numbers in many different countries. October 1952 saw the announcement of the MkII. The front of the car became less bulbous, with a lower prow and less prominent headlights. Inside, the instruments were moved to the right in front of the driver, and seats, furnishings and equipment were improved.

Production: *1946-48* 5 (approx.); *1949* 50 (approx.); *1950* 200 (approx.); *1951* 165; *1952* 114.

3 LITRE 1953-1957

It had become obvious that the type of hand-built machine offered by Lagonda would never sell in large quantities, so Brown went to the other extreme and created an idiosyncratic successor for the few. *The Autocar*'s pen portrait was succinct: "One of the most unusual cars tested in recent years. Having been driven once it will be bought immediately, finance permitting, or rejected because of various manifestations of heaviness".

The David Brown organisation had bought the Tickford body firm, who built a larger, wider body for the 3 litre, again styled by Feeley. William Watson was now back with Lagonda after the demise of the Invicta Black Prince (his engineering career alternating between the two marques) and with Ted Cutting was responsible for increasing the engine size and power. To cope with the higher weight and performance the suspension was further stiffened. Gone were the rave reports on the ride to be replaced by "a curious mixture of luxury touring car and out and out sports machine. The miles slip by leaving passengers glowing from that feeling of well-being that is derived from luxury, yet the driver is all the time enjoying the fine gear change, high geared steering and rugged precision of the controls. The Lagonda corners fast and true."

For the Series II 3-litre there was at last a floor gear change connecting directly to the box without the previous column linkage, but at low speeds clutch, steering and other controls were all heavier than what had become the norm. In fact there were only several hundred of "the few with finance permitting" who wanted a machine "which provided the pleasures missed by many owners of costly cars and which responded warmly to the right sort of hands". It was described as the modern vintage car, an appropriate title as the Watson connection went right back to the low chassis S-type Invicta of 1931. Those who did purchase seem to have become addicted. At the mid-'80s sale of the industrialist James Ellard's estate, five 3 litres (and some Invictas!) were found in his Aladdin's cave, and the Duke of Edinburgh so liked his early example that he later bought a Series II. Both series were available as saloon or drophead.

Production: *1953* 10 (approx.); *1954* 86; *1955* 89; *1956* 54; *1957* 26.

LAGONDA ACHIEVEMENTS

1948
"Mission to Milan" 2½ litre: Pomeroy, Walkerly.

1949
"Return to Le Mans" 2½ litre: S. Davis.

1950
Monte Carlo Pre-war V12: Franklin 97th.

1952
Monte Carlo 2½ litre B. Macartney-Filgate 70th.

1953
Monte Carlo 2½ litre C. Vard 113th.

LANCHESTER

LD10 in Park Lane, with Frank Lanchester and Daimler designer Simpson in AR 621. If the Lanchester brothers had been able to continue their innovative thinking, BMW might not now occupy these showrooms.

Bank directors, like other mortals, have to find their own routes to survival. But is it too much to hope that the day will come when they decide to take the longer view? In 1931 fear of what might follow the Wall Street collapse led to the calling in of overdrafts, and Lanchester were given under three weeks to find £38,000. The B.S.A. Directors learnt of the problem and made an offer which was accepted by the Lanchester board. Henceforward the name of the British motor industry's most illustrious pioneer was to be no more than a badge on cheaper Daimlers. I learnt of the consequent loss to the motoring world because my father worked for one of Lanchester's most faithful customers, the Jam Sahib of Nawanagar. As a teenager I was able to visit His Highness's motor house at Jamnagar, and laid out before me were magnificent examples of the company's products – coupés, landaulettes, limousines, sedancas and tourers on the straight-eight and earlier six-cylinder chassis – together with later Daimler eights specially fitted with the Lanchester radiator.

It has been suggested that if the horseless carriage Act of 1865 (speed limit of 4mph and a person to walk 60 yards ahead of any road locomotive) had been repealed, say, twenty years earlier (1876 rather than 1896) English engineers would have been the first producers of road vehicles. There had been work on steam carriages as early as 1830, but the legislation proved a major disincentive. Instead Daimler and Benz in Germany and Panhard in France led the pioneers. Frederick Lanchester's interest came through his ambition to produce an engine light enough for powered flight. He realised that the motor car was the sensible starting point but did not like what he had been able to glean from those Europeans, and therefore started again from first principles. Laurence Pomeroy wrote an erudite summary after the end of Lanchester production in 1956: "The great

Cyril Corbishley (at the wheel) and Dr C.
Hardman after the 1953 Monte Carlo Rally. They
finished 52nd after a snow chain from another car
broke the windscreen.

Dr Frederick Lanchester was the first Englishman to produce a practical self-propelled
four-wheeled vehicle and it owed little to the
conglomeration of gas engine, locomotive
and horse-drawn practice of other efforts. It
used not only the tension spoke wheel
invented by Cayley but also a horizontally
opposed air-cooled engine with two crankshafts rotating in opposite planes to give
perfect balance, a foolproof epicyclic gearchange, and a worm-drive rear axle."

Despite the inevitable friction between
engineering ideals and commercial restraints,
pre-1914 Lanchesters with engines behind or
between driver and front passenger, and
seats in the space between the axles (instead
of crowded into any room that was left
behind a vast bonnet!), were unique engineering concepts. If side lever steering had
been more acceptable (it was liked by those
who tried it: "the lever can almost be forgotten because its operation is instinctive")
many motor accident victims would not have
been pierced by the dangerous steering
column, and the modern airbag would be
unnecessary. The cantilever springs were
famed for their soft, level ride and even today
a backache sufferer who has to traverse
rough roads might benefit from a 1905 Lanchester! In the 1920s the engine came
forward – accepted fashion had won again.

By 1930 George Lanchester (Frederick's
brother) was well aware of the need for a
smaller car. The quality of the 12/70 saloon
designed when he was at Alvis gives an indication of what might have come if 1931 had
not intervened. The Sprite was a ray of hope
under the postwar Daimler regime. Had
B.S.A. and Daimler not been affected by
management turbulence there might have
been a continuation of innovative thinking
worthy of Lanchester tradition.

TEN (LD10) 1946-1951

There was praise – "so superbly easy to
handle, light steering, stability, comfort" – for
the Ten in the first road impressions pub-

lished in January 1946. Apart from the advantages of the fluid flywheel, which have been dissected in the Daimler Conquest section, a study of specifications gives clues to the model's particular merits. The cruciform chassis laid out before the war (production was to start in October 1939) had the chassis rails below the rear axle, and a long 8ft 3in wheelbase. This compared with the Singer and Wolseley Tens with wheelbases of 7ft 11in and 7ft 6in. The Lanchester's rear wheels really were further back and the seats forward, witness the straight lines of the rear doors, a feature later to be shared with the Singer 1500. The turning circle was 35ft, which produced the most manoeuvrable car of that length until the arrival of the Jowett Javelin.

Later road tests confirmed these qualities. "The riding is notably level, the back seat especially comfortable", and the car was not let down by details: "Starting is never in doubt, driving seat adjustable for height and rake, reserve petrol tap on the facia, and comprehensive took kit". It was not, however, the sort of car, or the owners were not the sort of people, to fill the correspondence columns with praise, and, looking back, the downside seems to have been that the long-stroke ohv four-cylinder engine gave only adequate rather than abundant power. It needed low gearing to move those 23cwt. At 2,500ft per min. piston speed, the top gear speed was a paltry 55mph.

Design and development was only one part of the LD10 story for production was twice disrupted. Soon after the war sufficient space had been reorganised in the Browns Lane shadow factory to assemble the cars with the six-light saloon bodies from Briggs at Dagenham. For three years there were steady sales and many were exported, including a fleet at Jamnager ordered by the faithful Jam Sahib as office cars for his staff. The fluid flywheel eased the negotiation of sacred cows in the crowded streets. Then in 1949 there were difficulties with the supply from Briggs. It was decided to make the body within the B.S.A. group, and this led to the

coachbuilt aluminium-panelled 4-light "Barker" saloon, but there were delays in preparing for production and for some months no Ten was available. Secondly, at the end of 1950, assembly was moved to the refurbished Radford factory, which allowed Jaguar then to move into Brown's Lane. The LD10 was listed till June 1951. If it had had an uninterrupted run, and if it had been possible to keep prices at the earlier levels, its reputation could have been much higher.

Production: *1946* Briggs 550 (est.); *1947* Briggs 1,071; *1948* Briggs 791; *1949* Briggs 33; *1950* Barker 207; *1951* Barker 373.

FOURTEEN/LEDA
(LJ200/201) 1951-1954

By 1950 Daimler was getting into its stride after the massive war effort. Rebuilding plans were under way and the first new postwar chassis was on the road. With a 5-inch longer wheelbase than the Ten, still the cruciform frame (but with chassis rails now above the rear axle), and laminated torsion bars specifically designed to ease the task of the shock absorbers, it was to be the foundation of the medium range. Before the 1950 show Managing Director James Leek announced the Fourteen: "Suited to a wide range of varying conditions, economically priced, economical to run, and maintaining the Lanchester refinement. We aimed at and planned production in line with the layout of a new factory in our rebuilding programme."

The engine was a 2-litre development of the Ten's, still with a long stroke, and the new body was built with the same traditional method of wood frame and steel panels. But this was only the initial stage, as an all-steel shell of the same shape had been commissioned from Pressed Steel. The all-steel model was to be called the Leda and reserved for export. Reorganisation and sorting out the bomb damage all took longer than planned and the first batch of Ledas, bound for Brazil, did not come off the new production line until April 1952. As before, the fluid

The Hooper Dauphin in 1953. "Those with over
£4,000 available seemed to have preferred a
Bristol or a Bentley."

flywheel limited the market, but the Fourteen was still a durable uncomplicated car in its own right, more than an inferior Conquest, and played its part in the latter's evolution with the same bodyshell.

For some it was a happy choice. A Mr Mackenzie purchased a Leda in Scotland and drove it out to Greece in September 1953. He was delighted to find no faults on delivery, praised the body sealing on Yugoslavia's dusty roads, and concluded: "The Lanchester proved most untiring to drive, whatever the conditions, and the automatic chassis lubrication is a blessing on a long journey. The car only needed routine service at the end of the journey".

Whatever the car's merits, the production capacity so carefully organised was not fully used. Purchasers seeking a higher quality car (and who were not amongst the dwindling band of former Lanchester or fluid flywheel fans) did not sit down and conclude that the Fourteen or the Leda was for them. Even when the basic price was reduced after the Purchase Tax reduction in the 1953 Budget, the message still did not get through. If it had, new owners could have been agreeably surprised and found they had the most manoeuvrable car on the market with its clutchless transmission and a turning circle of just 33ft. The De Ville drophead was advertised and

shown at the 1951 Paris salon, but few were made. Cyril Corbishley, as a prelude to his valiant efforts with the Conquest and the Century, achieved respectable placings on both his drives to Monte Carlo.

Production: *1951* 150 (est.); *1952* 1,012; *1953* 910; *1954* 50 (est.).

DAUPHIN (LJ250) 1953

The Dauphin was written up as having a twin-carburettor Daimler engine in a Lanchester Fourteen chassis. This was the attempt to provide the less extravagant Lanchester provenance in deference to the spirit of the times. In fact it was the corporate chassis and therefore an early example of the Century (see Daimler) specification. Hooper craftsmen had created an elegant two-door saloon, with wings and windows following their "Empress" line as built on Daimlers and some Rolls-Royces. The Dauphin remained in the price lists for six months, but those with over £4,000 available seemed to have preferred a Bristol or the factory-built standard Bentley.

Production: Not known. Estimates vary between 3 and 10.

FIRST & SECOND SPRITES 1954-1956

The Sprite was announced before the 1954 show with four descriptive pages and drawings in *The Autocar* and five in *The Motor*. Whilst B.S.A. had partially bought Lanchester in 1931 to help the production of a cheaper range, there was still some public awareness of the Lanchester brothers' pioneering and technical achievements. It was therefore an appropriate name for a smaller unitary construction car with advanced features and without that Daimler image. The pioneers of the fluid flywheel became the first users of the Hobbs gearbox, a British automatic with the option of lever selection by the driver without using clutch or pedal. Instead of a fluid coupling the Hobbs mechanism had hydraulically operated clutches to select the epicyclic gearing. There was less power loss, making it more suitable for smaller engines.

The magazines record that there were two separate cars on the show stand, both in dual colours, one grey and blue, the other grey and green. Michael Brown commented: "The car looks businesslike. The evolution of Daimler proceeds steadily and the car is now some distance from its associations with formal occasions. This move into the field of performance without losing traditional regard has been done very skillfully".

The dumpy four-light saloon may not have been a good looker but it was a functional work-a-day design with no Daimler overtones which seemed on the right track to attract a new range of customers. Because of the use of aluminium alloy panels the weight at 23cwt was the same as the Ten and 5cwt lighter than the Leda, yet the 1,622cc engine (two-thirds of a Conquest) produced the same 60bhp as the previous 2 litre. The total price at £1,078 was competitive, nearly £100 less than the cheapest Rover.

During 1955 management changed their minds. They kept the engine and the Hobbs transmission, but reworked the structure to create a longer and wider car. The body was now similar to the Conquest and Leda but the subtlety of the classic shape was lost, with heavier window frames and an extension to the boot. It seemed as if the directors had taken fright and were fearful of breaking away from the heritage of the past. It remained a sound and carefully engineered car, again with alloy panels to keep the slightly increased weight (now 24 cwt) below the Leda, but at £1,228 the price was now more than the cheapest Rover. The two cars on the stand (silver and black and silver and maroon) were well received and pilot production began, but by the following year it was all over. In an official statement at the end of August 1956, chairman John Sangster stated that production of the Lanchester Sprite was to cease.

Production: First Sprite 3 (est.); Second Sprite 6 (est.).

The first four-window Sprite with Hobbs Automatic transmission and lift-up front under scrutiny at the 1954 Earls Court Show.

LANCHESTER ACHIEVEMENTS
1952
Monte Carlo Lanchester 14: C. Corbishley/Dr. C. Hardman 68th.
1953
Monte Carlo Lanchester 14: C. Corbishley/Dr. C. Hardman 52nd.

LEA-FRANCIS

If, when the buyer's market returned in 1952, there had been a thousand or so enthusiastic interested UK purchasers each year who were prepared and able to pay a reasonable premium for a well-engineered traditional sporting saloon, Lea-Francis might have survived. Instead, with incomes curtailed by taxation and other pressing priorities, people sought the best apparent value. In the showrooms they could look at Humber Hawks, Wolseley 6/80s and their like at less than half the price of a Lea-Francis Eighteen. Ford and Vauxhall sixes were even cheaper. Looking back from the 1990s it is again salutary to remember just how many of the "better" cars now on the roads were originally purchased with company money for executives and other employees who would have shopped elsewhere if they had been using their own resources. The following table illustrates the position in April 1952.

	Basic Price	Total with Purchase Tax
Lea-Francis Fourteen	£1,240	£1,930
Lea-Francis Eighteen	1,520	2,365
Armstrong-Siddeley	1,110	1,728
Ford Zephyr	575	895
Humber Hawk	725	1,129
Jaguar MkVII	1,088	1,693
Wolseley 6/80	720	1,121

Later in 1952, and again in 1953, the basic price of the Fourteen was progressively reduced to £890, and the Eighteen to £1,380, but demand barely increased. Automobile historians have suggested that purchase tax caused Lea-Francis' demand but, though that unwelcome imposition (66⅔% 1951-52, 50% after the 1953 Budget) didn't help, it seems to have been an additional rather than a root problem. Volume sales were only to be achieved by the cheapest and most efficient production methods unless the offering was a desirable artefact unobtainable elsewhere.

This material was garnered from contemporary magazines and other sources before reading Barrie Price's definitive *Lea-Francis Story*. There is no conflict in the accounts but it is worth seeking a copy of Price's erudite volume (B.T. Batsford, 1978) for further background detail. The company had built bicycles, motorcycles and some cars at different periods since 1895. It went wrong in the early '30s, by which time Richard Lea and Graham Francis had departed. In 1937 a new company was formed by George Leek and Hugh Rose, who had both earlier left Riley. It would have been difficult to forsee the postwar situation but, looking back, they seemed to have assumed that other motorists would always seek the type of car which they themselves favoured. They were both then in their fifties. Like others, they didn't appreciate that the middle-class monopoly of the road was coming to an end and that few future purchasers looking for their basic transport would be concerned with the finer points of engineering and handling.

The company made money from its wartime sub-contract work and fortunately the bombs that rained down on Coventry did not hit the Much Park Street factory. An advanced concept like the Javelin would have been a daunting task for ageing executives in a small firm. It is understandable that they chose to reintroduce the 1938 design, whose development had continued during the war on the cars used by the directors. Albert Ludgate joined the company in 1946 and was to take charge of engineering. The initial postwar saloon bodies were built by A.P. Aircraft Limited (A.P.A.) in Dane Road Coventry. In 1948 Charlesworth Bodies, also in Much Park Street, were taken over. Lea-Francis, making its own engines and many of its bodies, had become self-sufficient in contrast to Allard, Jowett or Healey, who had to go elsewhere for one or other (or in Healey's case both) of these vital components.

Relative self-sufficiency was an admirable

achievement but of less value by the end of 1951 when there were not enough sales to balance the books and insufficient capital to develop a more saleable product. The last chassis were constructed in 1952. Sales continued until the final cars were sold in th summer of 1954. The company kept going with a contract for naval gun-trolleys from the Ministry of Supply, and the service department remained busy. A 1956 letter to *The Autocar* praised speedy delivery of a reconditioned gear box for a 1948 Fourteen and older cars were bought in for reconditioning and re-sale. But by the end of the '50s the Ministry contract was completed. The results for 1956 and 1957 showed a small loss followed by a small profit, and then for 1958 a loss of £50,000. George Leek and Hugh Rose had both retired. After various vicissitudes and changes of ownership there was a happier ending. The spares and name were bought by Barrie Price at Studley. He continues to offer enthusiastic service for the older cars and has also developed a new Jaguar powered Lea-Francis.

THE ENGINE

Hugh Rose had been at Belsize, Crossley, Humber and Sunbeam before Riley and had had extensive design experience. Foremost among Lea-Francis attributes was his rethinking of the Riley layout, which was common to both postwar engines. As described in the Riley section, weight was the penalty of that tri-partite cylinder block, cylinder walls and two camshaft housings. Rose did not want to take the Jaguar and Lagonda route with overhead cams in the cylinder head; that means long chains and complications when the head has to be removed. Instead, he put two cams at the top instead of half way up the cylinder block, resulting in a lighter narrower block with two upper bulges like French baguettes to house those cams. Short pushrods then operated improved Riley-type valve gear and the desirable hemispherical combustion chambers were retained.

Engine characteristics are described in the sports car section, but road car usage is only part of the story. American midget car racers wanted another engine to supplement the 1,671cc Offenhauser which was in short supply. The secretary of their Association suggested that a Lea-Francis engine should be fitted to his own car. The 1½ litre was modified with four Amal carburettors and produced 118bhp, over 40bhp more than the standard engine, on a 15:1 compression ratio. In 1948 Ken Rose (Hugh's son) and Albert Ludgate took the prototype across the Atlantic in the venerable *Mauretania*. It was well received and a batch of 1,674cc units

A Fourteen Estate at Earls Court in 1951. The Croft-Pearsons took a similar car to Monte Carlo in 1950.

(with SUs replacing the Amals) were sent to the States. Both Offenhauser and Meyer-Drake reacted to the challenge and patriotism won the day, dashing hopes of a substantial order. Later this engine became the basis of Rodney Clarke's Connaught sports cars. A developed 2½ litre powered the Formula I Connaught in which Tony Brooks secured his triumphant win at Syracuse in 1955, the first British postwar victory in a continental Grand Prix. It's a tantalising saga. Some of the bigger UK manufacturers had indifferent 2- and 2½-litre engines, and here was this British company near the end of its financial resources but with this tested and proven masterpiece.

TWELVE/FOURTEEN (1½/1¾-LITRE) 1946-1953

The early cars had the pre-war 1,496cc engine but this was then enlarged to 1,767cc. A.P.A.'s four-light saloon was a composite structure built up from aluminium and steel. The first cars, announced in 1946, were high waisted, but the next year windows were enlarged and advertisements stated that the Fourteen was "acclaimed on the continent as the most elegant of the postwar cars". Torsion bar independent front suspension was fitted before the 1949 Motor Show and the following year the radiator was brought forward and the headlights recessed into the wings. Reports commented on the car's light and accurate steering: "A pleasure to drive over a really winding road, can be placed with exactness on every bend". A Mr Walter Calvert wrote from Manchester: "I have had a Fourteen for three years and have never yet taken the car out without thinking at some time during the journey what an excellent car it is. Its performance far exceeds the maker's claims".

Estate cars and vans, at first built by Southern Caravans at Yapton, later by A.P.A., were offered to take advantage of the purchase tax concession up to June 1947 on such vehicles.

A. Marshall in a Lea-Francis Fourteen Sports on Darracott in a Land's End Trial.

They were again popular when, for a period, owners contrived their registration as "private and goods" to subvert the edicts of petrol rationing. Running chassis were bought by other body builders. In September 1948 a new six-light saloon for export only was announced. This was the first fitting of the torsion bar suspension and began life with the 1,767cc engine. Opinions differ over style but many commented that it was a successful attempt to carry on the good looks in a wider, more modern body. Thirty two-door fixed head coupés were built by the aeroparts subsidiary of Westland Motors at Hereford.

Production – Twelve: *1946* 5; *1947* 8.
Saloons & Coupés Fourteen: *1946* 217; *1947* 431; *1948* 308; *1949* 219; *1950* 390; *1951* 363; *1952* 147; *1953* 25 sold; *1954* 4 sold.
Estate Cars & Vans: *1946* 104; *1947* 124; *1948* 243; *1949* 238; *1950* 190; *1951* 177; *1952* 4; *1953* 2.

EIGHTEEN (2½-LITRE) SALOON 1948-1953

In September 1949 came the announcement of the new Eighteen, a six-light saloon with a single-carburettor version of the 2½-litre engine developing 95bhp. Here was a roomy, well-furnished body panelled in aluminium in the Charlesworth works. It did not have all the structural stiffness of later creations but the total weight was a commendably low 26cwt.

The car had attractive handling and a good power-to-weight ratio. For those who lap up figures, at the benchmark 2,500ft per min. piston speed this Lea-Francis would be travelling at 71mph. For comparison, at the same piston speed the Riley-engined Healey's speed would be 65mph and the big Jaguar MkVII 69mph. This technical "tour de force" was insufficient reason for writing out that large cheque.

Production: *1948* 1; *1949* 21; *1950* 49; *1951* 12; *1952* 5; *1953* 1.

FOURTEEN/EIGHTEEN (1¾/2½-LITRE) SPORTS 1948-1952

Ruth Sands Bentley, then American *Autosport* correspondent, in a 2½ litre Sports, September 1955.

The Autocar tested the 1767cc Fourteen: "On the road a responsive, high-spirited power unit which runs as smoothly as a sewing machine at 5,000rpm and over. Here is the essence of this new British sports car, especially pleasing to anyone who finds delight in the working of well-made mechanism."

Two were shipped across the Atlantic in February 1948 when MG still only had the TC and neither TR2 nor XK120 were on the market. Why didn't they sell like those proverbial hot cakes and make the company's fortune? There is no clear answer. It was an amalgam of high price, insufficient publicity, a little-known name and possibly that an occasional four-seater with its hint of family lacked the image of freedom for the unencumbered couple. Only eleven Fourteen Sports models were sold in America. It might have been better to wait and concentrate on the more powerful 2½-litre with independent front suspension.

Those that did purchase were enthusiastic.

Duncan Macleod wrote from Portland, Oregon: "Collecting from the New York docks, I drove home in part through Canada, covering over 3,400 miles in six days. 8,000 miles later I still have not experienced even minor mechanical difficulty. My pleasure in ownership is doubly enhanced by the friendly courtesy and efficiency of the organisation which so carefully made it". This evoked a response from Mr Frank in Cheam: "I have been fortunate to own the 2½-litre Sports for the last year and would like to second all Duncan Macleod's praise. It is disappointing there has been such scant mention of this entirely delightful car".

Should the company have concentrated on the sports cars and found a way, like Morgan, of keeping going until they had been able to tap the latent worldwide demand? Peter Morgan's skill was to use a much cheaper, mass-produced engine in those difficult times, and to win rallies with a factory team, often driving himself. In 1951 the basic

The Eighteen, the final development of the six-light saloon, with 95bhp and a 2½-litre engine.

prices of the Plus Four, £535 for the 2-seater and £550 for the 4-seater, were less than half that asked for the Lea-Francis. The Jaguar XK was £1,078.

The cars were extensively rallied by private owners, and two competed in the 1950 Alpine Trial. Frye in a lone 18 was one of only four unpenalised cars in his class at the end of the first stage. Then a rock interfered with the silencer and rebounded against the petrol tank. The ensuing leak put them out. Hockley in a 14 miscalculated his time for one of the observed sections but still finished. There was nothing like the factory-supported Jaguar or Sunbeam mass assault on the Alps. Lea-Francis would have benefited from a major win in the Alpine or other rallies, which might have been achieved with a full team and more experienced drivers.

Production – Fourteen: *1948* 89; *1949* 25; *1950* 8; *1951* 4. **Eighteen:** *1949* 1; *1950* 54; *1951* 11; *1952* 9; *1953* 2.

LEA-FRANCIS ACHIEVEMENTS

1946
Brussels Concours 1½-litre saloon: Grand Prix d'Honneur.

1950
Alpine 1¾-litre Sports: Hockley 8th in class.
Monte Carlo 1¾-litre Estate: Mr & Mrs Croft Pearson & Ken Rose 103rd.
Lisbon 2½-litre saloon: S. Boshier, 2nd Concours d'Elegance.
Torquay 1¾-litre Sports: Davies 4th.

1951
RAC 2½-litre Sports: F. Bullock 19th, C. Follett 27th, C. Kite 32nd.
Daily Express MCC 1¾-litre Sports: F. Bullock 2nd in class.
Isle of Wight 1¾-litre Sports: F. Bullock 2nd, 1st in class. Ventnor Hill Climb 1st in class. 2½-litre Sports: C. Kite, Ventnor Hill Climb 1st in class.

1952
Adriatic 2½-litre Saloon: G. Riederer 1st in class.
Evian-Mont Blanc 2½-litre Sports: Mrs L. Needham 2nd in class, 2nd Coupe des Dames.

1953
Circuit of Ireland 1¾-litre Sports: M. F. Mackie, Novices Prize.

LLOYD 1946-52

As already noted in the Fedden chapter, not everyone was content to recreate the old. We have seen how some of the more innovative engineers and entrepreneurs preferred the relative freedoms of the smaller companies. The likes of Bentley, Healey and Watson hoped to make a living from a continuing demand for more sophisticated products.

Roland Lloyd chose a more difficult path. He wanted to use advances in engineering to make a better, and preferably cheaper, small car. Before the war his small factory at Grimsby had built a single-cylinder 350cc two-seater, intended as primitive basic transport. Around 250 were sold at 80 guineas. Then came wartime sub-contract work for Rolls-Royce and thoughts about a postwar product. The 1946 Lloyd 650 conceived by Roland, John Linegar, Jack Hannan and others broke new ground. The light tubular chassis had independent suspension on all wheels. Instead of shock absorbers the coil springs were inside cylinders filled with oil. The twin-cylinder 650cc two-stroke engine had its own sump with the lubrication pressure normally lacking in a two-stroke provided by a patented double-acting Lloyd pump. There was no need for DKW-type petrol and oil mixture. The engine was transversely mounted like the Mini's and drove the front wheels. Because the action of the clutch pedal completely disengaged the gearbox, there was the equivalent of synchromesh and an easy change on all three gears. All these components were made by Lloyd and they even produced their own brakes.

In their 1950 road test *The Motor* gave the engine output as 17.5bhp. They measured maximum speed at 47mph and consumption at 44 miles to the gallon at a constant 30mph. John Linegar, in a letter to *Classic and Sportscar* thirty-five years later in 1985, wrote that the above figures referred to the

Prototype 650 Roadster in 1945 before fitment of bumpers, second screen wiper and development of hood details.

early engine with iron cylinder block. The company would have preferred the testers to wait until the developed aluminium block was fitted. Linegar confirmed that these later engines were all tested and had to produce 27bhp before fitment. He continued: "In fact Lloyds would exceed 60mph and manage nearly 50mpg at 30mph". This seems to have been a case where journalistic haste may not have been helpful, but owners, if few and far between, were still pleased with their purchases. William Clarke wrote from Northern Rhodesia: "I would be obliged if you could put me in touch with other Lloyd owners. So far as I am aware I still own the only 650 in this country, and have no means of getting comparative figures. Despite heat, dust and typical colonial roads, the car is performing splendidly". It is hardly the letter of a driver limited to 47mph flat out over African distances.

The car's fate was a familiar story. It just was not possible to reduce the price below the mass-production offerings and make a profit. After 1952 Lloyd returned to precision work for other engineering companies. Total production figures were not negligible, three times as many as Healey's Elliott or Silverstone, thirty times as many as Invicta's Black Prince.

Production: 350

METROPOLITAN

In contrast to Leonard Lord, George Mason (see Healey) president of the American Nash-Kelvinator Corporation, commissioned extensive research when considering the manufacture of a small car for sale to motorists. Some 235,000 questionnaires were sent out. From the replies it became clear that there wasn't much interest in a vehicle with the configuration of the standard American but on a smaller scale (i.e. four even six seats, but small seats) and which made its way with a different kind of engine and handling. What did interest was a machine which reproduced the feel of the standard American offering but had smaller dimensions.

The brilliant and logical answer was half a car, or more precisely half a car and a bit: produce a front compartment with similar appearance to and dimensions approaching the standard American car, attach a much abbreviated rear end and it should be able to go like the American even with a much smaller engine. A prototype of such a vehicle was exhibited in 1950. Mason also realised that Nash did not have the experience to effectively mass-produce such a machine themselves. Early discussions with both Fiat and Standard did not lead to any agreement. Then, soon after the Austin-Morris merger, it was announced in October 1952 that "Austin were going to co-operate in producing the new NXI light car for Nash at Longbridge. Another famous British firm, Fisher & Ludlow, would build the bodies". The car was to be sold and serviced by Nash dealers in the USA and Canada and it was calculated that 100,000 would need to be sold to make the venture worthwhile. In January 1954 Nash amalgamated with Hudson to form American Motors.

1200 & 1500 1954-1961

Nash's NXI Exhibit had a low grille surrounded by a heavy chrome bumper and totally enclosed rear wheels. The British version of the Nash "Metropolitan", as it was now christened, was announced in March 1954 as a 2-door hardtop and a convertible. The basic Nash shape was retained, echoing their larger cars, but the grille had been moved above the bumper and shallow cutouts had been provided for the rear wheels. To give an idea of the scale, the width across the bench front seat was 49in, plenty of room

The Nash NXI Exhibit with low grille surrounded by a heavy chrome bumper and totally enclosed rear wheels.

for two, or three with a squeeze. Austin's A30 was 41in and the standard Nash 55in. The length of the car behind the front seat (with a children's seat and luggage locker) was 52in compared with 85in in the Nash. Weight was 16cwt compared with the A30's 14cwt and the Nash's 28cwt.

By skilfully combining British and American components the engineers did manage to produce a small vehicle which handled like the standard American. Because of the low weight, the 1200cc A40 engine provided good top gear performance, and a three-speed version of the A40 gearbox with a simple steering column change sufficed. To provide the desired suspension softness the front suspension was an amalgam of A30 lower wishbones and hubs and long coil springs Nash-style between the Nash upper wishbone and the top of the wheel arches. At the rear there was a standard A30 axle and leaf springs mounted with large American-type bushes.

The car was equipped as standard with a good wireless and a sophisticated heater complete with thermostatic control to maintain a set temperature. Upholstery styles and bright colour schemes followed the larger models.

In 1956 the radiator grille was simplified. The 1489cc BMC B series engine was fitted and gave even more flexibility. *The Motor's*

The second series Metropolitan with the 1,489cc A50 engine, available in Britain with right hand drive from October 1956. *The Motor* tested a similar but left hand drive car in May.

testers summed up: "Comfort is a pronounced virtue. Springs and upholstery combine to soak up shocks in a manner which is remarkable for a small car. Ride is superior to most British and continental models whereas roadholding and sensitiveness of control are of a markedly lower standard. Steering is extremely light even at walking pace with the turning circle diameter 5ft less than the average Detroit counterpart".

Later that year it was possible to buy the car with right hand drive in England. The Metropolitan was a textbook example of how to plan and achieve an objective. There are pictures of ships sailing across the Atlantic, their deck-space crammed full of these little cars. This continued until 1961 when American Motors, who were beginning to lose out to the US giants, did not renew their contract with Austin. Over 100,000 were sold and Austin earned their money. It was in stark contrast to the A90 Atlantic story and that car's unsuitability for the market for which it was conceived.

Production: 104,000 estimated – no separate yearly totals.

MORRIS

Early in 1946 William Morris (Lord Nuffield) told Miles Thomas that he was going to stand down and give him full responsibility for the whole Nuffield organisation. We shall never know what was in Morris's mind during the following month when he had still not given up the Chairmanship and became increasingly critical of Thomas. Morris never wrote his own story. We can only surmise from biographies and Thomas's autobiography. We know that Morris and his wife Lilian had no children and therefore no prospective retirement pleasures in a family circle. We know that he had a tedious digestive condition which both caused pain and affected emission control, making social life hazardous. Discomfort could more easily be forgotten through the demands of hard work, and embarrassment camouflaged within the hierarchy of power. As decision time approached, standing down may have become less attractive.

There is also evidence that Morris became irritated by Thomas's full-throttle approach to life. Thomas not only coped with Nuffield Products, he took on Government commissions, was a fluent speaker and writer (talents that eluded Morris) and something of a bon viveur with no digestive worries. He was also a family man who had won the heart of Morris's former secretary. It would be understandably human if Morris began to think that he could not hand over his life's work to this genial, popular man who had everything. Or did he half hope that Thomas would take the initiative and find a way of deposing him? But Thomas was not that kind of personality. As an only child brought up without older male influence after his father's death, he seemed to prefer the approbation of a father-figure; and you did not shoot Pater.

Whatever the Boss's thinking, the hiatus of 1947 leading to Thomas's departure in

Miles Thomas at Coventry – could he have built better cars than those achieved by the combined BMC?

From left: Miles Thomas, H. Mullens (then director Nuffield Exports), Lady Thomas and record-breaker George Eyston.

November hindered the development of the postwar cars. Nor was this an untypical saga. Morris's energetic dictatorship may have produced a million cars between 1912 and 1939 but this was achieved with the loss of other potential successors. He had fallen out with Frank Woollard in 1932 and Leonard Lord in 1936. In 1940, Oliver Boden, over-worked to exhaustion, had collapsed from a fatal heart attack.

Morris had always preferred the intuitive mind to the trained graduate thinker. Now, unlike Ford or Mercedes who were already building multi-disciplined management structures and training programmes, there was no reservoir of talent. At the age of seventy Morris himself took up the reins again and became the agent by which his own creation lost its independent existence. In December, a month after Thomas, seven other directors learnt they were no longer needed. The remaining managers struggled with the elderly chairman's preference for the older designs. It was thanks to Reggie Hanks, a practical engineer apprenticed at the Swindon railway workshop who now became Morris's deputy, that the Issigonis Minor made it to the 1948 Earl's Court Show. But Hanks, despite his competence and persistence, was never to wear the crown.

The old love-hate relationship between Morris and Leonard Lord had not died. They had maintained some contact and there is a picture of them chatting and smiling together in front of the new cars at that '48 Show. After conflicting statements and denials the British Motor Corporation was formed in November 1951 with Austin and Lord as the dominant partner. William Morris remained, but not for long, and the able and forward looking Nuffield engineers had to play second fiddle to Longbridge. Issigonis departed to Alvis, chief engineer Vic Oak took early retirement. Whatever Leonard Lord's mistakes and misjudgements (discussed in the Austin chapter), he did go on to hammer out an organisation which re-employed Issigonis and manufactured the Mini and 1100 successes in the 1970s.

And Thomas? Would he have built better cars if he had taken command and Nuffield Products remained separate? Might he even have looked elsewhere on the merger trail and picked up the good pieces from Jowett, Lea-Francis or Singer when they went to the wall? The evidence is inconclusive. Thomas did go on to achieve the chairman rôle, but always as super-employee (reporting to State or American parent), never as all-powerful Dictator. Were there further strands to William Morris's thinking? Was he also testing and watching Thomas to judge whether he had the ruthless decisiveness which the motor industry demanded? Had he from years back seen Lord as the heir if Thomas failed the test? And, overreaching his personal worries, were the actions in 1947 those of the master tactician, the dismissals part of the plan to clear the decks for Leonard Lord?

EIGHT SERIES E 1945-1948

Recessing the headlamps into the front wings of the 1938 Series E had a significance far beyond the simple sheet-metal changes. This evocation of the streamlined shape hinted that we too in England would one day share the American dream. But the car still had the tax-induced narrow-bore engine, the big 17in wheels and leaf springs of the previous 30 years. It was back in production by the end of 1945 with prices raised from the pre-war £128 to £235 and £66 purchase tax. Many thousands were bought by drivers all over the world for whom there was little else and who did not yet appreciate the possibility of creating a less fretful small car.

Yet one should not underestimate the car's capability or driver and passenger fortitude in the 1940s. In 1948 a Canadian couple, Mr & Mrs Elliott, celebrated their 50th wedding anniversary by driving their Series E 7,000 miles across the North American continent. In 1949 a Mr Solberg took his family 5,000 miles round South Africa. On several days they drove 600 miles. Both journeys were free of mechanical trouble.

Eight Series E competing in driving tests on the Eastbourne Rally.

Production: *1945-46* 13,500 (est.); *1947* 24,658; *1948* 21,500.

Ten Series M 1945-1948

It is tempting to pair the M and the E, but the Ten was a different design with its own niche in history. It was introduced the year before the war as the first Morris without a traditional chassis frame. Instead there was one metal structure, with consequent weight saving, to which the separate components were attached. That the Morris engineers, Boyle and Oak, backed up by Hubert Charles and Issigonis, were aware of world and export needs is confirmed by their experiments with independent suspension for the M. In fact it wasn't used until the MG Y-type saloon, but they did achieve safer leaf springs controlled by an anti-roll bar doubling as radius rods on either side.

There was a new overhead-valve engine (which was to power the MG sports cars) and in 1945 the car attracted the attention of the Indian engineering firm of Birla Brothers. Miles Thomas was a quick mover and soon off on the Short flying boat to Karachi and Calcutta. G.D. Birla wanted to make motor cars starting with an established design under a licence agreement. He was preparing for the threatened import duties on completed vehicles. Thomas suggested a half-way house involving shipping all components for assembly, with the understanding that Birla Brothers would gradually produce more and more items themselves. Thus was born Hindustan Motors, who are still making the Ambassador, based on the later Oxford. The Series M became the Hindustan Ten, with a new horizontally slatted radiator grille later adopted for the English car.

The only international competitive entry I have found for the Ten Series M was a Dutchman, de Jong, who started from Stockholm in the 1950 Monte Carlo Rally but was

The Series M became the Hindustan Ten with horizontally slatted radiator. The Birla brother's creation is pictured in India with a pre-war Austin behind.

This Minor MM was used as *The Autocar*'s Press Car by S.C.H. Davis, Colonel Barnes (of the RAC) and photographer W. Banks to cover the 1949 Monte Carlo Rally.

not placed. A Mr Newell won his class in the 1951 Circuit of Ireland.

Production: *1945-46* 16,000 (est.); *1947* 20,072; *1948* 17,560.

MINOR MM & SERIES II
1948-1956

If Miles Thomas had been there to keep the pressure on the development of the Minor and the spares and service back-up, would it then have reached towards the Volkswagen Beetle's 20 million rather than the 1½ million which were produced? The young Issigonis knew how he wanted to interpret Thomas's wish for a new low price 4-seater saloon after the war. Vic Oak had the sense to let him get on with it with the help of draughtsmen Jack Daniels and Reg Job. They were able to take clean sheets of paper and work out the new ideas, partially influenced by Maurice Olley's suspension work for General Motors. The aim was to get the engine weight forward and down between softer, well-controlled independent springs suspending smaller 14in wheels, and steer with an accurate rack and pinion. Independent rear suspension was ruled out as too expensive. Unitary construction made use of experience with the Series M.

The engine was not part of the Issigonis brief. The intention had been to develop a new flat-four unit, but Morris engines were

still something of a separate fiefdom and demurred after making a working prototype. It would have needed too much development work, as Jowett found to their cost, though numerous Volkswagen and Subaru owners would confirm the effort would have been worthwhile. A well developed flat four is an agreeably smooth-running device.

So Morris had this little jewel of a car, comfortable, with superb handling and balance, and into it they plonked the old 918cc sidevalve 27bhp Series E engine. It was like selecting the best carbon fibre tennis racquet and then going onto the court in wellington boots. Issigonis, Oak and Thomas did not like it, but the decision not to use the flat four had been taken too late to develop an alternative before the launch. At least they did not leave it there, for they went on to install the overhead-valve version of the

Minor (crew unidentified) in Tanganyika during East African Safari Rally.

918cc engine, which powered the Wolseley 8. Prototypes were on the road by 1951 and the extra 6bhp made all the difference to the Minor. If only they had been quicker: when BMC was formed the order came to use the 803cc Austin A30 engine which was already in production. At least it had overhead valves but it wasn't as powerful or smooth-running as the Wolseley 8.

Comparison between Minor and Volkswagen sales to America in the early 1950s is illuminating.

	Minor	Volkswagen
1952	2,100	-
1953	1,570	2,000
1954	500	6,600
1955	700	31,000
1956	-	55,000

In 1953 Volkswagen were selling just that one model, the "Beetle", for which they then set up a nationwide dealer organisation with rigid requirements for the training of mechanics and the quantity of spares in the parts department. Leonard Lord had earlier only had mediocre success with the A40. The Minor may have been a more suitable car. Could BMC, or indeed Nuffield, have done a Volkswagen if they had set about it the right way?

The Minor was occasionally used in competition but it was not until the end of our decade in 1956 that an appropriately larger engine was fitted. In the Minor 1000 the car's potential was at last confirmed.

Production: *1948* 1,215; *1949* 28,454; *1950* 48,121; *1951* 42,290; *1952* 47,420; *1953* 57,667; *1954* 73,659; *1955* 88,298.

OXFORD MO 1948-1954

The advertisements heralding the new range in October 1948 gave prominence to the Oxford, "Britain's answer to the demands of world motorists." Historians have not been kind to the car, but what have been their standards of judgement? Listen instead to Donald MacRow writing of working journeys in Nigeria in 1951: "It was advisable to be in Warri by nightfall and it was on that appalling corrugated road, never more than eight feet wide, that Francis drove his Oxford over 18 miles in 18 minutes. We later covered the same road in a Chevrolet. Give me the Morris every time." And again: "The Morris rarely made less than 40 miles in each hour. Never was the policy of high gears and a square engine better vindicated. Even on the corrugations, which at one measured spot were five inches deep and four to a yard, the suspension was excellent".

The car was not created just for UK conditions or, like the A40, to have a shot at the American market. A great deal of effort went

Francis Usher's Oxford with an A70 Estate crossing a tributary of the River Niger on a typical three manpower pontoon ferry in 1951.

into developing and testing a stronger version of the Minor front suspension to cope with the colonial roads of that time. Those torsion bars (in effect coils straightened out) were long, strong and decently located. They did not break and an early shock absorber problem was overcome. Of the rack and pinion steering Lawrence Pomeroy wrote "the beautiful accuracy and sensitivity of that mechanism".

The intended larger flat four engine suffered the same fate as the planned unit for the Minor, and a new 1,476cc sidevalve was hurriedly designed. Without the restriction of the horsepower tax, now repealed, there were wider cylinder bores, hence MacRow's reference to the square engine. A square sidevalve is simple and smooth. The stumpy pistons give less of a thump because of the imperfect explosion space. Pomeroy again: "Showed absolutely no sign of resenting continuous use of full throttle but it is apparent that the robustness and simplicity of the side valves involves some penalty in efficiency".

The design was a sensible choice for many colonial conditions where high speeds were not possible and reliability was cherished, but the detractors have a point. It only developed 41bhp (eight more than the Wolseley 8 engine). John Bate's pithy *Wheels over Black Cotton*, a delightful tale of African motoring, says it all: "I have nothing against a good side-valve but the Oxford at anything above sea level was lethargic to the point of stupor. Rowlocks should have been fitted as standard equipment or, at best, a mast through the centre of the roof for sail application. Such a pity as the car itself was a delight to drive, well-sprung, steering and road holding well nigh perfect with body size very adequate. Why wasn't the overhead valve Morris Ten fitted, punched out a bit, or the current Wolseley engine? Morris lost a heap of orders over the engine performance in a car that otherwise might have outsold all in its class and size".

At least there were reasons why those two engines were unsuitable. The overhead-valve Morris engine was "punched out" to power MGs and the Wolseley 4/44, but it was a more complicated design which would have been reflected in a higher price. The ohc Wolseley engine was heavier, again more complicated, and not trouble free. But this does not explain why no other unit (even just an overhead conversion) was produced between 1948 and 1954. Was it the lethargy of those last years of Nuffield Products? And did Leonard Lord not want the car to succeed at the expense of "his" Austin? The only development was the introduction of a Traveller (with similar outline to the Minor) in 1952, praised as "a load carrying vehicle which still handled well".

Would Thomas have turned the MO into the car that swept Africa? It was on sale a decade before the ubiquitous Peugeot 404, six years before the 403 and concurrent with the excellent but less roomy 203. The car may have been deficient but it was still a popular car for long drives. It was John Godley's choice for his drive to New Zealand to attend the centenary celebrations at Christchurch which had been founded by his grandfather. Except for the consequences of an incorrectly filled shock absorber near Isfahan, there were no other troubles in 17,000 miles.

Production: *1948* 5,809; *1949* 25,366; *1950* 32,902; *1951* 31,706; *1952* 28,245; *1953* 31,955; *1954* 27,000 (est.).

SIX MS 1948-1954

If all the Oxford needed was more power, then surely, with two more of the same-sized cylinders and an overhead camshaft, the Six should have been a winner. It wasn't. Even

Lord Nuffield, then in his 70s, welcoming an export Oxford at Fremantle in 1949.

though Morris Engines had the similar Hispano engine (which they had made under licence in the first war) as a guide, they fluffed the detail design so that the exhaust valves got far too hot and had to be replaced every 12,000 miles.

Issigonis was less involved but the body engineers still had to fit a heavier and longer engine into his forward engine location, the basis for the whole range. The revised structure was too weak and some early cars broke their backs where the front bulkhead joined the extensions for the engine. This was eventually sorted out, but the combination of fitting lower-geared cam type steering (there wasn't room for the more accurate but space-taking rack) and understeer resulting from the weight up front meant that the car was always a handful in traffic, and did not corner well. On the credit side the Six was superbly stable in faster straight-line motoring, a "motorway cruiser" before motorways, and, at steady speeds, commendably economical.

Hans Keller, the enthusiastic Swiss Morris distributor, entered the 1949 Alpine. Somehow he wound that understeering five-seater saloon up and down the hairpins of 29 peaks

Nuffield production lines, with Morris Oxford and Wolseley 4/50.

Hans Keller in a Morris Six in the Nice acceleration and braking test, Alpine Rally 1949.

including the Stelvio, Iseran and Galibier, and the machine was still in good enough fettle to record the fastest time for the 3-litre class in the final acceleration and braking test at Nice. He was quicker than Donald Healey in a two-seater Silverstone. The factory didn't stop trying and by 1950, owners had discovered that applying the Stellite hardening process to exhaust valves would lengthen their life. Let the last word go to Mr Akers writing to *The Autocar* in February 1957: "I purchased the Morris Six new in April 1950. To date I have covered 143,000 miles. I have been driving now for 35 years and sampled more than 40 types; the overhead camshaft Six has given me more satisfaction than any other vehicle. It is the tenth Morris I have owned and undoubtedly the last. I am very disappointed the model has been superseded, therefore OMM 505 will probably remain with me for another 100,000 miles."

Production: *1948* 4; *1949* 3,596; *1950* 5,546; *1951* 1,247; *1952* 838; *1953* 830; *1954* 123.

COWLEY & OXFORD SERIES II 1954-1956

Oxford MO front suspension, but with independent rear suspension still denied by cost considerations, the whole to be clothed in a roomier body, sums up the Series II sketched out by Issigonis before his departure to Alvis. With Austin and Morris now working

together as BMC, the 1½-litre engine dilemma was solved by the Austin-designed B Series overhead-valve corporate engine. The result was a competent if bulky machine, marred by the off-set steering wheel and remote dash board, which would presumably have been much better if the effort and expenditure that had gone into the A50 had been retained to produce one corporate 1½-litre model. But at that stage two dealer networks still had to be satisfied and they did not want to sell the same vehicle.

Thanks to John Pressnell and John Williams' recent research on the Issigonis Alvis saloon we can believe that his preference would have been to use that duplicated expenditure to develop the four-wheel independent suspension that was to be delayed until the Mini and 1100. The car's enduring fame comes from its choice by Hindustan to become the Ambassador, which is now being re-imported into the UK as a cheap new car. The Cowley was a less well-equipped version of the Oxford.

Production – Cowley: *1954* 5,086; *1955* 10,178; *1956* 2,500 (est.). **Oxford:** *1954* 27,069; *1955* 41,546; *1956* 20,000 (est.).

ISIS I 1955-1956

Morris reverted to the name Isis (Oxford's river and first used in 1929) for the larger edition of the Oxford replacing the MS Six. It was the last Six that was mostly Morris, for

BMC's C Series engine was designed and built by Morris Engines. The owner purchased power for the basic price of £565 (only £40 more than the Oxford), but the Austin, Ford and Vauxhall equivalents cost the same or were cheaper. Like the MS the same woolly cam steering wasn't as precise as the rack and pinion and, whilst the torsion bars still did their job, the suspension wasn't as well balanced on the heavier car.

The road testers were critical: "combination of suspension and steering does not appeal to the driver who corners fast; must be driven with care when surface is wet." (*The Autocar*). "On wet or bumpy roads rear wheels display marked reluctance to transmit full power available." (*The Motor*). Then Mr Charnley wrote from Rangoon in 1956: "Suspension produces excessive steering wheel kick… also rattles, a disturbing knock underneath and then poor brakes in really heavy rain."

Export markets had already experienced the all-independent Volkswagen on their rough roads and were beginning to get to know the swing-axle Mercedes. Mr Rowland writing from Australia summed it up: "All too many of the world's motorists have to travel over inferior roads where distances are great and petrol expensive. These circumstances require all-round independent suspension, simple, rugged and accessible construction, and low fuel consumption. These requirements are not incompatible."

The Isis had both the rugged simplicity and economy (33.4mpg in the Australian Mobilgas run) but was let down by those old-fashioned leaf springs. Given the choice between Isis and Mercedes 180 or 220 to cope with the potholes and gullies from Tehran to Peshawar in the mid-'50s, driver (and passengers) would have shunned the English product. It could have been a different story for it was just at that time that the Issigonis-Moulton team were proving with the Alvis prototype that hydrolastic all-wheel independent suspension worked on a powerful car. If only it could have been fitted to the Isis in 1956 rather than eight and ten years later to

the BMC 1800 and 3 litre. Yet there were those who did try with the car. Messrs Manussis and Davies drove an Isis from Nairobi to Cape Town and back in 116 hours. Their "record" was 32 hours quicker than an earlier attempt.

Production: *1955* 3,183; *1956* 4,500 (est.).

MORRIS ACHIEVEMENTS

1948
7,000 miles in America 8 Series E: Mr & Mrs Elliott.

1949
Monte Carlo Minor MM: Mrs Wisdom 47th, 2nd Coupe de Dames. S.C.H. Davis, Press Car.
Alpine Six: H. Keller 4th in class, 1st in class Acceleration Test, Nice.
5,000 miles in South Africa Mr Solberg.

1950
MCC 1,000 Miles Minor MM: H Coombs 10th, 1st in class.
17,000 miles to New Zealand John Godley, March-November.

1951
Daily Express MCC Minor MM: G. Le Grys 1st in class.
Circuit of Ireland Ten Series M: P. Newell 1st in class.
12,000 miles through USA Oxford: Ted Henderson.

1952
10,000 miles non-stop Minor: Goodwood, Sussex.

1953
Monte Carlo Minor MM: K. Frazer 2nd in class. Coachwork competition.
Daily Express MCC Minor MM: G. Perry 17th, 1st in class.
Redex Round Australia Minor: F. Kleinig 1st in class.

1954
Monte Carlo Minor: H. Arndt 107th, 20th in class.
Redex Round Australia Oxford: John Crouch 19th.
7,000 miles around USA Oxford: H. McDougall.

1955
Monte Carlo Oxford: E. Lambert 1st Comfort Competition.
RAC Minor: K. Ballisat 1st in class.
Ampol Round Australia Minor: Bode 1st in class.

1956
Mobilgas Economy Run Australia Isis: 1st in class.
Nairobi-Cape Town-Nairobi Isis: J. Manussis, Nairobi Record, 7,056 miles at average 60.7mph.

MURAD

Wadia Murad's one and only Murad in its prime.

Before and during the war a Lebanese engineer, Wadia Murad, built up a machine tool company in Britain which successfully competed with the established giants. Being fully aware of overseas demand after 1945 he set out to achieve similar success in the car industry. With assistance from the designers of Britain's postwar racing car, the BRM, a prototype was conceived and built at the Murad factory at Stocklake near Aylesbury.

Wadia Murad did not, like Roland Lloyd, seek to break new ground but rather to incorporate the best of the then "state of the art" techniques. An ordinary-looking 1496cc ohv four had oil pipes running through an additional chamber in the cooling system so that, on starting up with the radiator thermostat closed, water was concentrated on heating the lubricant. To maintain a constant supply to hydraulic tappets, oil was trapped in the adjacent passages. The gearbox was mounted in the centre of the car between the separate front seats to avoid complicated gear lever linkages and provide a clear front

floor. The independent front suspension's coils were mounted as near as possible to each extremity, and the consequent wide base provided stability and good spring movement. The design was also an early user of rubber bushes to replace grease nipples.

The Murad was not fully tested by the magazines but they did report favourably after short drives in the prototype. Nor did it get to Earl's Court. For some months in 1948 it was listed (though unpriced) in *The Autocar*'s Buyer's Guide. There was nothing wrong with the design – the problem was production. Government officialdom interfered with new factory plans. Tussles over directives to move to "development areas" led to costly delays. Wadia Murad could not risk more of his depleted capital and the project ground to a halt. However, he himself continued to use that prototype for another 25 years until he was in his 70s. It still exists.
Production: 1

RILEY

At the turn of the century William Riley expanded the family's weaving business first to manufacture bicycles and then cars. There were no succession problems. With Mrs Riley's assistance Mr Riley also manufactured five sons. The company prospered between the wars with Victor as managing director. Percy and Stanley led the design team. In 1926 Percy introduced his 1089cc "Nine" engine with the masterly camshaft and valve layout continued in subsequent designs. The following year Stanley was responsible for the innovative Monaco body, which started the trend of pushing the rear seat forward to provide inter-axle seating and space for a built-in luggage compartment. Alan was on the body side and Cecil dealt with financial and other business matters.

Through the '30s the family were dedicated to making well-engineered sporting saloons, their fame enhanced by the competition and track successes of racing variants and by their contribution to the single-seater ERA. Rileys were attractive, but there was no cheap Minx-type car for the volume trade and by the end of 1937 the sums were not adding up. The expenditure on racing and constant development was not matched by profit. Victor, by then 62, was face to face with commercial realities. Discussions with Triumph did not progress and would in fact have been joining like with like, not necessarily leading to volume. In February 1938 Sir W.H. Peat arrived as official receiver and administrator. After some uncertain months William Morris purchased the assets and Victor (they had known each other for many years) was reinstated. The company limped to the haven of war work with Morris influence on the 1939 12 and 16hp models. When the end of the fighting was in sight the Coventry factory was left alone with sufficient finance to initiate the RM Series.

RMA 1½ LITRE 1946-1952

The initial descriptions in 1946 of the Riley "Twelve" (as it was called when the RAC

A 2½-litre RMB in South Africa.

149

L.O. Sims and R.E. Stokes in a 2½-litre RMF placed 41st at Monte Carlo in 1955.

rating still ruled) concentrated on the new design's "secret", its roadholding and steering. The school of thought which had advocated front wheels connected by rigid axles suspended by stiff springs as the best design for getting a sporting car round corners was losing ground. The discomfort was becoming less acceptable. Two years before the Morris Minor was on sale the Riley team, now led by Harry Rush (Percy had died in 1940, Stanley had retired), showed that by constructing a really rigid frame and carefully designing and stressing the attachment points for separate wishbones and torsion bars, it was possible to achieve independent suspension which combined comfort and control. The package was completed by a rack and pinion mechanism which accurately communicated the driver's steering input.

The engine was a continuation of Hugh Rose's 1935 development of the Percy Riley design. It was still narrow in bore, with chain-driven camshafts either side of the cylinder block operating high inlet and exhaust valves

via vertical pushrods. That valve position, with openings at 90 degrees to each other, enables the chamber to be hemispherical, the shape which encourages the best explosion, but with only 1½ litres it gave adequate rather than abundant power for the weight of a heavy chassis and wood-framed body. In 1948 Pomeroy took Sports Editor Walkerley's car to Italy (to meet up with the Lagonda in Milan): "It will hold 70-75mph right across the continent and I'm not the first to exclaim with astonishment at the magnificent cornering and roadholding power. For mountain climbing one would appreciate the extra litre but we climbed steadily, if we did not storm, the Simplon and then dropped down to the shimmering heat of the Lombardy plain".

Production: *1946* 750 (est.); *1947* 2,788; *1948* 1,908; *1949* 1,498; *1950* 1,356; *1951* 1,164; *1952* 700.

RMB SALOON 2½ LITRE 1946-52
RMC ROADSTER 2½ LITRE 1948-50
RMD DROPHEAD 2½ LITRE 1948-51

The 2½ litre had a 7in longer wheelbase than the RMA and extra strength in the frame to take the weight and power of the larger engine. The merit of the machine is underlined in contemporary references. *The Motor* covered 6,000 miles during two continental tests "over every sort of road surface". They wrote of: "so much usable performance offered for so relatively low a price" and of "the low centre of gravity and absence of roll contributing to driver and passenger freedom from worry".

For the bigger engine Harry Rush had further developed the Riley-Rose design concept. The hemispherical combustion chambers were all the better for the extra volume and the camshaft and pushrod housings either side of the larger cylinders made for a stiff, strong structure. On the debit side it was a heavy unit, but that strong block together with the careful arrangement of water circulation to all high-stress areas and effective lubrication contributed to long engine life. *The Autocar* reported on a car after 128,000 miles and found only moderate wear in the cylinder bores.

There was no major rally win, but private owners were placed in international events. Bremner was 21st at Monte Carlo in 1953 and Sims 22nd in 1954. Nijhof was 2nd in class in the 1952 Tulip. At Le Mans in 1950 Lawrie and Beetson had a trouble-free run in a roadster to take 17th place ahead of a Frazer-Nash and a Riley-engined Healey. Around 500 dropheads and 500 roadsters were made before the formation of BMC.

Production: *1947* 608; *1948* 1,272; *1949* 1,518; *1950* 2,232; *1951* 1,457

RME 1½ LITRE &
RMF 2½ LITRE 1952-1955

It was a fortunate combination of circumstances which permitted the postwar flowering of this fondly remembered design. The same team were still working together in Coventry and the parent organisation was preoccupied with its own new Morris and Wolseley models. In 1949 the Nuffield claws were extended, with Riley production transferred to the MG factory at Abingdon. Components used by other Nuffield (now BMC) cars – the group hypoid rear axle and open propeller shaft in place of the Riley torque tube, and full hydraulic instead of hydromechanical brakes – were incorporated by 1952. There were detail body changes: a larger rear window, different instruments, better heating. Before the 1953 Show the 1½ litre was altered with running boards deleted and a new wing line.

Journalists liked the RM series. Michael Brown bought a 1½ litre in 1952, writing of it at 10,000 miles and again in 1955 after 60,000 miles which had included the reporting of several European rallies. His affectionate comments were leavened by noting the drawbacks of those attractive low lines. It was not a car for the repeated entry and exit of shopping trips, nor would a driver be happy hauling that heavy steering in and out of car parks. But once installed with legs straight, floor gear lever conveniently to hand, screen not too far from the eyes, and looking out over the sculptured bonnet to clearly visible side-lights, Brown always felt "an absurd reluctance to leave the driving seat for that of another car".

It was a different experience to sitting on the bench seat and manipulating the steering column changes of the contemporary Consul, Oxford or Vanguard. But the Oxford was less than half the price, a foot shorter and 4cwt lighter than the 1½ litre yet had more inside room and more luggage space and entry and exit was easier. With Victor Riley dismissed and designer Harry Rush the victim of a road accident in 1949, any new car had to be a BMC design, but with the bonus of the Riley name, then just as well respected as BMW. The opportunity to produce a modern sporting saloon whilst BMW were still concentrating on two-cylin-

der vehicles and veering towards bankruptcy was not taken.

Production – 1½ litre: *1952* 450 (est.); *1953* 1,096; *1954* 1,790; *1955* 29. **2½ litre:** *1952* 1,059; *1953* not known.

PATHFINDER 1953-1957

In 1949, before BMC, Gerald Palmer had returned to Nuffield from Jowett to look after future Wolseley, Riley and MG designs. It was decided that the bigger 2½-litre four-cylinder Riley engine, plus Riley badges and radiator, should be engineered into the new big Wolseley as an alternative to the BMC C-type six. The result was christened Pathfinder and put on the market at the end of 1953. The new car still had torsion bar front suspension, but the accurate rack and pinion had been replaced by woolly cam steering which did not appeal to Riley devotees. The all-steel body was much bigger, with masses of room for passengers and luggage. It was fine for a Wolseley but not an appropriate

successor to the compact RM.

Unfortunately the rear suspension was not right. In an attempt to improve on the old-style leaf springs, there were coil springs with long radius arms and a diagonal Panhard rod to take the torque. In a heavy, hard-cornering car there are considerable forces on such a rod. Let Pamela Smith who had often written in *The Autocar* of her travels with her husband take up the tale: "There was new snow on the peaks but John was not relishing the view, being entirely occupied with the behaviour of the car. Yesterday's squeak was with us again only now it was accompanied by a tendency for the Pathfinder to weave from side to side at speeds over 50mph. Auto-Fink in Ulm didn't speak much English but they could hear the squeak. They had the car jacked up and two men under it. After some ten minutes there was a loud yell. A blackened face came out proclaiming 'Chassis kaput!' Two electric welders got to work. The bracket connecting the Panhard rod to the chassis had broken in two".

Other owners reported similar fractures, (Lurani had had a similar problem racing the

LEFT John Bremner in a Pathfinder placed 69th in the 1956 Monte Carlo. Joan Johns' upturned Austin A90 is behind. **RIGHT** Ian and William Sutherland in their Pathfinder were placed 42nd in the same event.

Healey saloon). The engineering was not good enough. Change has its victims. In three years BMC had not been able to reproduce the skills and dedication built up by the Riley family and Harry Rush over 30 years. There were substantial changes to the rear suspension, eventually reverting to leaf springs. Then there were problems with the brakes, which sometimes failed and some-

times locked on. These happenings were not in the Riley tradition. The Pathfinder did not inspire confidence and was not the right design to sell to the market sector in which BMW were able to re-establish themselves two years later with their 1500/2000 models.

Production: *1953* not known; *1954* 889; *1955* 2,719; *1956* 1,475.

RILEY ACHIEVEMENTS

1948
Durban-Johannesburg 2½ litre: J. Hoare, 6hrs 15mins.

1949
Monte Carlo 1½ litre: W. Gerlach 68th, A. Van Splunter 89th.
Rallye de Soleil 2½ litre: A. de Heredia 1st in class.
Alpine 2½ litre: A. de Heredia 3rd (3,000cc class), 1st Flying 5km (88mph) (beating the Healeys).
Montlhéry 2½ litre: R. Porter, 1hr at 94mph.

1950
Monte Carlo 1½ litre: G. Hayward 40th. 2½ litre: F. Cooper, Plaque for Coachwork.
Le Mans 2½ litre Roadster: R. Lawrie 17th.

1951
Monte Carlo 1½ litre: J. McLauglin 41st. 2½ litre: E. Brinkman 33rd.
RAC 1½ litre: H. Sweeney 11th. 2½ litre: E. Brinkman 6th.
Tulip 2½ litre: J. Searle 5th in class.
Daily Express MCC National 1½ litre: G. Hayward 1st in class.

1952
Monte Carlo 2½ litre: A. Warren 62nd, G Fender 80th.
RAC 2½ litre: R. Lane 2nd, A. Warren 3rd in class.
Tulip 1½ litre: A. Meredith-Owens 5th in class. 2½ litre: B. Nijhof 2nd in class.

1953
Monte Carlo 2½ litre: J. Bremner 21st, A. Warren 38th, L. Sims 57th.
RAC 2½ litre: A. Warren 30th, T. Darque 32nd.

1954
Monte Carlo 2½ litre: L. Sims 22nd, A. Warren 38th, J. Bremner 39th.

1955
Monte Carlo Pathfinder: L. Sims 41st.
Montlhéry Pathfinder: 100 miles at 108mph.

1956
Monte Carlo Pathfinder: W. Sutherland 42nd, L. Sims 65th, J. Bremner 69th.

SINGER

The Super Twelve, for "the man in the know", was in production again in 1947.

In the 1920s Singer began to acquire and expand, intending to mass-produce a popular model. This was five years before Billy Rootes took the same trail, yet Rootes was successful until the '60s and Singer (who had been his first employer before he enlisted in 1915) became little more than a Rootes model name in 1956.

George Singer had died in 1909 and ten years later the company was managed by William Bullock, reputed to be just as forceful and energetic as Messrs Black, Lord, etc, in their day. Both Calcott and Coventry Premier had been purchased by 1926, and Singer was then Britain's third largest manufacturer after Austin and Morris. The company also made most of its own components, but Bullock badly needed more space to further expand the production of the successful Junior, the first inexpensive British car with an overhead-camshaft engine. Like Rootes, he had personally visited American factories and realised that the key to survival, even to overtaking Austin and Morris, was volume. So, in 1927, the fateful decision to

purchase the 34-acre BSA factory at Small Heath, Birmingham was taken. There was a six-storey building which, though inconvenient, was to be used for making bodies, and what was then thought to be the largest covered floor space in England for assembly. With no thought of recession it must have seemed just the place for an ambitious man set on becoming another Ford. Bullock pressed on with innovative new models. In 1933 the 9hp 2-seater with body design by Eric Neale (who was later responsible for Jensen's Interceptor 541 and the A40 Sports) was the first of the sports cars. The 1934 Eleven was available with Flui-drive (based on the Vulcan-Sinclair, not Daimler, system) and had trailing-arm independent front suspension. Leo Shorter (ex-Sunbeam), H.M. Kesterton and A.G. Booth were a strong engineering team.

However, slumps are the death-knell to many ambitions and Bullock did not escape in the 1930s. Sales declined. Morris and now Ford themselves were both succeeding with their cheap Eights. The overheads and interest charges on Small Heath were eating into profits. Fate then delivered a further blow. An alert press photographer snapped the three Singers piled in a heap in front of gaping crowds during the 1935 Tourist Trophy. The picture made the front pages! It was not good publicity and it didn't help that the fault in a steering component had been in the metal, not in Singer's design. At the 1936 AGM the shareholders revolted. Bullock was ousted at the age of 58 (the same age that Black was removed from Standard), never to work again in the motor industry, though he lived on until 1968.

The new directors changed tack and decided to concentrate on "a smaller range which were more expensive and better equipped than the lowest priced types of the same size, but were not so extravagantly designed as to become specialist vehicles". In other words the ambition to compete head on with Austin, Morris and Ford was dis-

William Bullock – ousted by shareholders in 1936.

missed with Bullock. Innovation was also a casualty and this meant a return to leaf springs. H.M. Emery and A.E. Hunt became managers, with Leo Shorter also playing a bigger rôle. A socialist accountant, Charles Latham (ennobled in 1942) became chairman. The range was rationalised to the Nine, Ten and Twelve.

From 1940 to 1944 Singer manufactured 14 million aircraft and munition parts. At the AGM in Holborn on December 8th 1944, his Lordship reported a trading account profit of £221,233, and a dividend of 6%. Shareholders must have been well pleased and confident that the company would soon find a profitable place in the postwar motor industry despite the continuing costs of Small Heath and the need to repair bomb damage.

SUPER TEN & SUPER TWELVE 1946-1949

A 1944 article in *The Motor* (the magazine was running a series on 1938/39 models) is helpful in establishing what Leo Shorter and his team were doing to justify the "rather more expensive than lower-priced types" label. Singer cast their own cylinder blocks using an iron alloy which they had developed themselves and laboratory tests confirmed owner experience that 70,000 miles without rebore was easily attained. This was way above the average for those days and was helped by other benefits deriving from the single overhead camshaft valve gear, which had originally been adopted in Bullock's day for reliable long service rather than high power output. As Mercedes and others have found, the symmetry of the cylinder block casting in an sohc engine means less distortion.

There were other good details: The upper sprocket for the chain driving that single camshaft was removable so that the head could be taken off for decarbonising without upsetting the timing, and the valves were so arranged that plenty of cooling water always reached the critical valve seats and guides. The older journalists who kept the magazines in being during the war were able to take a Super Twelve works hack (which had already done 50,000 miles) on a wartime journey and were delighted with the performance and cornering characteristics on those empty roads.

The company still made many of its own components and development had continued alongside war work. An improved 1193cc Super Ten was in production again by the end of 1945. There was a new gearbox with a smooth precise feel to the central lever, the result of re-thinking the selector mechanism. The springs may have been old-fashioned leaves but even they had been re-thought, with slightly curved ends for a more progressive movement. At a basic price of a little over £100 more than the Austin or Morris offering you were buying much more car if you cared and could afford to look. The Super Twelve wasn't in production till 1947. It was a larger edition of the same general concept: 10in longer wheelbase, 4in wider and with a 1,525cc engine. Its price was not excessive at £100 less than the equivalent Humber, Jaguar and Rover.

Both cars were advertised in the British motoring press for "the man in the know", and "as the car-wise have known for some time, both are uncommonly well worth waiting for". The trouble was that whilst these models did so much to re-establish Singer's reputation in export markets after the problems of the 1930s, there were few at home who had the opportunity to get to know them and their excellent qualities. They were shipped all over the world, and *The Autocar* even has a picture of two gleaming Super Tens outside the premises of a Chinese garage with "China Motors – Singer Sales" inscribed above the entrance. Small Heath may not have been an ideal factory but thousands of cars were still produced and profits continued through the 1940s.

Production – Super Ten: *1946* 1,542; *1947* 5,149; *1948* 3,204; *1949* 602. **Super Twelve:** *1947* 174; *1948* 734; *1949* 390.

SM1500 & HUNTER
1948-1956

Like Rose with the Lea-Francis engine, Shorter put all his considerable experience into the evolution of the new SM1500, which the company were able to finance from wartime profits. All who had contact with the car including the magazines' road testers praised the design for its balance of virtues – good roadholding with comfort, pleasant driving characteristics, lively performance with economy – all allied to Singer long-term reliability. Yet, when the UK buyer's market returned, the cars piled up at the factory, unwanted. Why?

Posthumous critics have pointed to the body, commenting that it was ugly and ungainly, but without considering the reasons behind that shape. Showroom looks were not Shorter's priority, his aim being to create the most satisfactory vehicle for those who travelled inside, particularly overseas, where the demand at that time was for seating for six. People wanted to travel huddled together, so different from today's demand for individual seats. Singer didn't have experience of unitary construction so they opted for a separate chassis which they could make themselves, purchasing just the body shell, in this case from Pressed Steel. You can put a low body on to a separate chassis if you have footwells either side of the frame (the Riley solution), but three people on the same seat need a flat floor front and back the opposite to today's dividing console. Shorter also wanted decent head-room for those rear passengers, so its not surprising that the result was 4in higher than Ford's Consul or the Fiat 1400. The next achievement was placing the rear seat ahead of the wheels, which improves the ride, but this meant the car was nearly a foot longer than the Ford and 8in longer than the Fiat. Finally Shorter saw no point in surplus width, Ford and Fiat were wider.

So the SM1500 looked different – higher, longer and narrower than its contemporaries – but it was in fact the more natural shape to

T.N. Blockley and SM 1500 in the 1951 Circuit of Ireland.

best provide for the needs of that time. One cannot entirely excuse Shorter and his team. Rover showed what could be done to break up the slab sides of a not dissimilar design, but what seems to happen is that creators get used to shapes which they live with day by day and are thus unable to visualise the initial impact on others. This is where a less involved chairman might have been useful, for in those years immediately after the war his Lordship was both leader of the London County Council and Lord Lieutenant of Middlesex! Did he really have time to observe and reflect on Singer's plans? It also shows the value of today's clinics to judge public reaction to a new design. One of the problems was the undisguised vertical line of the back door, the consequence of the better seat position (most rear doors had cut-outs for the wheel arch), which emphasized the height. Rover had lines and curves to mitigate this effect.

The critics forget that it was a considerable achievement to combine such roominess with good handling. It could have been even better if Lockheed had been able to perfect Peter Thornhill's hydro-pneumatic suspension struts (which had contributed to the Fedden somersault). They gave good results fitted to early UK prototypes, but in hotter climates the suspension sagged or rose according to temperature. Others have

written that the car was too expensive but the figures do not support this assessment. At £625 (£799 with purchase tax) it wasn't another Lea-Francis at £998. It's true that it was nearly £200 more than the Consul or the Morris Oxford but you were getting much more car for your money. The car was much liked for its toughness in Commonwealth countries and was a favourite of South American farmers. It was also used as a taxi in Japan. At home the buying public's awareness of the SM suffered from the Government's restrictions on sales.

Despite Ralph Sleigh's efforts in the 1953 Tulip Rally ("Sleigh, outclassed in speed, threw the Singer round the downhill hairpins faster and faster, convincingly showing its well-known cornering abilities") there had been no major rally successes to be trumpeted across the national press. And not enough people read the motoring journalists' reports of their journeys. Sammy Davis, covering the Monte Carlo Rally in 1950, wrote of the SM1500 "astonishing its driver by the way it puts up a good average speed over a long journey; the road surface does not come through to the crew who most of the time have no idea whether it is good or bad." In November 1951 John Cooper and Michael Brown took another SM twice across the Pyrenees en route to Barcelona and were delighted with its behaviour: "Outstanding

Export SM Roadster in the 1953 Libyan International Rally. The Author's Fiat 1100 is to the left of the drophead Ford Zephyr.

stability, not a vestige of vice in its make-up. How that car was hard driven, day after day, without the slightest protest, is a matter for affection in one's motoring heart".

Sadly, despite all the enthusiasm, when that buyer's market returned in 1953, and the SM (and other cars) were readily available, there were simply not enough British buyers "in the know" to realise that it was well worth looking beyond that uncompromising shape in the showrooms. Eventually British motorists woke up to the car and started writing to the magazines. J. Brown from Essex: "Recently my SM1500 passed the 50,000 mile mark. It has never failed me, never been in a garage for any repair or adjustment whatever". K. Woods from Kent: "An interesting experience to drive all Singer models from 1950 and note the development which has been carried out with great care and determination to make the car as good as possible in its price range. Anything up to 100,000 miles can be obtained before reboring. No back axle or gearbox trouble on any of the six cars operated over 200,000 miles. Very long distances can be covered without fatigue".

The SMs would have been better appreciated if they had completed these mileages on English roads two or three years earlier. The Hunter was introduced in August 1954 with traditional radiator grille but still the same slab sides. The 1955 road test once again pointed to the benefit of getting the rear seat forward and the rear wheels back: "shows up well on a winding road, passengers are not thrown about, and comments from the rear compartment during a fast journey were most favourable". But you had to be travelling in the car to experience these advantages. Sales did improve in 1955, though not in sufficient volume to achieve a profit. UK buyers still did not seem to realise what was available for £688 (£975 with purchase tax). over £100 less than the 1½-litre Riley or the Rover 60, the Javelin being no more.

The Autocar's **Michael Brown and John Cooper with SM 1500 south of the Pyrenees en route to the Barcelona Show in 1951.**

Production: *1948* 2; *1949* 700; *1950* 5,000; *1951* 6,400; *1952* 4,000; *1953* 1,558; *1954* 1,880; *1955* 2,519; *1956* 2,000.

P.H. Bibby in a 4AB
Roadster on the
Morecambe Rally of
the Lancashire Auto
Club in May 1952.

ROADSTER 1946-1954

The re-introduction and development of the 1939 Roadster after the war was a success for Singer. There would never have been a large market for such a car but for those all over the world, particularly in sunnier countries, who wanted a small reliable four-seater open tourer, it fitted the bill exactly. Money was not wasted on cosmetic changes. Because the price was kept down, the Singer, at £450 in 1948 (£576 with purchase tax), outsold rivals like the MG YT, Morgan and Lea-Francis, and even the A40 Sports.

There were three stages of development: 1074cc engine and leaf springs (4A); 1074cc engine and independent front suspension (4AB) introduced at the 1950 Show; and 1497cc engine plus ifs (SM) introduced at the 1951 Show. The ifs cars can be recognised by the shape of the wings. There is much less of a side valance, they do not wrap so tightly round the circumference of the wheels. As often happens, the later models did not win all the laurels. On test the 4A averaged 35mpg and "the leaf springs showed up strikingly well on unsurfaced country tracks." Mr Wolff wrote from Johannesburg: "The 4A displays an outstanding appetite for miles. A few weeks ago 412 miles were covered com-

fortably in 8½ hours and mpg was 33. The hood is particularly good; we were completely dry after driving through a storm which produced three inches of rain in ¾ hour. Its old-fashioned suspension system irons out corrugations at 50mph".

With the arrival of the SM version, the Roadster was written up as a car which above all was fun to drive, particularly with the twin-carburettor option. The steering was praised: "Light and positive, only the smallest movement – an inclination of the body almost – is needed to swing round fast mainroad bends; very little reaction to road shocks through the wheel". There was no nonsense about taking away that lovely gear lever which was so pleasing on the Super 10 and had to be sacrificed for sake of a flat floor on the SM saloon! Mr Kenney wrote from Wayne, Pennsylvania: "The Singer is better than ever at 36,000 miles. I have ranged in it from Massachusetts to Florida. It is a very charming car for open air touring and is also eminently satisfactory for sleeping. With top up and windows mounted I have survived hail storms without inconvenience. I have seen an old Singer which was still going strong at 175,000 miles, so they must be a good bet".

It was a pity that French distributor

Jacques Savoye's entry for the 1952 Le Mans was not accepted. If not amongst the winners, the Roadster's usual reliability should have achieved the 24 hours. In the 1953 Ulster Tourist Trophy an SM Roadster driven by Tyrer & Reece "circulated with impressive steadiness" – the 1935 TT debâcle avenged? Otherwise it was left to the Australians to enter the cars in their reliability trials, and it is sometimes forgotten that the SM engine and gearbox were the heart of the HRG which achieved so many successes in those postwar years. The inimitable John Bate (rowlocks for the Oxford) did not forget "a red HRG, an engine that revved smoothly to high levels with corresponding performance. Why didn't the sons of Nippon copy that gem of a Singer engine? What a lovely gearbox to mate with such a power unit too".

There were attempts to use "the gem" as a basis for other machines. In 1952 there were pictures of a fibreglass 2-seater which

Mrs Norma Williamson with Roadster in the 1955 Round-Australia Trial.

Vaughan Motors announced they were going to produce in California, but the project faltered. Michelotti designed, and the Swiss Ghia company at Aigle built, a pretty coupé on the Roadster chassis. Then for Earl's Court in 1953 Singer themselves had further developed the chassis, with smaller wheels and larger tyres, a larger petrol tank, extra instruments including a rev counter and temperature gauge, and the extra space which was needed round the foot pedals; and, still looking ahead, clothed it with one of the first fibreglass bodies in the U.K. This SMX was 1½cwt lighter and the *Daily Mirror* enthused, "if there is a car of the future at the Show it is the new Singer Roadster". Even *The Times* took up the theme: "perhaps most significant is the Singer SMX". It was significant as a pointer to the future use of plastics in every vehicle; but at the time the cost of turning the prototypes into production cars using a new process was too high and the SMX became a victim of the company's other problems.

Reporting on the Paris Ghia Coupé, *The Autocar* had written "a heartening approach indispensable if this British chassis is to offer opposition to Porsche." At the beginning of 1955 the elements for such opposition were visible, when the fruits of further cooperation between HRG and Singer were announced. Singer provided the bottom half of the engine with new crank and rods, also the gearbox, steering and other parts. HRG had designed a new tubular chassis with full independent suspension and disc brakes and a new alloy twin overhead camshaft cylinder head. Had Singer survived as an independent company, there are indications that they would have taken over series production and decades of Porsche-beaters could have emerged!

Production: *1946* 500; *1947* 586; *1948* 1,103; *1949* 1,919; *1950* 2,836; *1951* 1,500; *1952* 500; *1953* 450; *1954* 580; *1955* 400.

THE LAST YEAR

In April 1954 Maurice Curtis, who had been a successful general manager at Sentinel in

Ghia body on the Roadster chassis at the Paris Show in 1952.

Shrewsbury, took over at Singer, with Hunt becoming chairman and Shorter remaining as Technical Director. Curtis was fully aware of the need for change and particularly for a new and more attractive body design, but did not have time to implement his priorities. A moderate loss for 1954 was followed by the announcement of a £140,000 deficit in November 1955. The ordinary shares rose to 4s 4½d, but then fell back. Something was in the wind. In December it was announced that, with the exception of Curtis, the directors were recommending acceptance of an offer from Rootes by which both classes of shareholder would receive cash and new preference shares. At a meeting in Coventry on December 29th these shareholders rejected another offer by George Cohen, Sons & Co., also known as the "600" group, and Rootes won the day. Billy Rootes returned to his first employer, was photographed with employees who had been there with him in 1914, and confirmed that production of Singer Cars would continue. In fact the Hunter was produced for another year with price reduced and the next Singers were Minx-based.

Did it have to happen? *The Autocar* reported that Singer's gross assets were over £2 million, yet the total debt wasn't much more than £½ million. The factory was already doing sub-contract work for other companies and there were other prospects in hand. It seems likely that the elderly directors (Shorter was 70, Hunt in his 60s) were weary of the struggle. They knew how much work was needed to modernise the factories. (Ex-Rootes engineers remember visits to the gloomy Singer plants – "cramped floor layouts with consequent heavy handling costs, machines making engine parts almost all belt-driven".) Those directors probably believed they were doing their best by the shareholders (not forgetting their own stock) and giving employees the chance of future employment. Curtis alone spoke out, and then resigned. He was the only younger man and had not had enough time to bring in allies. Had he done so, and if the banks had been co-operative, a new team might have carried out their own modernisation and reorganisation and the company survived till more affluent times.

The pity of it was that, at the Motor Show just a month before the Rootes offer, there was a maroon Hunter which didn't look so

high. The interim expedient of fluted edges to the wings and body sills on the existing bodyshell mitigated the effect of those slab sides. If you looked inside there was new leatherwork and an exquisite solid walnut dash. Alongside was a beautifully finished display chassis and sectioned engine which had all the details of a new twin overhead camshaft head (an iron version of the HRG design) shown in operation connected to an electric motor. Outside the hall there were further complete cars available for demonstration. The magazine descriptions showed that the whole car had been meticulously engineered in the Shorter fashion. It was to be called the Hunter 75, with deliveries to start in January at £811 (£1,218 with PT), still cheaper than the Rover 60 or a 1½-litre import like the Borgward Isabella TS. Those who did get to drive the 75 were enthusiastic. *The Motor*, after a Goodwood test day, wrote of "a veritable wolf in sheep's clothing". But when January came there were no 75s and never would be. One of Rootes' first actions had been to order the smashing up and scrapping of all existing twin-camshaft cylinder heads and blocks. It was the pre-war Talbot story again. Rootes did not like advanced engineering when the adequate would suffice.

1953 fibreglass SMX, the car of the future at Earls Court in 1953, but it was not to be.

SINGER ACHIEVEMENTS

1948
SM1500: Reporting Alpine Rally for *The Motor*.

1950
Monte Carlo SM1500: A. Greenhalgh 62nd.
MCC 1,000 Mile SM1500: G. Duff 12th & 1st in class.
SM1500: Reporting Monte Carlo Rally for *The Autocar*.

1951
Daily Express/MCC National 9 Roadster: A. Anderson-Wright 1st in class.
SM1500: *The Autocar* journalists' transport to Barcelona.

1952
Circuit of Ireland 9 Roadster: Miss Andrews, Ladies' Trophy.

1953
Tulip SM1500: R. Sleigh 4th in class at Ballon d'Alsace 6-mile circuit.
SM1500: Reporting MCC Rally for *The Autocar*.
Redex Round Australia 9 Roadster: H. Thompson 2nd in class.
Ulster Tourist Trophy SM Roadster: G. Tyrer 13th.

1954
Monte Carlo SM1500: J. Bolton 174th.

1955
Mobilgas Economy Run Hunter: R. Hellyer 3rd in class.

STANDARD

Bubbenhall today is an attractive Warwickshire village unaware of the drama of January 1954 when Alick Dick and his fellow directors at Standard-Triumph asked their world-renowned 58-year-old leader for his resignation. It was a classic example of the downfall of a dictator without resort to the sword. Over the years any potential coterie of support had been alienated and an attempt to make a fight of it at a public meeting was out of the question. A face-saving formula was accepted. *The Autocar* of 8th January 1954 reported: "Widespread regret is felt at the necessity for Sir John Black to relinquish his position as chairman and managing director. This is the result of the road accident in which he was involved in November". As we shall see, this was far from the whole story.

Son-in-law of William Hillman, Black had already shown his abilities in his first wife's parental company but had baled out in 1929 when Billy Rootes appeared on the scene. At the invitation of Standard founder Reginald Maudslay he was soon installed at Canley, where production was around 7,000 cars a year and the bank was showing concern at the size of the overdraft. Maudslay had started manufacture in 1903 using the name "Standard" to represent "a good standard of components". In 1907 he had lost control to Charles Friswell, owner of Friswell's Automobile Palace in London, but was able to buy back the company in 1912 with help from Siegfried Bettmann (who became chairman for a year – see Triumph) and others when Sir Charles's distributing business (he was knighted for imperial services) was in trouble. Maudslay died in 1934. Black then became managing director and things started to happen. He found his iron man in Ted Grinham, chief engineer since 1931 and appointed technical director in 1936. Together they lashed production up to 50,000 cars a year by the end of the 1930s, achieving competent if unexciting vehicles fashioned by the body makers so there was no need for a Standard styling department. Transverse-leaf independent front suspension was a technical advance in 1939, and Standard also supplied components, including engines, to SS, as Jaguar was then called.

John Black, then Captain Black, with Reginald Maudslay at the opening of the Davies Street Showrooms in 1932.

It was a fine achievement, but Black was gaining a reputation as a dictator and those executives who couldn't take the pace didn't think it was so fine. Then to war and more heroic efforts – 1,000 Mosquito fighters, 20,000 Hercules engines and much else – plus a knighthood for the dictator.

In 1944 Sir John purchased the remains of Triumph and, in time, Walter Belgrove, creator of those lovely pre-war Dolomites, became the chief of the new styling department. The shadow factories were taken over and it was agreed that Standard would produce the Ferguson tractor. Sir John was absolute master of his company, 50 years old, respected for his achievement but not liked, and with everything still to play for. Why, ten years later, was he isolated and depressed at his retreat in Wales with the company going downhill when he should have been preparing for an orderly hand-over of a prosperous firm prior to honourable retirement? Most of the problems common to the industry affected Standard, but there was also the Black management style. Subordinates were frightened to stand up and be counted. They did not sufficiently criticise and question when the boss adumbrated his ideas on future products. Too often, instead of careful market research, it was "what Sir John wants", and the results (e.g. the Mayflower – see Triumph) did not show up well in the sales charts. Nor was there harmony within management. It seems there was discord between Grinham and Belgrove, and Sir John liked it that way. He believed tension was creative and anyway left him as top dog. We now know that these are not the best ways to develop fault-free top-sellers, as is demonstrated in the following figures for pre-tax profits.

	Austin/BMC	Standard	Ford
1946	£1.0 million	£0.3 million	£3.2 million
1948	1.1	0.9	5.5
1950	5.2	1.3	9.7
1952	5.2	1.6	9.6
1954	17.9	2.2	19.0

One answer was to merge with another company but other industry leaders did not fancy tying the knot with such a personality! Relationships had not been improved by the decision to negotiate separately with the Standard workforce, which led to a 42½-hour working week, full union recognition, and the company's withdrawal from the Coventry Employer's Association. No one firm can be an island in industry and, whilst it was an advanced agreement for its time, the fall-out in the future did not help successor managers.

The Black régime continued through the imperfect Vanguard launch, the more successful small Standard and on to the TR sports cars, which could so easily have become another sad story had not one Ken Richardson (see Triumph) been prepared to speak his mind to Sir John in 1952. There had not been enough Richardsons in previous years – those heroes, often unrecorded, of the human story who risk their own livelihoods by speaking out. By crushing his subordinates Sir John had removed the checks which could have muzzled the progression from dictatorship to the borders of megalomania.

Typical of his autocratic decision-making was when in October 1953 he informed fellow directors that he had signed a new agreement with Ferguson soon after they had been discussing withdrawal from the partnership because of proposed Ferguson links with Massey-Harris. A few weeks later he was injured in an early production Triumph-engined Swallow Doretti sports car. Richardson was demonstrating the performance outside the factory and hit a lorry, but there is absolutely no evidence that this was a commissioned assignment – in fact the Doretti made by Tube Investments with chassis constructed from one of their strongest steels wasn't the best choice for assassination! Sir John was recovering at home during much of November and bounced back in December more dictatorial than ever. The final straw was when he decided to sack Ted Grinham. The other directors did stand up and were counted, hence the journey to Bubbenhall.

The last (83,139th) Eight, presented to oldest employee Albert Smith by Sir John Black on 9th July 1948.

There is no record of the longer term effects of Sir John's injuries. We know that he did hit his head. Would today's brain-scan have revealed pressure which aggravated his innate tendencies?

Alick Dick, who had shown his managerial abilities during the war and gone on to become successively Black's personal assistant and then his deputy, became managing director at the age of 37. It was an unenviable task. A merger might still have secured the future, but discussions with both Rootes and Rover were unfruitful, so Dick turned to Massey-Harris-Ferguson. For a time it looked as if the Canadian combine would take over Standard-Triumph but that didn't work either, and after our decade Dick was finally free of the tractor contract bought back by Massey-Harris. With the money thus received Dick opted for self-sufficiency and all the ramifications which were to lead to the Herald project launched in 1959. Dick's efforts have to be commended but he had started from too weak a base. By 1960 the company was overdrawn and rapidly losing more money. The Leyland takeover was announced at the end of that year. At least there was something worth taking over.

EIGHT, TWELVE & FOURTEEN
1945-1948

For the first three years the new car announcements came from the Triumph side of Sir John's postwar empire. the pre-war Standard range was pruned and production was concentrated on the separate-chassis 1009cc sidevalve Eight and the one larger car available at the same price with either 1609cc 12hp or 1766cc 14hp units, both side-

Margaret Pearson and Aileen Secks with a Standard Fourteen in a Cemian Motor Club Rally.

valve. Reliability had been underlined in wartime service use, so the engineers were able to concentrate their efforts on the all-new design which would become the Vanguard.

The Eight looked upright and had the narrow track and short wheelbase of its generation (the track of the Morris Minor was to be 5½in wider and its wheelbase 3in longer), but still benefited from its pre-war independent front suspension. The result was a machine which didn't pitch and roll as much as its contemporaries and which could absorb the worst jolts of poor surfaces. The postwar edition was fitted with the four-speed gearbox used in the rest of the range. There were both tourer and drophead versions, which appealed to those in warmer climates. In its 1946 "Cars for the World" issue *The Autocar*'s eulogy wrote of: "The quite remarkable Standard Eight in as much as it does not feel or sound like a small car and has an ability to cover the ground in surprisingly quick time".

Yes, it was better than some of its rivals but not good enough to meet the needs of all the countries to which exports were being shipped. There were opposing views in the same 1948 edition of *The Motor*. C. James wrote from Subukia in Kenya: "The popular Eights are practically useless no the roads we have here. We need a car with 9in ground clearance (the Standard's was 7in) and an engine capable of climbing mountain roads", whilst on the same page "an English car owner" from South Africa used to smoother roads asked: "Have you stopped to look at the Standard Eight Sedan? What more could one wish for? They have everything a 1947 model could have". Later, in *The Autocar* in 1953, Eric Scaife wrote from Bloemfontein: "Although a polio victim, I average 1,000 miles a month in my very dependable Standard Eight. I get an average of 45mpg, and usually cruise at 47mph".

The larger car had a similar specification and neatly filled the gap left by other manufacturers between their 1¼- and 2-litre models. With the 1776cc engine it was cheaper than other possibilities like the Austin Sixteen, Jaguar 1½ litre (with an ohv version of the same unit) and the Wolseley 14/60, none of whom had ifs. It was a tough reliable well-finished product built on a strong chassis. Montague Bradley wrote from South Africa: "The Standard Fourteen purchased in Port Elizabeth in 1947 has now done 11,000 miles. We recently motored the 508 miles to Cape Town in one day. We covered the first 101 miles (on tarred road) in two hours dead, after that it was gravel which was muddy and treacherous. On another occasion I covered 1,200 miles in five days in the Cape Midlands. It was on this trip that I

J. Ramos Castello
Branco and C. Cardoso
in a Phase I Vanguard
came 19th in the 1951
Monte Carlo Rally.

A later 1952 Vanguard
in Alberta.

struck one of the worst stretches of corrugated road, nearly 40 miles of it, and found
that the car took it best at 60mph".

Some of these basically 1939 designs were
more than just stop-gaps. Strong frames and
simple side valves (provided there were
enough ccs) had their own value in the conditions of the time.

Production – Eight: *1945-46* 18,791; *1947*
22,580; *1948* 11,728. **Twelve:** *1945-46* 3,955;
1947 4,331; *1948* 1,673. **Fourteen:** *1945-46*
5,726; *1947* 8,774; *1948* 7,729.

VANGUARD PHASES I & II
1948-1955

Postwar Government policy was to encour-
age motor manufacturers to concentrate
their efforts on one model suitable for worldwide export. Sir John went part of the way,
determining early in 1945 to commission one
new Standard but then use some of the new
components in Triumphs and the Ferguson
tractor. Ted Grinham, whose war efforts had
been with other companies, returned as technical director in October and Walter Belgrove set about implementing Sir John's wish
for scaled down American styling for the car
which was to be christened Vanguard after
Britain's last battleship.

The genesis of the one-piece flowing stern
and the three-window side plan can be seen
in any picture of a Plymouth, Ford or Nash of
that era. However, all those models had separate wing outlines whereas Belgrove was
one of the first to develop the full-width
cabin and continuous wing line. Belgrove's
achievement was to provide an extra inch of
ground clearance and an acceptable appearance on a wheelbase 6in shorter than the
Fourteen's. The snag was the placing of the
rear seat over the wheels, with entry impeded
by the wheel arch, the antithesis of the
Singer solution. A supposedly tough X-braced
chassis was retained, for rough colonial

Production and Engineering staff before their visit to America in 1950. From the left: F.K. Lord (Plant Manager), H.G. Webster (Chief Chassis Engineer), H.S. Weale (Production Director), A. Hammon (Manning) and H. Griffith (Fisher and Ludlow).

tracks, and there was a new coil ifs system.

Grinham, with Lewis Dawtrey, Harry Webster and the rest of the engineering team, had anticipated the abolition of the horse-power tax. Their new 2-litre engine (at first 1849cc, later 2088cc) had a short stroke, and replaceable cylinder liners conceived (with other details) after study of the Citroën Light Fifteen. With suitable gearing the result was low piston speed and the attendant benefits (67mph at 2,500ft per min. compared, for example, with the Humber Hawk's 57mph). The 1948 *Motor* road test reported: "Particularly in the speed range of 50-70mph the engine seems to go to sleep and the car literally streams along on part throttle as though aided by a strong following wind". This unit became one of Britain's best, and powered the Ferguson and Triumphs up to the TR4. The interior of the car was fitted out to meet the fashions of the time, with front bench seat, styled instruments and dash, and a column gear change for the three-speed all-synchromesh 'box.

The Vanguard was announced to the Press as early as July 1947 with a fanfare of congratulations to Sir John. It was acclaimed at the European shows, and in November there was talk of a first-year target of 100,000 cars. Production began in April 1948 at the laudably low price of £425, £100 less than the Fourteen. On 9th July the last (83,139th)

ABOVE Vanguard Spacemaster in the 1955 Redex Round-Australia Trial. BELOW Vanguard Spacemaster in Ampol Round-Australia Trial, 1956, possibly either Lefoe or Scarlett. BELOW RIGHT Twenty years after the photograph on page 163, John Black, with Alec Dick.

Eight was presented to veteran employee Albert Smith.

Why were these figures never achieved? Why didn't Sir John have the soaring success which could have propelled the company into an unassailable position? First there had been insufficient market research. If there was to be concentration on one model, it should not have been a 2 litre. Fiat, Peugeot and Simca all achieved a million sales with one full-size model introduced during the life-span of the first Vanguard, and they all had engines of less than 1½ litres. John Dugdale's August 1948 *Autocar* article described "an automobile of whopping appeal" but then gave a hint of the troubles to come: "During 1946 and 1947 the prototypes went on test, though strangely enough not to the continent". This was the second problem: the engineers had little personal knowledge of world conditions and there had been no testing overseas. When the early cars were driven on some of the European roads, particularly the notorious Belgian pavé, there were both chassis and shock absorber fractures. In fact the basic structure was strong, and it wasn't too difficult to reinforce the weak points once they had been identified, but it would have been so much better for the Vanguard's reputation if this had been done before rather than after sale. Nor was the initial sealing good enough for African and Australian conditions, and it is much better if this is not left for customers to find out.

Many of the cars gained their owners' affection once the worst faults had been hammered out. They liked the reliable lusty

engine (which was particularly appreciated in the estate car and later van and pick-up versions, where it did not baulk at heavy loads) and therefore put up with the rolling gait on fast corners. In 1950 overdrive was available, selected manually by moving the existing gear lever (relocated to the left of the column). It only operated on top gear, but this went some way to answer critics of the three-speed 'box, and it reduced engine speed to below 3,000rpm at 60mph. By 1951 Imperia in Belgium were assembling a modified saloon (with longer, finned rear wings and extra chromium) and making a drop-head. The car was also built up in Switzerland and further afield in Australia and India.

The Phase II came in March 1953 with notchback style, a smaller tank repositioned behind the seat (12 gallons but the Phase I had been well endowed with 15 gallons) and much more luggage space. There were numerous detail improvements, including further chassis reinforcement, and a cheaper two-door estate alternative; but by 1953 sales figures confirmed that reliance on one 2-litre vehicle with the Standard name was not going to produce the results which the politicians had proclaimed. 1954 brought two further developments. The tractor diesel engine was fitted to modified saloons and estates, and overdrive then gave the driver a double economy bonus. W. Crossland from Richmond wrote of "a carefully measured 38.7mpg over 1,600 miles". Contrast this with the 1952 test of a petrol overdrive estate which averaged 23mpg. Unfortunately sales were not encouraged by bureaucratic diesel regulations and the additional cost, an extra £200. The other advance was the addition of a solenoid to the overdrive, which could then be operated electrically on both second and top gears by a simple switch on the steering column. Second and overdrive second provided the equivalent of clutchless changing in town conditions.

The Phase I was not a sporting saloon yet did not disgrace itself in occasional rally appearances. Despite continuing criticism of cornering ability – too much roll – the sturdy

Phase II was taken up by the Australians, who did not have to cope with so many winding roads. Spacemasters, as they were called, were second in class in the 1953 and 1954 Redex Round-Australia Trials. Then in 1955 Malcolm Brooks was announced as the winner after the two Volkswagens posted first and second at the finish both had 500 marks deducted for structural damage. The VW crews then appealed successfully against these deductions and the Spacemaster was demoted to third place. However, the team prize was won. In 1956 Standards were 4th and 6th in the "unofficial" Ampol Trial. As John Hall wrote from Victoria, "Standards are the most consistently good trials performers in Australia". There were also good reports from Africa. In 1955 a Mr Hart wrote from Tanganyika: "Especially suited to our very rough conditions, the Vanguard handles and pulls well in deep mud, a type of surface met with only too often in the rainy season. Its good clearance is of great use on rutted roads and a great point in its favour is the lack of need for any special tools", and in 1956 Neville Smith from South Africa summed up: "I have been the proud and enthusiastic owner of three Vanguards. They have exceptionally good ground clearance, heaps of power, roominess and stout bodies, all at a fair price. I am an accountant and my work takes me on foul roads over mountains to quarries and numerous other business trips often of 300 miles. My next car will be another Standard".

Production (UK Factories only): *1948* 7,623; *1949* 38,605; *1950* 45,362; *1951* 38,186; *1952* 23,818; *1953* 26,579; *1954* 22,515; *1955* 13,080.

EIGHT & TEN 1953-1960

By the beginning of the 1950s, with hopes for Vanguard sales unfulfilled and North American buyers not queuing up for the Mayflower, the engineering team were concentrating on a new small car to widen the range. It was decided to tackle the sub-one-litre class but by the time the first of the family was introduced in September 1953 the Minor was already a well-established favourite and the A30 was coming up in the popularity stakes. (The Citroën, Renault and VW offerings were well on the way to their millions.) It needed to be a superlative Standard to swamp the market and bring in the big profits – to reach those seven-figure sales. After studying the small Renault and rejecting that layout, the first prototype was conceived with utilitarian side valves and a three-speed gearbox without synchromesh.

This route to minimising costs was not taken. Grinham and colleagues' achievement was to undercut the price of rivals with a conventional four-door saloon (basic price £55 less than the equivalent Minor) using an efficient 803cc ohv unit and four speeds. They did it by eliminating all inessential fittings, heater and every ounce of unnecessary trim, and still managed a unitary structure which did not boom or vibrate offensively. Plus points were the early use of a hydraulically-operated clutch, much appreciated for its lightness by motorists chained to stop and start local journeys, exceptional fuel economy (the Brisbane to Melbourne car achieved 41mpg whilst averaging 49.6mph), and a turning circle as low as 32 feet. On the debit side the cam and peg steering was not as pleasing as the Minor's precise rack and pinion and motorists were not conditioned to the starkness and to paying extra for things like hubcaps (12/6 each). The verdict on this first Eight was that the penny pinching had gone too far. Plain painted door interiors and no opening boot lid put off prospective buyers. When the 948cc Ten version was described in March 1954 it did have a boot lid, full upholstery, thicker seats and winding windows, but it was more expensive (£14 more than the Minor) and fuel consumption was down to 35mpg. A four-door estate was on the stand at Earl's Court.

In May 1955 the basic Eight received winding windows and door trim and was christened the Family Eight. The following year the range was completed with the

Tulip Rally 1956. A squadron of Standards, now Eights rather than Tens, were led home by an A30 (5th in this picture) to take the next four places.

Family Ten, with bigger engine but without opening boot. In July the estate became the Good Companion. At the Show Super Eights and Super Tens had more refinements, including optional "Standrive" using Newton's centrifugal clutch, and the heaters which had previously been an extra cost.

Ken Richardson realised that in some rallies these small saloons would have a better chance of success than the Triumph TRs. It began in 1955's wintry March with Jimmy Ray and Brian Harock's resounding win in the RAC Rally, resounding because they only lost 258 marks, over 200 less than the second finisher. The light and nimble modified Ten was skilfully conducted on the icy and snowy roads of Wales and Yorkshire, often maintaining progress when more powerful vehicles ground to a halt. (Standard-Triumph dominated that event, with a TR2 2nd and Ken Richardson himself 3rd in another Ten.) In May Maurice Gatsonides,

last mentioned swirling the big Humber up the Mont des Mules and who had joined Standard as European technical representative, was in reach of winning the Tulip. With St John Foster he was 16th at the end of the road section; then came the Zandvoort races with handicaps related to estimated performance. This is a précis from the *Autocar* and *Motor* reports: "Until the last minute of the last race first place in general classification was in doubt. The first race developed into a scrap between the Standard Ten and Greta Molander's SAAB, for nine laps the two passing inside and outside on corners, but the Standard held together and Gatsonides was home on handicap as leader of the rally by seven seconds."

Sadly for Standard the two Mercedes and Banks' Bristol excelled in later races and Gatsonides was demoted to 4th place. For 1956 the handicapping system favoured the smaller vehicles and a squadron of Standards, now Eights rather than Tens, were led home by an A30 to take the next four places. These small Standards were competent, well-engineered offerings but failed to gain that

Dennis Taylor finished 43rd in the 1954 Monte Carlo Rally in an Eight.

superlative soubriquet. By the time the Herald was announced in 1959 some 350,000 had come off the assembly lines, just over half the production of the A30/A35, and nowhere near those millions of other rivals.

Production – Eight: *1953* 9,336; *1954* 40,210; *1955* 30,522. **Ten:** *1954* 11,291; *1955* 37,440.

VANGUARD III 1955-1958

Consider the Standard situation at the beginning of 1955, a year after the departure of the chairman and managing director. There were doubts about the future of the lucrative tractor contract and the TR2 was making its mark to compensate for the poor showing of the Mayflower and Renown. The small Standard saloons were not excelling, and sales of the ageing but now well regarded Vanguard II were falling. We know from research by Richard Langworth and Graham Robson that the sales department "had already signalled the need for a 1½-litre saloon". Had there been an integrated design for a mid-range 1½ litre (Standards and Triumphs of this capacity were to come but only as variants of other models), there would not have been so much at stake over the prospects of the next Vanguard, and a satisfactory Phase

III would have found its place at the top of a range. Instead the car was set an impossible task. Even if rapturously welcomed, rocketing sales would have then been difficult for any 2 litre.

Grinham and his team listened to pleas for lower fuel consumption from Australian buyers (where sales had benefited from the Spacemaster successes), and opted for unitary construction to be built by Pressed Steel, based on experience with the small car. Wheelbase was 8in longer than the Phase II so that the rear seat could be lower and forward of the axle, thus improving the ride and getting over that old Vanguard bugbear of clambering in over the wheel arch. The familiar engine was also further forward, and the whole car lower and 1¼cwt lighter than its predecessor. The objective was achieved with markedly better economy:

Vanguard I	with overdrive	25mpg
Vanguard II	without overdrive	22.5mpg
Vanguard III	with overdrive	30.8mpg

Reactions to the handling and roadholding were less favourable: "On wet roads the 57½/42½ distribution of kerb weight (i.e. front bias) makes it easy to spin the wheels when accelerating in low gear", "Changes in road camber, and gusty winds, seemed to call for

Maurice Gatsonides and Vic Gossington in the 1956 Safari with the Vanguard III.

Gatsonides placed 8th in the 1956 Monte Carlo Rally in this Vanguard III.

appreciable steering correction" were comments from *The Autocar* and *The Motor*. Pomeroy spoke up for the model, describing a journey back from the Turin show in 1956: "The trip (657 miles from Turin to Paris) was made fully laden without anything which a French jockey would call 'le forcing', and with so little fatigue to driver or passengers that within the hour we were enjoying dinner of a quality which is hard to find outside Paris. We thought we deserved it but the real credit lay with the Vanguard which was not only untiring but tireless". David Scott drove out to the Leipzig fair that same year: "For hour after hour the speedometer hovered around the 80mph mark. No whine of anguish came from the 2-litre engine, whose labours were eased by the overdrive". In other words it was a sat-

isfactory machine for long journeys and hard work, preferably with weight in the tail; but not a vehicle of universal appeal.

Then there were the looks. It was decreed that Belgrove's suggestions should not be followed up and the job went to an American, Carl Otto. Historians have credited him with the final style, but an article in *The Motor* of the time wrote that "it was decided not to proceed with the Otto design and the ball was then passed to Standard's own styling studios". Whatever the full story there were too many billowing curves with upper-works bulging out over ill-defined wheel arches and then tucking in at window level. The effect was to exaggerate rather than disguise the large wheels and high ground clearance. Ford's Consul MkII and Peugeot's 403 had wider tracks, more interior width, straighter, sharper profiles with arches wrapping round smaller wheels – and smaller engines. In contrast the Vanguard III could look as if it was on stilts. Was it the last victim of Sir John's methods? Would a design team that was not at war with itself have given more attention to the car's looks before it was released to the public? Would they have honed the shape till it echoed the flattering colour advertisements with their impression of a lower line and wider track?

After further tussles with Grinham, Belgrove departed in 1955. A drawing of his proposal (with vestigial front and full rear wheel covers) shows that he was fully aware of the need to mitigate the effect of those large wheels. Three years later, when Harry Webster had taken over from Grinham, Michelotti worked a miracle with a few deft changes, but by then the car was in its twilight period.

The Phase III was rallied in 1956. Maurice Gatsonides and Marcel Becquart reached Monte Carlo in 14th place at the end of the road section, and then managed to lift the Vanguard to 8th place by dint of superb driving and timekeeping on the regularity circuit. This was achieved with precious little tread left on the tyres, yet the car still won the road safety and comfort competition! In June, with Vic Gossington, Gatsonides entered the same car in the East African Coronation Safari but only managed 3rd place in class.

Other variants were the well-liked estate, which became the staple workhorse of expeditions who wanted more comfort than a Land Rover, and the garish Sportsman. This sports saloon seems to have been another casualty of the interregnum before Dick and Webster had got the new act together. Conceived as a Triumph, it was sold as a Standard with 90bhp engine, bigger brakes, front anti-roll bar and a Renown-type grille complete with Triumph-type badge. *The Autocar* liked the performance but pointed to shortcomings which were unacceptable at the price. It was soon withdrawn.

Production – III: *1955* not known; *1956* 10,000. Sportsman: *1956* 700 (est.).

STANDARD ACHIEVEMENTS

1948
JCC Eastbourne Twelve: P. Thornton 1st class Award.

1949
Lisbon Vanguard: V. Teixeira 2nd, 1st in class.

1950
Monte Carlo Vanguard: C. Edge 21st, T. Wisdom 43rd.

1951
Monte Carlo Vanguard: J. Castello Branco 19th, C. Edge 37th.
Isle of Wight Vanguard: Dr J. Spare 1st in class.
MCC 1,000 Mile Vanguard: C. Edge 9th, G. Milton 11th, Mrs J. Cooke 2nd Ladies Award.

1952
Monte Carlo Vanguard: P. Bolton 41st.
RAC Vanguard: Dr J. Spare 7th closed car class, M. Ward 9th closed car class.

1953
Monte Carlo Vanguard: G. Milton 55th
RAC Vanguard: R. Dickson 11th.
Redex Round Australia Vanguard/Spacemaster: E. Nelson 2nd in class.

1954
Monte Carlo Eight: D. Taylor 43rd.
Redex Round Australia Vanguard/Spacemaster: D. Whiteford 2nd in class. Eight: Brisbane-Melbourne average 49.6mph.

1955
Monte Carlo Ten: J. Wallwork 78th, 3rd in class.
RAC Ten: J. Ray 1st, K. Richardson 3rd, Ray, Dickson & Richardson Team Award.
MCC Hastings Ten: P. Cooper 1st in class. Vanguard: J. Harrison, Team Award.
Tulip Ten: M. Gatsonides 4th, 1st in class.
MCC Hastings Ten: P. Cooper 1st in class. Vanguard: J. Harrison Team Award.
Circuit of Ireland Ten: E. McMillen 1st in class.
Redex Round Australia: Vanguard/Spacemaster: M. Brooks 3rd, G. Kook. Brooks, Kook, Edmonds, Team Prize.

1956
Monte Carlo Vanguard III: M. Gatsonides 8th & RAC Trophy.
RAC Ten: P. Cooper 5th.
Alpine Ten: D. Barker 32nd, 1st in class.
Tulip Eight: J. Wallwork 2nd, P. Hopkirk 3rd, D. Taylor 4th, I. Sutherland 5th, Wallwork, Hopkins, Taylor, Team Prize.
Morecombe Ten: P. Cooper 1st in class, Mrs Hall Ladies Award.
Ampol Round Australia Vanguard/Spacemaster: J. Lefoe 4th equal, 2nd in class. R. Scarlett 6th, 3rd in class. Ten: K. Thallon 2nd in class. Vanguard III.
Highland Three Days Ten: T. Threlfall 1st.
Vanguard III: L. Pomeroy to Venice.
D. Scott, To the Leipzig Fair.
Ten: K. Wharton, Australia, 818 miles between dawn and dusk.

SUNBEAM &
SUNBEAM-TALBOT

A.G. Douglas Clease (then *Autocar* Associate Editor) on right with cap in front of 2 litre during first post-war Alpine Rally, 1947. The Roosdorps and their Triumph Roadster are on the left.

The decline of Sunbeam and Talbot in the 1930s was another tragedy for the British motor industry. Sunbeam had evolved from John Marston's sheet metal and cycle company founded in 1859, Talbot had been set up by the Earl of Shrewsbury and Talbot in 1902 at first to assemble cars from French Clément components. If both companies had continued the quality of that late '20s and early '30s engineering there would have been two more postwar competitors to BMW, Jaguar and Mercedes, but it was not to be. In 1919 they had become part of the Sunbeam-Talbot-Darracq combine headed by the British-owned Darracq company with headquarters at Suresnes, a north-western suburb of Paris. It was an excellent idea to build a European group but then the designer and managing director at Sunbeam, Louis Coatalen (who had come to England from France to work first at Humber and then

Hillman), borrowed £½ million to finance the company's racing and record breaking activities. At first Coatalen's activities were successful. In 1923 Henry Segrave won the French Grand Prix and Malcolm Campbell and Lee Guinness both broke world records; but then Coatalen's ability waned and he spent more time back in France complaining of ill-health. Unfortunately he left behind an untenable situation. Excellent they may have been but the Sunbeam touring cars were not making enough money to repay that half million when it became due in 1934.

Meanwhile Talbot was pressing on with an excellent range of meticulously engineered six-cylinder cars designed by the Swiss genius

Georges Roesch. The cars were selling well and the firm was making a profit but, when Sunbeam defaulted, a receiver had to be appointed for the whole STD group, which meant that Talbot had to be included.

The predatory Rootes brothers saw their opportunity and purchased both companies in 1935. Charles Marston's Villiers Engineering took over the Sunbeam factory and there was then one attempt to make a better Sunbeam with Roesch-designed engine in a Humber chassis, but it did not go into production. The Talbots continued, but suffered from Rootes ideas on rationalisation as they were gradually fitted with cheaper Humber components. Roesch could not take it and resigned. Sunbeam-Talbot Limited was formed in 1938 with H.C.M. Stephens, who had been responsible for the last Sunbeam, as chief designer. The Rootes brothers have been heavily criticised for these takeovers. If they were at fault, it was not so much the act of takeover but rather their failure to forsee that they would need Roesch's engineering calibre if they were going to maintain their position in ten and twenty years time. The postwar Sunbeam and Humber Hawk could have been much better cars if they had been fitted with a development of the pre-war Roesch Talbot engine in place of the pedestrian Hillman-Humber-Commer unit.

TEN &
2 LITRE 1946-1948

They were not much to write about! The cars were still based on the low underslung chassis of the pre-war Aero-Minx with simple leaf springs. At least Donald Healey had made subtle improvements to the basic layout during his war-time sojourn with Rootes. The 1,185cc sidevalve engine came from the Minx, the 1,994cc unit had been used in pre-war Hillman and Humber models and in Commer trucks. Redeeming features were the pretty bodies, with the development of the pillarless construction first seen on the mid-'30s Humber Vogue and Aero Minx and continued on the 1937 Talbot Ten. The combination of

that larger widow area, traditional grille and traditional furnishings, plus memories of the two illustrious names, encouraged owners to believe they had bought something different for their extra money.

Dropheads and four-seater tourers were also available and in 1946 *The Autocar*'s associate editor, Colonel Douglas Clease, took his Ten tourer back to battle-scarred France. The leaf springs did not break when the driver failed to avoid imperfectly filled bomb and shell craters. The unstressed sidevalve coped with 60mph cruising on indifferent fuel. It didn't boil tackling the Alps, four up, in the lower gears. In over 2,000 miles the Sunbeam-Talbot was trouble free: simplicity does have its value.

Enter Norman Garrad who had worked and rallied for Talbot in the '30s and, in 1946, became sales manager of Sunbeam-Talbot. He used a 2-litre tourer as a Press car to cover the 1947 Alpine Rally. His demands were more strenuous than Douglas Clease's French jaunt and he returned to Coventry with a long list of problems. This outing deserves a place in motoring history. The 2 litre's deficiencies in braking and handling in extreme conditions led to the establishment of Rootes' competition department under Garrad.

Production – Ten: *1946* 1,500; *1947* 1,812. **2 litre:** *1946* 200; *1947* 522.

80 SALOON 1948-1950, 90,
90 MkII & IIA, SUNBEAM MkIII,
SALOON 1948-1957
DROPHEAD 1948-1954
ALPINE 1953-1955

The new models were announced in July 1948. Both engines had been converted to overhead valves. With some input from the Loewy studios, Ted White had evolved another pretty body which was to become recognised as one of the most attractive shapes of the 1940s. On the debit side the chassis still had leaf springs and the gearbox was controlled, in deference to the American fashion, by a steering column lever. This may

TOP Sheila Van Damm, Françoise Clarke and Anne Hall with MkII A in the 1953 Monte Carlo Rally, when they only managed 90th place.
ABOVE The Duchess of Newcastle, Lorna Doone Snow and Reina Whittelle prepare their private entry for the 1954 Monte Carlo Rally.

TOP Mechanical problems were rare, but Godfrey Imhof's and Raymond Baxter's Mk II A broke a half shaft near Lyons on the 1954 Tulip Rally.
MIDDLE Competitions Manager Norman Garrad with Lorna Doone Snow and Sheila Van Damm.
ABOVE Sheila Van Damm, Françoise Clarke (on left) and Anne Hall (on right) back at Lympne after winning the Coupe des Dames and 11th place in a Mk III in the 1955 Monte Carlo Rally.

have been satisfactory as the corporate Rootes Group component on Hillmans and Humbers with their bench front seat and room for a third front passenger. It was inappropriate for the narrower body on a sporting saloon with separate front seats. The economy of rationalisation together with the contemporary feeling that a column change evoked a

ABOVE John Cutts and Stirling Moss at Monza during the 1953 Alpine Rally, when they were placed 14th and 4th in class behind three Lancias.

LEFT Sheila Van Damm and Anne Hall descending Gavia Pass during the 1953 Alpine Rally on their way to the Coupe des Dames and 24th place.

ABOVE RIGHT Jimmy Ray (in the back seat) John Cutts and John Waddington on their way to 10th place in the 1956 Monte Carlo Rally.

BELOW Stirling Moss and John Cutts on the Stelvio in the 1954 Alpine Rally when Moss got his Gold Cup. The car was the same MKV 21 as in 1953.

RIGHT 1955 Monte Carlo Rally winner Per Malling closing the bonnet of the Mk III after fitting a new fan belt in 40 seconds on the second lap of the final circuit test.

BELOW Mk III beats five new Rapiers! George Hartwell and 'Tiny' Lewis came 21st and 3rd in class in the 1956 Alpine Rally.

LEFT Peter Harper and David Humphrey in a Rapier between Comegliane and Dob-biaco in the 1956 Alpine Rally. They finished 23rd and 6th in class.

RIGHT George Murray-Frame (on right) and John Pearman before the 1956 Alpine Rally. They collided with a Porsche and Murray-Frame missed a Silver Award.

modern image overruled the benefits which would have accrued from a more positive floor change.

Garrad's report on the 2 litre had convinced engineering director Winter of the value of competition. After some persuasion the Rootes family gave their backing. Garrad became the inspiration and mentor of the Sunbeam-Talbot teams which were to spearhead British success in the early '50s as did the Austin-Healeys later in the decade and the Minis in the '60s. The table of achievements shows that the cars featured somewhere in the results of all the major rallies. They were entered from year one, when George Murray-Frame and Leslie Onslow Bartlett, driving an early production 90, won their class and a Coupe des Alpes for a penalty free run in the 1948 Alpine. Garrad himself was 4th in the class. The 80 tends to be discounted because of its small engine but three cars all finished in the first 50 in the 1949 Monte Carlo Rally.

The cars' accomplishments were by no means the easy rides which the numerous successes may now suggest. Despite Garrad's relentless attention to detail the margin between success and failure was always tiny. In the 1952 Monte, making up time after a snow bank encounter in the final test, and ignorant of the secret check location, Moss (with Cooper and Scannell) went too fast. Had they been just six seconds slower, they would have beaten Sydney Allard. In the 1954 Alpine Rally, with John Cutts as co-driver and driving an Alpine, Moss was in line for a Gold Cup provided he achieved a penalty-free run for the third successive year. In the speed test on the Munich-Salzburg Autobahn, Alpines were set the task of achieving 87mph for the flying 1½ kilometres. This shouldn't have been a problem. The previous year the car, admittedly modified, had achieved 120mph driven by Sheila Van Damm and Moss at Jabbeke, but just before the Autobahn test the rain came down in torrents and there was a strong headwind. Moss blanked off the radiator and increased the pressure in the tyres to over 50lbs. Even then his recorded speed was only just enough. He had passed the timing clock with just one fifth of a second in hand. And

poor George Murray-Frame, also in line for an Alpine Gold, was one fifth of a second too slow: two fifths of a second difference which denied Murray-Frame a gold cup on his mantlepiece for the rest of his life!

Per Malling and Gunner Fadum nearly didn't win the 1955 Monte. The fan belt broke towards the end of the mountain circuit. There was no time to fit a replacement before the last control, after which cars had to go straight to the Parc fermé where they could not be touched before the final tests round the Grand Prix circuit. To make matters more difficult cars were not allowed to stop on the first lap and that belt operated both water pump and dynamo. Malling spent the previous evening fitting belts to other Sunbeams. Fortunately there was enough charge in the battery to start the engine, one lap was completed, Malling jumped out, managed to keep calm and fitted that new belt in 40 seconds. Try it sometime!

Lessons from all these events had been fed back to the engineering departments, and the MkIIs, introduced in September 1950, were quite different underneath. The chassis now had strong cruciform bracing connecting the side members and a much stouter front cross-member to provide the mountings for the Hillman/Humber style coil-sprung independent front suspension. The engine was now 2,267cc, the same size as the sidevalve Hawks'. Douglas Clease was pleased with the MkII drophead which he used to cover the 1951 Alpine: "Between the earlier models and the present version there is no comparison. Climbs which were hard going in 1949 were romped up in the 1951 edition. Descents were easier and faster too, the brakes being more adequate, the steering lighter and more decisive".

The MkIIA was announced in September 1952. Main improvements were to stopping power. It had been found that the rear brakes (and the tyres) kept much cooler on rally cars with the pretty rear spats removed, and these were now deleted. At the same time brake drum width was increased, better linings fitted and the wheels perforated. The final edition was the MkIII, with Talbot name deleted and engine power increased from 77 to 80bhp. It seems that the engineers did not always get it right, for just three months before Malling's heroic effort the descriptions of the MkIII specifically mentioned that a new thin-section fan belt had been fitted! But there were other worthwhile improvements. Fitted with the new optional Laycock overdrive the MkIII could cruise at 70mph at only 3,000rpm. At last the testers were enthusiastic about the steering where previously they had only been luke-warm: "Steering is light and positive, road shocks are not transmitted".

Prodded by Garrad, Rootes had evolved, in the words of *The Autocar*, "a lively, neat and nimble sports saloon", and they had done it mainly by using standard components. But all that effort was heading for a dead end – except for the greatly enhanced reputation of the Sunbeam name. The MkIII remained on sale till 1957 but the time was coming when fewer people would want a 28cwt car which only seated four and needed greasing attention every 1,000 miles.

The Alpine evolved from the two-seaters which the Bournemouth Rootes dealer, George Hartwell, had created by modifying dropheads. The factory liked the idea and by 1953 had their own version. Numerous details were changed. Plates were welded to the chassis and there was an additional cross-member, detachable for easy sump removal. Stiffer springs, a larger anti-roll bar, higher gearbox and steering ratios and more engine power indicate the work that was done to increase suitability for hard motoring in the Alps.

Production – 80: *1948* 650; *1949* 1,387; *1950* 1,831. **90 and MkIII:** *1948* 500; *1949* 1,650; *1950* 2,570; *1951* 5,916; *1952* 4,889; *1953* 2,449; *1954* 1,889; *1955* 1,532; *1956* 1,556; *1957* 200. **Alpine:** *1953* 900; *1954* 800; *1955* 1,000.

RAPIER I 1955-1957

The Rootes family would not spend money on developing a separate Sunbeam, the sort of car which would compete with the 2.4-litre

Leonard Miller and Raymond Baxter (polishing nearest to camera) at the start of the 1956 Alpine. They slid into a wall during the descent of the Stelvio and did not finish.

Jaguar and which Georges Roesch could have produced ten or even twenty years earlier. The next Sunbeam had to be cobbled together from the corporate parts bin, in this case the Hillman Minxs', because the new Humbers were much wider machines unsuitable for a sports saloon derivative.

Were the accountants right? The Minx-based Rapier, which came at the end of our decade, sold in larger quantities than the Jaguar and was able to benefit from all that good publicity achieved with the 90 and the MkIII. At first they were beaten by the older cars (note Hartwell's 21st place in a standard MkIII and Harper's 23rd in a Rapier in the 1956 Alpine) but they soon became a potent force. It was in the longer term that Minx, and later Hunter, derivatives were not able to match the emerging BMWs, SAABs, Volvos and even Fords.

Production: *1955* 14; *1956* 900.

SUNBEAM & SUNBEAM-TALBOT ACHIEVEMENTS

1946
Journey through France Ten Tourer: A. G. Douglas-Clease.

1947
Alpine 2-litre Tourer: N. Garrad, Press car, Press Cup.

1948
Alpine 90MkI: G. Murray-Frame 1st in class & Coupe des Alpes, N. Garrad 4th in class.
JCC Eastbourne 80: N. Garrad 1st class award.

1949
Monte Carlo 80: P. Monkhouse 34th & 4th in class, N. Haines 41st, G. Hartwell 49th.
Alpine 90 MkI: P. Monkhouse 3rd in class, Monkhouse, Garrad, Douglas-Clease, Foreign Team Challenge Trophy.

1950
Monte Carlo 90 MkI: G. Hartwell 46th, N. Garrad 66th, M. Pearman 68th.
Alpine 90 MkI: G. Murray-Frame 1st in class; Murray Frame, Hartwell, Garrad, Team prize for Tests.

1951
Monte Carlo 90 MkII: T. Wisdom 27th; M. Gatsonides, Best equipped car in Concours de Confort.
Alpine 90 MkII: G. Murray-Frame 3rd in class. 90 MkI: G. Griffiths 4th in class.
RAC 90 MkII: G. Hartwell 2nd in class.
MCC Daily Express National 90 MkII: C. Offley 2nd in class. 90 Supercharged: G. Hartwell 1st in class.
90 MkII: A. G. Douglas-Clease (*The Autocar*) following the Alpine Rally.

1952
Monte Carlo 90 MkII: S. Moss 2nd, E. Sneath 24th, G. Hartwell 28th.
Alpine 90 MkII: G. Murray-Frame 8th, M. Hawthorn 9th, S. Moss 10th. Above all Coupe des Alpes & Team Prize.
RAC 90 MkII: E. Sneath 10th in class, C. Offley 11th in class.
MCC Daily Express National 90 MkII: Miss S. Van Damm Ladies Prize.

1953
Monte Carlo 90 MkIIA: S. Moss 6th, P. Harper 17th, E. Maguire 23rd, A. Imhof 24th, N. Garrad 26th, P. Bolton 27th, J. Skeggs 29th, C. Edge 44th, G. Hartwell 51st, L. Johnson 58th. Moss, Imhof, Johnson, Team Prize. B. Proos Hoogendijk 1st Concours de Confort.
Alpine 90 MkII: S. Moss 14th, G. Murray-Frame 18th, J. Fitch 20th, Miss S. VanDamm 24th & Coupe des Dames.

Above all Coupe des Alpes. S. Johnston 1st in class, Miss S. VanDamm 2nd in class. Johnston, VanDamm, Garrad, Team Prize.
RAC 90 MkIIA: R. Adams 2nd & 1st in class, G. Hartwell 9th & 3rd in class, Miss S. VanDamm 23rd & Ladies Award.
MCC Daily Express National 90 MkIIA: F. Downs 1st, A. Milner 7th.
Jabbeke Alpine: Miss S. VanDamm 120mph.
American Mountain 90 MkIIA: D. Bakrag 1st in class, N. Garrad 2nd in class.
Montlhéry Alpine: L. Johnson 111 miles in 1 hour.
Australian Alpine Alpine: 1st.
Tulip Alpine: VanGelderan 2nd in class, Payne 3rd in class.

1954
Monte Carlo 90 MkIIA: S. Moss 15th, L. Johnson 50th, C. Lesage 63rd, Miss S. VanDamm 77th, J. Kemsley 78th. Moss, Johnson, VanDamm, Team Prize. B. Proos Hoogendi"jk, 1st Concours de Confort.
Alpine 90 MkII: S. Moss 3rd in class & Gold Cup (Awarded for three successive Coupes des Alpes). G. Murray-Frame 4th in class, Miss S. VanDamm 5th in class & Coupe des Dames, Orr 6th in class. G. Hartwell 7th in class.
RAC 90 MkIIA: P. Harper 4th, G. Hartwell 9th.
MCC Daily Express National 90 MkIIA: R. Davis 2nd in class, A. Whatmough 3rd in class.
Tulip 90 IIA: Miss S. VanDamm 10th & Ladies' Cup.

1955
Monte Carlo MkIII: P. Malling 1st, P. Harper 9th, Miss S. VanDamm 11th & Coupe des Dames, J. Fairman 52nd. Malling, Harper, VanDamm, Team Prize.
Alpine Rally cancelled.
RAC MkIII: Miss S. VanDamm 2nd in class & Ladies Award.
MCC Daily Express National MkIII A. Whatmough 2nd.
Viking MkIII: Miss S. VanDamm 3rd (She thus won the Womens' European Championship for 1955.)

1956
Monte Carlo MkIII: P. Harper 4th, J. Ray 10th, Miss S. VanDamm 122nd. Harper, Ray, VanDamm, Team Prize.
Alpine MkIII: G. Hartwell 21st & 3rd in class. Rapier: P. Harper 23rd, E. Deane 28th.
RAC MkIII: P. Harper 2nd in class.
MCC Daily Express National Rapier: G. Howe 2nd in class.
Tulip Rapier: J. Melvin 11th & 2nd in class, D. Dawson 19th.
Mille Miglia Rapier: P. Harper 2nd in class, Miss S. VanDamm 3rd in class.

TRIUMPH

Early 1800 entered for Concours d'Elegance in Monte Carlo in 1947 and won first prize in class.

The purchase of Triumph was described in the Standard chapter. The company had been founded in 1897 by Siegried Bettmann and Maurice Schulte, both from Germany, who had journeyed to England to take part in the Victorian trading boom. Bicycle manufacture was followed by elementary motorcycles in 1902. Richard Langworth tells us that Bettmann alone thought up "Triumph". "I looked out for a name which could be understood in all European languages". Claude Holbrook joined the firm in 1919 and the first Triumph car, the 10/20, was on sale in 1923. In the later 1920s the Super Seven was successful, more expensive, and better equipped competitor to the Austin. There was design input from Stanley Edge who had created the Austin with Sir Herbert. In the '30s Holbrook took over from Bettmann as Managing Director and went upmarket, embarking on the extensive range of 1¼ to 2 litre sports saloons which competed with Riley and which eventually led (as with Riley) to the arrival of the Receiver. This was the Donald Healey era but his string of competition successes was not enough to save

the company. In 1936 Holbrook and his fellow directors sold the motorcycle business to Ariel. They had reasoned that they could not concentrate on both products. Their choice led to the success of Triumph motorcycles under Edward Turner (see Daimler) with Bettmann for a time as chairman, but these profits were not available to Triumph cars when their problems came.

The company was sold to Thomas Ward, a Sheffield steelmaker, at the beginning of September 1939 (two days before the declaration of war) with one of the factories then being taken over by the Air Ministry for H.M. Hobson to manufacture carburettors. In November 1940 much of the remaining factory area was blasted by German bombers, their crews no doubt unaware, as with the Daimler Radford works, of the German connection. There was thus little remaining of the Triumph company, but Sir John Black wanted another marque name, preferably with a sporting image, with which to compete with Jaguar, where his pre-war take-over had been rebuffed. With the purchase made and the bomb-damaged factory sold, Triumph in 1944 became a wholly-owned subsidiary of Standard.

1800, 2000 TDA, RENOWN MkI TDB, MkII DTC, LIMOUSINE 1946-1954

Sir John was determined to have his own Standard-Triumph body styling department after the war. First there was Frank Callaby, who had checked the outside designs submitted to Standard in the '30s. He reported to Ray Turner who as chief mechanical engineer was under Ted Grinham. A year later Walter Belgrove, already mentioned in the Standard chapter as creating the pre-war Triumph, and who had worked for Standard during the war, was appointed the new department's chief body engineer.

Sir John had decided that his first Triumph would be a distinctive saloon based on the packaging and general dimensions of the existing Standard – the Twelve/Fourteen. Graham Robson tells us that the razor-edge idea came from Ray Turner, but we also know that Black had commissioned a razor-edge saloon for a Jaguar chassis from Mulliners of Birmingham in 1939. Early in 1945 (before Belgrove was in post) Callaby was given just one morning to sketch out a possible style for the boss to take to Mulliners so that a prototype could be produced. Their effort, with detailed work by Leslie Moore, was not totally acceptable. When Belgrove took command he drew up his own "razor edge", keeping much of Moore's cabin and developing the attractive wing-line that was to become the model's hall-mark. To cut short a long story, in which the departmental tensions (see Standard) played their part, the Belgrove car with some Callaby-Moore-Turner features was on display to Swiss buyers as early as February 1946.

Handling and roadholding were only mediocre. On the merit side this Triumph was a comfortable vehicle, light and airy to ride in with, to many, a pleasing appearance. Because the wood-framed, alloy-panelled body built by Mulliners didn't use up precious steel Sir John had provided an extra bonus to appease the car hungry. The model mirrored changes on the Standard side. The Vanguard engine and three-speed gearbox (keeping the right-hand column change) were fitted in April 1949, and then before

Mulliners stretched the structure to produce a limousine Renown in 1951.

that year's Earl's Court Show the same body was built on a longer version of the Vanguard box-section chassis with coil spring front suspension, lighter steering and left-hand column change. The car was christened the "Renown" after another battleship, and continued until 1954 with the last sales helped by a reduction in price. Mulliners stretched the structure to produce a limousine version in 1951 but it did not sell – another of the Managing Director's mistaken impulses? – and at the 1952 Show the MkII saloon had the longer 111in wheelbase.

The Renown's appeal was always going to be limited but the later products, particularly those fitted with overdrive after 1950, were well liked. *The Autocar*'s Michael Brown took an overdrive car to cover the 1952 Monte Carlo Rally: "Choice fell on the 2-litre Triumph somewhat to the bewilderment of acquaintances who saw the car as the attribute of the City gent or county family. Consider, though, you can see out in a way largely forgotten in modern motoring. The ground clearance is 8in and the overdrive means that power isn't surging through the transmission when surfaces are slippery". Later, describing the journey, "The blizzard that caught competitors between Le Puy and Valence (this was the year of Allard's win, remember) met us on the southern descent of the Col de la Croix Haute beyond Grenoble. It was now that we appreciated the steady co-operation of the Triumph over bad surfaces, for this surface was wicked. Every so often the packed snow had been churned up and the car would hit a morass of snow at about 35mph. It would wallow, axle deep, with wheels spinning, but the bonnet stayed out front and the rear responded to correction. This was the British product at its best and one grew absurdly fond of the car as time after time it did just what was asked of it."

The final gilding, as on the Vanguard from the end of 1953, was electrical operation of the overdrive with the higher ratio also available on 2nd gear.

Production – 1800: *1946* 400; *1947* 1,400;

1948 2,000; *1949* 200. **2000 & Renown:** *1948* 250; *1949* 1,750; *1950* 3,199; *1951* 3,338; *1952* 2,011; *1953* 407; *1954* 380. **Limousine:** *1951* 100; *1952* 90.

1800TR, 2000TRA & TRX ROADSTERS 1946-1950

Sir John's other requirement was for an exciting sporting car which would have some of the appeal of the pre-war SS100. In 1944 (long before Belgrove was free) he asked Frank Callaby for some ideas which would include a dickey seat like the pre-war Dolomite. One of Callaby's offerings was approved and detailed plans were drawn up with help from Arthur Ballard. This body also had a simple wooden frame to be built in the Standard factory and fitted to a shorter version of the saloon's tubular chassis with the 1776cc engine. The Roadster as it was called (there was never a nautical baptism) did not sell as well as its four-door saloon sister but had its own brand of charm for those who were not primarily concerned about performance and liked an open car which could be made snug with winding windows and a good hood. Laurence Pomeroy had one for his own use: "On this trip we were three up with luggage for three weeks and the Roadster was somewhat tail-heavy. A convertible is however a particular blessing when touring the continent in fine weather. Nowhere does it give more advantage than in mountainous country and many of the small villages between Menton and the Italian plain would have been invisible if we had been in a fixed top saloon".

Pomeroy so liked the model that, to use his own words, "he came into possession of" (not an outright purchase?) the succeeding Vanguard-engined edition, which was on show at Earl's Court in 1948. This 2-litre car (with three-speed gearbox) had better top gear acceleration and at 2,500ft/min piston speed was cruising at 70.5mph compared with the 61.6mph of the first edition. The Roadster in either version was certainly no SS but it was a much better proposition for

Roadster 1800 outside the Prince George Hotel in New York, with bumper modified for American conditions.

The new 1800 Roadster on show in the "Car Mart" London showrooms in May 1946. On left are Colonel Maude and Sir John Black.

TRX Roadster at the Paris Show in 1950.

long journeys than the sports two-seaters of the time. It was also tough. J.C. Breakell wrote from Accra, Gold Coast: "When I brought my 1949 Roadster to this country heads were shaken and dire prophecies made about the probable results of the damp heat of this climate. The car, though now back in England, survived four years and the body is as good as new. I have nothing but praise for the endurance of this car in a country where conditions are notoriously severe".

Unfortunately not enough purchasers followed Mr. Breakell's example. Only 184 Roadsters were exported in 1949, the last year of production. They were never available with the Vanguard chassis or with overdrive. Instead Sir John, still knowing what he wanted, had asked Walter Belgrove in 1947 to design a new luxurious full-width style three-seater. The TRX, based on the Vanguard chassis with twin-carburettor engine, and finished in metallic grey and dark red leather, was the centrepiece of the company's stand at the 1950 Paris show and then went on to Earl's Court. Overdrive was standard and everything was power-operated – seats, windows, hood, headlamp covers, radio aerial – just like a modern Mercedes SL. Today the style seems too high and narrow from the front but the side profile is still considered stunning by many. Belgrove's creation was way ahead of its time, and all that componentry might not have achieved today's reliability. Inevitably it would have also been expensive. The published total list price was £200 more than the Sunbeam-Talbot drophead and the Jupiter and the same as the XK120 and the Riley drophead. The problem was that the company was fully occupied with potentially higher volume sellers. After discussions with Italian coachbuilders it was decided not to proceed. What would have happened if the car had gone into production? It is one of the fascinating unanswered questions of the decade.

Production – 1800: *1946* 400; *1947* 900; *1948* 1,100. **2000:** *1948* 200; *1949* 1,800. **TRX:** *1950* 3.

MAYFLOWER SALOON & DROPHEAD 1949-1953

Companies do not now introduce a new product without extensive market research. It was not so in the 1940s. Having launched the 1800 saloon, and before the longer-term public reaction to that car was known, Sir John decided that the razor-edge style plus classic radiator shell was the best way to tackle the supposed market for small cars in America. It would be different to anything else on offer and have echoes of the large Rolls Silver Wraith which the Americans liked. To reiterate the thinking shared by Leonard Lord (see Austin), it was known that US factories were not yet satisfying their home market for new cars and there were few cheap used cars around, so it was assumed that the American housewife would appreciate a small, economical, easily-parked second car for domestic duties.

Mulliners had shown their ability with razor-edged cabin design and it was their Leslie Moore who achieved the difficult assignment of an acceptable shape on a short wheelbase (84in compared with the later Renown's 111in). This body was built by Fisher & Ludlow and welded to a simple box-section frame. The Mayflower, as it was to be christened, did achieve the airiness and good visibility of the larger saloon but, if you compare measure by measure, there was only a little more room (interior width at the front) than in the more conventionally styled A40.

Then there's the mechanical specification, which was a singular mixture of the good and the bad. With no attempt to achieve sports-car feel or handling the coil front suspension gave comfortable riding on normal roads, and in the words of *The Autocar*: "It is not until the car is tried over really rough stuff that the excellence of the springing can be fully appreciated". This was backed up by "pleasantly light steering" and a compact turning circle at 34 feet. To power the Mayflower Ted Grinham developed the 1247cc long-stroke sidevalve used in the pre-

ABOVE S.R. Allen's Mayflower performing in the North Midland Autumn Sporting Trial: "It is not until the car is tried over really rough stuff that the excellence of the springing can be fully appreciated." LEFT An early production Mayflower tested by *The Autocar* in April 1950. "One can crawl along at 6mph in top gear and accelerate away without a falter."

war Standard Ten. This was no athletic modern unit but, married to the three-speed Vanguard gearbox and with low gearing, did provide top gear flexibility. In fact it was hardly necessary to use the gearbox. It was possible to start off in second gear, change into top below 10mph and stay in that gear.

So there really was everything for town use – flexibility, visibility, light controls – but there was a price to pay when the first Amer-ican buyers took their cute little English car out onto their highways in 1950 (over two years after the A40). They found that the comfortable cruising speed of 55mph just wasn't fast enough for the distances they had to cover out of town.

It was the same story as road conditions improved in Europe, which can be illustrated by comparison with a design that was then on the stocks at Turin. At its 55mph the small Triumph's pistons had already reached 2,500ft per min. In the new small Fiat, the Millecento, the pistons would not reach that speed until the car was travelling at 80mph! The Mayflower's slogging characteristics were better appreciated in other countries where slower speed abilities were needed.

K.N. McCall wrote from Risalpur in Pakistan: "The Mayflower has maintained a monthly average of 1,000 miles, most of it over bad roads, with seven or eight climbs of 7,000 feet, a tough journey to the ceasefire line in Kashmir, a run through the Khyber Pass and two trips to Swat State – in fact a long succession of climbs. The engine showed no sign of heating or strain and the springing was excellent. More than ever am I a confirmed admirer, but a four-speed gearbox would be an improvement".

The UK journals added their comments. Bunny Tubbs wrote a realistic summary in *The Motor*: "The Mayflower is ideal for this gentle sort of work, being light of steering, flexible in top to an 'American' extent, and absurdly easy to drive".

With the advent of the small Standards, which achieved a higher volume, this small Triumph was dropped. It would never have been a universal seller but there is evidence that demand was still there if a way had been found to achieve profit from moderate production. It had taken time for motorists to understand the Mayflower's peculiar virtues. Even in America buyers did turn to small cars in the later '50s and there was a pointer to the potential when a Mayflower won first prize for the "Light Car of Distinction" at New York's World Motor Sports Show in 1953. Another might-have-been was the drophead coupé shown at the 1950 Show. Mulliners converted the saloon but it became a costly operation. Ten were built, three with left-hand drive.

Production – Saloon: *1949* not known; *1950* 2,779; *1951* 13,113; *1952* 10,132; *1953* 7,793. **Drophead:** *1950* 10.

TR1, TR2 & TR3 1953-1962

There are copious articles and books on the TR sports cars by Richard Langworth, Graham Robson and others. So this section only summarises the story and its relationship to Standard-Triumph's problems in the postwar decade.

Cancellation of the TRX did not dampen Sir John's appetite for a sporting success. His next plan was to take over Morgan, but at the end of 1950 the Malvern directors made it clear that they did not wish to surrender their independence. It seems that Sir John then listened! Did he at last realise that he did not have a monopoly of wisdom over the sort of cars that sell?

During 1951 divers voices told him of the gap between the MG and the XK120 on the American market, and early in 1952 Grinham and Belgrove were commissioned to investigate a simple 2-litre two-seater. So minimal was the budget that they could only use or modify existing components. One of the biggest hurdles was to convert the Vanguard gearbox to four speeds whilst retaining the same casting. As late as July the car was commissioned with instructions to build two prototypes for display at the Show in October. It was an almost impossible mandate, but there on the stand was that one (two had been unattainable) stumpy-tailed car retrospectively known as TR1. Press and public reaction suggested the idea was right, especially if the basic price could be substantially less than Donald Healey's beautiful Hundred which was also at that Show; but there was a mountain of development work still to be climbed.

Sir John was hesitant after the experience of the previous postwar Triumphs but then came one Ken Richardson, recently redundant from BRM and invited by Grinham, to drive that prototype. Richardson was not a man to pussy-foot and made it clear to Black and Grinham that the roadholding and handling were awful. Mercifully, for the future of the company, the directors did not take offence and the *Motor* records that Richardson joined Standard-Triumph on November 5th, 1952. There followed months of testing and development, Richardson caning the car round the MIRA high-speed track, Len Dawtry, Harry Webster and John Turnbull modifying, strengthening and redesigning back at the factory.

By creating the essentially simple shape of

Earl's Court 1952. "There on the stand was that stumpy-tailed car retrospectively known as TR1."

The Wadsworth and Dickson TR2 at Le Mans in 1954 ahead of a Cunningham and a Panhard. The fuel consumption of the 15th place car was an incredible 34.6mpg.

the TR Walter Belgrove confirmed the manifold genius which had also embraced the TRX complexities and the attractive lines of the pre-war Dolomites. At the Geneva Show in March 1953 his appealing long-tail development, the definitive TR2, was exhibited. Development continued and early on Monday, 18th May at Jabbeke in Belgium a car with overdrive, undershield and cockpit cover recorded nearly 125mph for the kilometer.

By the end of the year around 250 TR2s had been assembled with bodies from Mulliners.

In March 1954 John Wallwork and Peter Cooper took their own private entries to 1st and 2nd places in the RAC Rally. Two months later Richardson joined forces with Maurice Gatsonides for the Mille Miglia, and averaged 73mph for the whole 1,000 miles, finishing 27th overall and 10th in class. At Le Mans fuel consumption of the 15th-place car

Best TR2s in the 1954 Alpine Rally. From the left: Richardson, Slotemaker, Gatsonides and Kat. They were 4th, 2nd and 3rd in their class.

was an incredible 34.6mpg. Pomeroy wrote: "The TR2 won the hearts of all spectators by regular running with an absolute minimum of pit staff. There can be no doubt that the overall performance of this, the cheapest car in the race, caused a most favourable impression". Pomeroy also described the drama when Wadsworth stopped and lit a cigarette on the last lap. He'd calculated that if he had crossed the line before others finished he would have to do another lap by himself.

By then the basic price was up to £625, only £125 less than what had become the Austin-Healey Hundred. After the initial demand sales did not boom, and in the first part of 1955 potential exports were diverted to the home market. Customers had been put off by the ride and by brake problems, but, with the uplift that seemed to spread through the whole company after Alec Dick's accession, the engineers continued to work at the car and gradually new adherents were won.

The TR3, with more power and overdrive on 2nd and 3rd as well as top, followed on at Earl's Court in 1955. Then at the 1956 Show, the TR (displayed with a clear perspex body) became the first British production car with disc brakes. The battle had been won and sales soared, the start of a successful line of Triumph sports cars.

Production – TR1: *1952* 1. **TR2:** *1953* 248; *1954* 4,891; *1955* 3,489. **TR3:** *1955* 910; *1956* 5,000 (est.).

TRIUMPH ACHIEVEMENTS

1950
Tulip Roadster: L. Odell 13th.

1953
Renown: Press car for Monte Carlo.

1954
Mille Miglia TR2: K. Richardson 27th.
Circuit of Ireland TR2: Miss M. Walker, Ladies' Trophy.
RAC TR2: J. Wallwork 1st, P. Cooper 2nd, W. Bleakley 5th. Miss M. Walker Ladies' Award.
Tulip TR2: G. Grant 17th, 2nd in class.
Alpine TR2: M. Gatsonides 2nd in class & Coupe des Alpes, J. Kat 3rd in class, K. Richardson 4th in class. Gatsonides, Kat, Richardson Team Prize.
Le Mans TR2: E. Wadsworth 15th.
Jabbeke TR2: K. Richardson, One mile 124mph.

1955
Midlands TR2: T. Gold.
Circuit of Ireland TR2: R. McKinney 1st, D. Titterington 2nd, B. McAldin 3rd. McKinney, Titterington & Adams Team Award.
RAC TR2: H. Rumsey 2nd & 1st in class.
Tulip TR2: K. Richardson 17th, 2nd in class.
Le Mans TR2: Dickson 14th, K. Richardson 15th, Brooke 19th.
Liège-Rome-Liège TR2: K. Richardson 5th & 1st in class, Léidgens 6th & 2nd in class, M. Gatsonides 7th & 3rd in class.
London TR2: R. James 1st, V. Domleo Coupe des Dames.
Highland Three Days TR2: R. Daglish 1st.
Mobilgas Economy Run TR2: R. Bensted Smith 71mpg.

1956
MCC Hastings TR2: R. Dalglish 1st, D. Taylor 3rd.
Circuit of Ireland TR3: R. McKinney 1st.
Alpine TR3: M. Gatsonides 8th & 1st in class, P. Hopkirk 13th & 2nd in class, J. Kat 14th & 3rd in class. Gatsonides, Hopkirk, Kat Team Prize.
Liège-Rome-Liège TR3: Léidgens 5th & 2nd in class.
Morecombe TR2: J. Waddington 1st, A. Birkett 2nd.

WOLSELEY

The pleasing radiator shape and the illuminated name badge with the cunning anti-theft spring clips are no more. The gospel of the 1960s and '70s was to amalgamate. The British companies were to get together and produce just one range which in time came to be identified, like Mercedes and Peugeot, by numbers. Loyalty to marque names like Wolseley was a matter of history, an understandable reaction to the late '50s when BMC produced five similar 1½-litre cars with different badges and trim.

Rover became the chosen one because of its image and history. Wolseley lost out as long ago as 1899 with the death of Frederick Wolseley a year after designer Herbert Austin had completed the first Wolseley motor cars. Thereafter the company never stood on its own feet and like an orphaned child remained affected by the early loss. It was bought by the Vickers armaments and engineering combine in 1901 after Austin's good performance in a voiturette in the previous year's 1,000 mile trial. One can imagine the Vickers directors, encouraged by Austin's friend Hiram Maxim, concluding that they should get involved in this motor thing. But in those early experimental years it was no good unless the motor enthusiast, who was prepared to live with the unrelenting struggle, was in control. Those directors fell out with Herbert Austin. They took on John Siddeley and fell out with him. Then in the '20s when the debts were mounting the motor business didn't seem such a good thing and the Receivers were called in. Management buy-outs weren't thought of, and there was no forceful personality to plead the cause. If Siddeley (or a Black or a Lord) had been given a free hand and Vickers had put in more cash from their considerable resources, would Wolseley have become another Mercedes? At least Vickers deserve praise for spurring both Austin and Siddeley to establish their own companies and one hopes that their involvement with Rolls-Royce won't follow a similar pattern – nice when the going is good, off-load when it becomes difficult.

The successful companies were the creation of a new class of pioneers (some ex-cycle trade, some not) rather than the next development taken aboard by the old-established Victorian engineers. When Wolseley was put up for sale in 1927, it was purchased by one of the cycle pioneers, William Morris. The embryo organisation that became

Winston Churchill, Mrs Churchill and Miles Thomas visiting the Wolseley works during the war.

The six-cylinder 18/85 Series III, staple transport of Government departments in the late '40s and early '50s.

Nuffield Products did not then trumpet the need for one marque so that in the 1930s Wolseley was able to take its place as a de luxe Morris or Morris GL or SE, to use more recent designations.

Managed by Miles Thomas, they made appealing cars. Then came the war. After Oliver Boden's demise, Thomas became Nuffield vice-chairman. With Harry Mullens (one of the few Etonians to achieve high office in the industry) in charge, 22,000 tracked vehicles and, literally, millions of fuses and thousands of mines and shells were produced. Later, after rebuilding the destruction resulting from high explosive and incendiary bomb attacks, the company made the wings for the Horsa glider which played a significant part in the invasion of Sicily and Europe. It was a magnificent contribution to victory but there was no essentially Wolseley product like the Humber Staff car or Daimler Scout car to enhance the image. As a subsidiary, the company was everyone's handmaiden rather than thinking about furthering its own future. Thus it moved into the postwar decade re-established as the producer of the high quality range in the Nuffield line-up. The loss of independence in 1900 was to shadow the company to the end. In the 1950s the constituents of Nuffield Products became submerged in BMC. Gradually the corporate policy-makers took over,

and the time came when they saw little value in the Wolseley name.

12/48, 14/60, 18/85 & 25 1945-1950

The last pre-war six-cylinder Wolseleys were pre-eminent examples of the British motor industry at its best despite the limitations of the horsepower tax. The cars were imposing and smooth, not much good for rushing round the Alps, but comfortable at a more sedate pace on a long journey, and the choice of Ministers and officialdom. In 1939 the 18/85 plus sliding roof cost £325. Debate as to which car should be first in production postwar was curtailed by a large order for the 18/85 from the War Office as early as April 1945. The first one left the factory on 4th September with price increased to £530 (£678 with PT).

The car was the hero of Bertie Browning's 30ft plunge into the River Gada during the record-breaking run to Cape Town with Humphry Symons at the end of 1939, but a better evocation of the natural charisma comes in the account of a more leisurely journey. Wilson McArthur's *Auto Nomad in Barbary* describes a drive along the coast of North Africa in one of these Wolseleys just after the war. Harold MacMillan when Housing Minister seemed content with the

Andy Hutchinson in a Wolseley Eight (with the ohv 918cc engine which would have been fitted to the Minor) competing at Syonfin hill-climb near Belfast.

The vast 25 Limousine, "an appropriate hire and funeral car also used by local dignitaries and other potentates."

18/85 in which he was usually photographed! The 14/60 with a smaller six and the 12/48 with four cylinders had the same body, but lacked the creamy power of the larger car. The 25, an even bigger six, was only made again as a vast limousine, an appropriate hire and funeral car which was also used by local dignitaries and other potentates.

Production – 12/48: *1945-46* 2,000; *1947* 1,719; *1948* 445; *1949* 12. **14/60:** *1945-46* 1,600; *1947* 1,953; *1948* 1,551; *1949* 520. **18/85:** *1945-46* 1,710; *1947* 1,396; *1948* 2,147; *1949* 1,600; *1950* 300. **25:** *1947* 14; *1948* 35; *1949* 13.

EIGHT & TEN 1946-1948

As the big Morris sixes were not re-introduced after the war, there could have been a natural dividing line between the small Morris and the big Wolseley. But the small Wolseleys seemed to fight for their separate existence. The Eight had to surmount two hurdles before arriving on the scene in March 1946. The original announcement was scheduled for the second week in September 1939, but by then Britain was at war. In early 1945 the prototype was stolen. It had the same structure and body as the Morris Eight but the extra £100 on the Morris's price paid for an ohv engine (which would have gone into the Minor), the Wolseley radiator and all the furnishings and fittings – leather seats, wooden dash, better sound insulation, etc. – which then, much as now, meant superiority. Electrics remained 6 volts.

The production of a Ten with all dimensions – wheelbase, width etc. – only one or two inches bigger than the Eight and with just another 200cc of engine capacity is only explicable when it is realised how every single £ mattered in those early postwar years. The Eight was an easy adaption of an existing Morris and the answer for those who wanted the cheapest possible first and running costs, but also sought the status of that radiator grille and the illuminated badge! The Ten cost another £80 but this was the cheapest proper Wolseley on which all the development work had been done before the war. And "proper Wolseley" still meant something. It had 12-volt electrics, rear-hinged doors with no-draught ventilation louvres at the tops of the windows, pressings in the side-panels, a four-dial instrument panel, wood cappings for the door trim, a steering wheel adjustable for length and rake, and the marque bulkhead separating engine and body; all these things just as on the bigger Wolseleys, and the Eight had none of them! The Ten used the equivalent Morris engine but had its own chassis and a body with some unique metalwork.

Production – Eight: *1946* 1,053; *1947* 2,407; *1948* 1,884. **Ten:** *1946* 850; *1947* 1,264; *1948* 601.

4/50 1949-1952

We are now back to the problems already outlined in the Morris section. People wanted a more powerful Oxford (John Bate and his rowlocks, etc.). Why wasn't the 4/50, overseen by Charles Van Eugen, who had been at Lea-Francis before Hugh Rose, just that car? The simple but insufficient answer is the ageing William Morris and his yearning for traditional grilles. Insufficient because

there was a market for a Wolseley (even with a smaller grille) but not for that great cliff face resisting the air flow and necessitating the replacement of the easy-access front opening bonnet by small centre-hinged panels.

The design was a confluence of anomalies. The easy-access Oxford engine seldom needed attention. The more difficult to reach ohc Wolseley unit required more maintenance including regular checks on valve adjustment – and even then there were the potential valve problems. Pomeroy's "beautifully accurate and sensitive mechanism" on the Oxford had been surrendered to the space needs of the bigger engine and replaced by the imprecise Bishop cam steering. The Wolseley now had individual front seats but still the steering column gearchange designed expressly for bench seats!

According to the road tests, the Oxford's top speed was 69mph, the Wolseley 71mph, and the fuel consumption was the same; though it has to be admitted that the Wolse-

De Rijk and Keiuper from Holland in the acceleration and braking test at Monte Carlo in 1951, the only recorded entry of the four-cylinder Four-Fifty in this rally.

F. Wharton and E. Richardson in their Wolseley 6/80 after winning class D in the 1954 East African Coronation Safari.

ley had better acceleration (5 seconds quicker to 50mph). The car was planned "for the more critical section of the postwar buying public to which the Wolseley has always appealed". But only 9,000 sold compared with 160,000 Oxfords. If only the effort put into the 4/50 had gone towards a better Oxford!

Production: *1949* 3,225; *1950* 3,214; *1951* 11,342; *1952* 1,129.

6/80 1948-1954

The "cliff face" grille was more acceptable on the 2¼-litre six-cylinder overhead-camshaft car. This imposing machine cost just £70 more than the 4/50 and was at least 10mph faster. English police forces still bought English cars and chose the 6/80 as a cheaper alternative to Riley and Jaguar. We now know that the police acted as development

engineers. They applied the "Stellite" hardening process to the exhaust valves from the beginning, yet, despite rigorous checking and adjustments at service intervals, these still only lasted for 20,000 miles. After two years telescopic shock absorbers were fitted, a pair on each side at the front, and one each side at the rear on an inclined mounting to compensate for the deleted anti-sway bar. The police cars had both bar and angled mounting. With stiffer springs they were impressively stable. Physical fitness coped with the steering.

By the end of the model run, with feedback from police and private owner experience, there had been improvements to the cooling system and the interior heating and ventilation, a smaller turning circle and a lower compression ratio. Van Eugen's team had produced a better car but it still wasn't good enough to stand up to the other overhead-camshaft "cliff face" – the Mercedes 220, of similar 2¼-litre capacity, which was now returning to world markets. Pomeroy did his best for the Wolseley in 1952: "I would like to award a hypothetical medal for the vast

improvement they have made on the 6/80. To be critical, I continue to think that a combination of most marked understeer with a small diameter steering wheel is unfortunate, and the car would not be my choice for crowded city streets. On the open road, however, it handles reasonably well and goes quite exceptionally well, a maximum of 85mph being achieved with an exceptionally sweet running engine". Was he really thinking, "Come on now, it's better, but burn the midnight oil till you have sorted the faults and achieved the first of a line of medium-sized Wolseleys whose imposing radiator will herald a car which will outperform and outsell Mercedes over the coming decades"?

A few private owners struggled with that steering to Monte Carlo but there were no significant placings. Wharton (not Ken) and Richardson won their class in the 1954 Safari. Ralph Sleigh's account of his 1950 attempt on the trans-Sahara record when he had to race to get medical aid for his sick co-driver demonstrated that a 6/80 with valves in order was as tough as they come. They were ahead of past efforts on the first leg, covering 832 miles in just under 24 hours.

Dr. A. Mitchell and J. Roberts in their Wolseley (no. 97) pass J. Banks and M. Porter (Bristol no. 96) en route to Monte Carlo in 1955. The Wolseley did not finish.

Meanwhile the 6/80 soldiered on at home in the workaday world. D.F. Davies wrote from Glamorgan: "My work necessitates driving a 6/80 approximately 3,000 miles per month at a cruising speed of 50-60mph. The car is trouble-free and petrol consumption during the month is 22.6mpg".

Production: *1948-49* 2,300; *1950* 5,864; *1951* 6,224; *1952* 5,637; *1953* 2,887; *1954* 1,971.

4/44 1952-1956

The pattern of future Wolseleys within the Nuffield range seemed to be established. It would be confirmed with the arrival of the Series II Morris Oxford with its emphasis on more passenger space in a well-engineered but utilitarian travelling machine. Gerald Palmer returned from Jowett to lead the design team for new Wolseleys and other individual marques. There was room in the market place, without eating into Morris sales, for a more compact fully equipped four-seater provided it didn't have the faults of the 4/50. The 4/44, with Palmer's new unitary bodyshell, was that car. The M Series Morris engine, now developed and enlarged to 1,250cc for use in the MG sports car, replaced the imperfect overhead cam and was positioned well forward. With an irregularly shaped oil sump bulging out to the front under the crankcase a steering rack could be fitted between the back of the sump and the cross-member to which the suspension, now coils instead of torsion bars, was attached. Result: no more woolly cam-type steering. The smaller but agreeably responsive engine meant lower gearing than the 4/50 but everyone seemed to like this car for its combination of comfort, roadholding and pleasing steering. Nearly 30,000 were sold to those who were prepared to pay £100 more than for the Oxford.

Production: *1952* 3; *1953* 5,706; *1954* 10,879; *1955* 10,976; *1956* 2,280.

6/90 1954-1959

If the 4/44 was a satisfactory smaller car, the same cannot be said of the 6/90 which replaced the ohc 6/80. The car was based on the Riley Pathfinder's separate chassis frame. Being a year later into production, at least it only had to suffer the troublesome coil rear suspension with deficient Panhard rod location (see Riley) for two years. Later cars which followed our decade had conventional leaf springs.

The 6/90 had the sturdy new ohv BMC engine, but the unit's bulk condemned host cars to that cam-type steering again. The front suspension continued with the torsion bars of the Riley and the 6/80, and the bodywork was similar to but higher than the Pathfinder's. This last separate big Wolseley design became a comfortable and reliable performer, particularly after 1956 with the introduction of servo-assisted brakes and

optional automatic transmission, but it never evoked the strong pro and anti responses of its predecessor. It lacked character, and the biggest problem was the steering, to which every test referred: "Strong self-centering action combined with a front-wheel loading in excess of 1900lb gives steering which demands substantial muscular effort despite low gearing. City parking, country lanes and continental mountaineering all tax the physical resources of the driver". This tester looked to the arrival of power steering, which would come in the next decade. It was a pity that BMC's engineering resources were spread over four large cars – Austin, Morris, Riley and Wolseley, all with differing engines or suspensions – at a time when Ford, Jaguar, Rover and Vauxhall were concentrating on improving just one model.

Production: *1954* 82; *1955* 2,958; *1956* 3,373.

WOLSELEY ACHIEVEMENTS

1947
Tangier-Cairo 18/85: W. McArthur (Auto Nomad to Barbary, Cassell 1950)

1950
Trans-Sahara 6/80: R. Sleigh (Savage Sahara, Allan Wingate 1956)

1951
Monte Carlo 4/50: D Rijk. 6/80: J. Finnigan Did not finish.

1952
Scottish 6/80: T. McDonald 1st in class.

1953
Monte Carlo 6/80: Dr A. Mitchell S. Veitch Did not finish.

1954
Coronation Safari East Africa 6/80: F. Wharton 1st in class.

1955
Monte Carlo 6/80: Dr A. Mitchell, A. Roberts Did not finish.
Montlhéry 6/90: 100 miles at 101mph.

1956
Tulip 6/90: W. Bennett 1st in Class.
6/90: Motor staff car covering Monte Carlo, R. Bensted-Smith.

CONCLUSION

The Industry "which was not created by committees" is now controlled by committees and management hierarchies. The decisions made by those forceful autocrats did not lead to a long-term future for their companies. There are times when only dictators can carve progress from confusion but then, if the lessons of history are forgotten and they continue with unfettered power, they self-destruct. Because each and every human being is prey to human fallibility, the large survivor companies are those which are now controlled through the interplay of different management disciplines. We may not enthuse over the bland product which results but the checks and balances have prevented the intuitive unresearched decision.

With hindsight it is easier to discern the different flaws in those companies (and their designs) which are now in oblivion. None of them had a strong mix of all disciplines: Each was only good in parts. Talented designers were not matched by comparable strength on the financial, marketing or production side. There were companies where those strengths were available but the engineering lacked flair. Within the Industry there were all the elements of success but their disposition was random. It is tempting to think how the cards in the pack could have been re-shuffled, to imagine engines of Lea-Francis or Singer quality in an Oxford or Hawk, developed Lagonda handling for the A70 and A90 or Javelins engineered and tested by Mr Simpson's team at Daimler. But this is fantasy: reality suggests that, even if superhumans had existed with the capacity to take the best components from a combined parts bin to create better joint products, such rationalisation would not have been acceptable to those separate industry chiefs. Vickers and Wolseley boss Sir William Peat had tried it in 1917 when he organised a motor industry conference. He suggested that the major car manufacturers should co-operate by each concentrating on one class of car to face the challenge from American and European rivals, but Rolls-Royce would not play because they feared Wolseley domination and the others followed Rolls' lead. After 1945 politicians did speak of rationalisation and even suggested volume production of standardised cars with design input from the whole industry. This potential bandwagon was not boarded by any significant organisation or political group but so much of the evidence indicates that the likes of Black, Lord and Rootes would have been reluctant to relinquish their personal power and that it really was only those despotic characters who could then wring the desperately needed production from the potential chaos. None of them – and certainly not that triumvirate – were going to sit round the conference table and plan an anonymous machine (which couldn't become Billy's or John's or Len's success story) when the world was waiting to grab every running vehicle which could be shoved through the gates. The pressures of the moment overruled the consideration of longer-term tactics.

The smaller producers on their own would have needed different conditions to go on and develop higher-volume export successes and eventual home market winners. Despite latterday enthusiasm for the better postwar cars, in 1945 the British people did vote for a Government which encouraged the cheaper car and which made life difficult for those companies who tried to do better by restricting materials and by restricting access to and use in the home market. Taxation also restricted the incomes of the few who could purchase. Enthusiasm for a sophisticated vehicle is curtailed when pockets are shallow and there are cheaper alternatives.

We may also regret that decision-makers at Alvis, within the Bristol/Hawker-Siddeley combine, and even at Vickers, did not opt to use their reservoir of talent and experience for a full-blown assault on the world car market. But at the time they anticipated the conditions that would prevail as the seller's market disappeared, and opted for the other defence-related activities that were available. Those other opportunities, the continuing orders for ships and planes and armoured vehicles, were the direct legacy of the island aspiration to rule the waves and maintain empire which, if needs be, had meant tackling European rivals. It was not anticipated that there would be decades without war in Europe and that the competition with those rivals would be with artefacts of peace. There was also a formidable tradition of armament manufacture, which had been the spur to many of the developments in the production of steel and machinery which Britain had pioneered. The cynic might even suggest that money for payment gathered by Government tax collectors rather than from individual customers was always a safer bet. We shall never know what would have happened if Vickers had hung on to Wolseley and used it as the cornerstone to create an earlier BMC, or if the Issigonis Alvis and Bristol 220 (backed up by the big Sapphire) had been developed to produce BMW and Mercedes beaters. At least the decisions taken helped Jaguar to prosper.

Enough of regret! It is much more fruitful to think of ourselves as world citizens and reflect on the total British donation to the planet's postwar motor industry. First of all we did win that fearsome war and forestalled the regimented imposition of Volkswagen or Mercedes (or, presumably, Fiat wrested from Agnelli control) on surviving households. (Purchase by personal choice is a different matter!) How would Renault and Peugeot have fared under the National Socialists? Second we did help to fill that transport vacuum at the war's end. Those pre-war horsepower tax influenced designs aided reconstruction from New Zealand to Iceland and the money they earned both paid for vital imports and contributed to the Government's health and social programmes. As already explained it wasn't an option to close the doors and live off war profits whilst perfect vehicles were developed. Third, and overlooking the human misery which resulted, in flattening so many factories British (and American) bombers forced the European manufacturers into reconstruction and gave their designers the breathing space to plan anew. Many of them were simply not in the position where they could mass-produce old-fashioned designs. Looking back we can see that our achievement in the 1940s, in war and in the early years of peace, was to prepare the way for others to follow. It was a destiny with which we became inextricably linked when we responded to Hitler's attack on Poland and later when Churchill rallied the nation. The fourth significant contribution came in the '50s when the Japanese asked for British assistance in improving their products. As recorded earlier, Austin and Rootes both responded and greatly reduced the time-scale of Japan's advance to their present excellence.

I hope that by listing those four contributions it may be better realised that the British did not wantonly waste that postwar opportunity. There were circumstances which could not be controlled by individuals, companies or nations. Many of us might prefer to be driving behind one of the badges which have been despatched to oblivion. This is understood but, when we lament what has happened, we need to remember the total British input into the industry's history and into the common pool of technical knowledge. Peugeot would not be manufacturing at Ryton if it were not for Billy Rootes' prodigious efforts. Mercedes, Volvo and others buy British components because they are effective. The cars that Honda and Nissan make at Swindon and Sunderland (appropriately in that same island which provided technical help forty years ago) are more than just the products of Japan. Rather they are the current Japanese interpretation of a machine to whose development the British have significantly subscribed. When we can resist fighting each other we all gain from mutual inter-dependence.

REPRESENTATIVE PRICES

		Basic Price	With Purchase Tax				Basic Price	With Purchase Tax
	ALLARD					**AUSTIN**		
1946	Competition 2-seater	750	("preliminary	1946		Eight	270	346
	4-seater	765	announcement", no			Ten	330	422
	Drophead coupé	850	Purchase Tax given.)			Twelve	450	576
						Sixteen	495	633
1949	J-type 2-seater	999	1,277					
	4-seater	900	1,151	1948		A40 Dorset	335	429
	Drophead & saloon	999	1,277			A40 Devon	345	442
						16	555	710
1952	Palm Beach 4-cyl.	800	1,246			A125 Sheerline	999	1,277
	Palm Beach 6-cyl.	865	1,347			A135 Princess	1,350	2,101
	J2X 2-seater	1,100	1,713					
	K2 2-seater	1,050	1,635	1950		A40 Devon	329	502
	Saloon	1,100	1,713			A70 Hampshire	507	649
	Safari	1,250	1,946			A90 Atlantic Convertible	615	787
						A90 Atlantic Sports Saloon	695	889
1955	Palm Beach 4-cyl.	720	1,021			A125 Sheerline	1,150	1,470
	Palm Beach 6-cyl.	750	1,064			A125 Sheerline Limousine	1,375	1,758
	K3 3-seater	1,100	1,560			A135 Princess	1,425	1,822
	Monte Carlo saloon	1,375	1,949			A135 Princess Limousine	1,550	1,981
	Safari	1,375	1,949					
				1952		A30	355	554
1956	K3 3-seater	1,537	2,307			A40 Somerset Saloon	467	728
	J2R 2-seater	1,722	2,584			A40 Somerset Coupé	497	775
	Monte Carlo saloon	1,782	2,674			A40 Sports	586	913
	Safari	1,784	2,674			A40 Countryman	516	804
						A70 Hereford	627	977
	ALVIS					A70 Countryman	775	1,207
						A125 Sheerline Saloon	1,307	2,034
1948	Chassis	665				A125 Sheerline Limousine	1,449	2,255
	Fourteen saloon	998	1,276			A135 Princess Saloon	1,617	2,517
						A135 Princess Limousine	1,667	2,595
1952	3 litre saloon	1,250	1,946					
	3 litre drophead	1,325	2,062	1956		A30 4-door	382	574
	3 litre sports	1,250	1,946			A30 Countryman	425	639
						A40	503	756
1955	TC 21/100 saloon	1,285	1,822			A50	546	820
	TC 21/100 drophead	1,360	1,928			A90	600	901
						A105	739	1,110
1956	(January) Graber	1,850	2,776			A135 Princess Saloon	1,790	2,686
	(December) Graber					A135 LWB Limousine	2,150	3,226
	(Willowbrook)	2,300	3,451					
						DAIMLER		
	ARMSTRONG-SIDDELEY			1947		2½-litre saloon	1,270	1,977
						2½-litre coupé	1,500	2,335
1946	Hurricane	900	1,151			27hp chassis	1,700	
	Typhoon	900	1,151			36hp chassis	2,025	
1948	Hurricane	975	1,247	1951		Consort	1,380	2,148
	Typhoon	975	1,247			2½-litre Special sports	1,775	2,762
	Lancaster	995	1,272			Regency	1,500	2,334
						Straight Eight	3,570	5,555
1952	Hurricane	1,110	1,728					
	Whitley 4-light	1,110	1,728	1953		Conquest	1,066	1,511
	Whitley 6-light	1,110	1,728			Conquest Roadster	1,180	1,673
						Straight Eight	3,570	5,059
1956	234	1,065	1,599					
	236	1,104	1,657	1954		Conquest	1,066	1,511
	346	1,215	1,824			Conquest Roadster	1,180	1,673
	Limousine	1,910	2,866			Conquest hardtop	1,235	1,751
						Conquest Century	1,172	1,662

		Basic Price	With Purchase Tax
	3½-litre Regency	1,640	2,324
	3½-litre Sportsman	1,870	2,650
	4½-litre Regency	1,960	2,778
	4½-litre Sportsman	2,190	3,104
	Regina	4,385	6,213
1956 June	Conquest	1,032	1,549
	Century	1,132	1,699
	104	1,885	2,829
	4½-litre	2,293	3,441
	DK400	2,793	4,191
	Hooper limousine	4,385	6,213
1956 October	Conquest	863	1,295
	Century	996	1,495
	Century automatic	1,119	1,680
	104	1,596	2,395
	104 automatic	1,719	2,580
	DK400	2,796	4,195

HEALEY

1948 November	Westland	1,500	2,335
	Elliot	1,750	2,725
	Sportsmobile	1,850	2,880
1950 September	Elliot	1,275	1,630
	Tickford	1,450	1,854
	Abbot	1,500	1,917
	Silverstone	998	1,276
1952 October	Tickford	1,218	1,896
	Abbot	1,268	1,973
	Alvis	1,400	2,179
1954 July	Alvis	1,250	1,772
	Austin-Healey 100	750	1,064
1955 June	Austin-Healey 100	750	1,064
	Austin-Healey 100S	1,125	(Export only)

HILLMAN

1946	Minx Saloon	310	397
	Minx Drophead	375	480
1948	Minx Saloon	385	493
	Minx Drophead	435	557
1952	Minx Saloon	470	733
	Minx Convertible	540	842
	Estate car	540	842
1954	Minx Special	458	650
	Estate car	540	766
	Minx de luxe	480	681
	Convertible	520	738
	Californian	520	738
	Husky	398	565

HUMBER

1946	Hawk	535	684
	Snipe	675	863
	Super Snipe	695	889
	Pullman	1,250	1,598
1948	Hawk	695	887
	Snipe	810	1,036
	Super Snipe	825	1,055
	Pullman	1,395	2,172
1950	Hawk	625	799

		Basic Price	With Purchase Tax
	Super Snipe	895	1,144
	Super Snipe Limousine	970	1,240
	Pullman	1,395	1,783
	Imperial	1,395	1,783
1952	Hawk	725	1,129
	Super Snipe	1,045	1,627
	Pullman	1,600	2,490
	Imperial	1,600	2,490
1954	Hawk	695	986
	Hawk Touring Limousine	775	1,099
	Super Snipe	985	1,396
	Super Snipe Limousine	1,065	1,510
	Imperial/Pullman	1,395	1,977
1956	Hawk	715	1,074
	Hawk de luxe	730	1,096
	Hawk Touring Limousine	795	1,194
	Hawk Estate car	885	1,329
	Super Snipe	950	1,426
	Super Snipe Limousine	1,030	1,546

INVICTA

1947	Chassis	1,850	
	Wentworth saloon	2,300	3,579
	Byfleet drophead	2,500	3,890

These remained the same until the end of 1949.

JOWETT

1948	Bradford Utility	335	428
	Javelin	640	819
1950	Javelin	595	761
	Jupiter	795	1,017
1952	Bradford Utility	426	663
	Javelin	725	1,129
	Javelin de luxe	810	1,261
	Jupiter	975	1,518
1954	Javelin	625	887
	Jupiter 1A	725	1,028
	Jupiter R4	545	773

LAGONDA

1948	2½ litre saloon	1,998	3,110
	2½ litre drophead*	2,198	3,421

*October: First appearance in price list

1951	2½ litre saloon	1,895	2,422
	2½ litre drophead	1,970	2,518
1952	2½ litre saloon	2,250	3,502
	2½ litre drophead	2,325	3,618
1953	MkII saloon	1,925	2,728
	2½ litre drophead	1,900	2,693
1955	3 litre 2dr. saloon	2,260	3,203
	3 litre 4dr. or drophead	2,400	3,401

LANCHESTER

1946	Ten	525	671
1951	Ten	725	927
	Fourteen	895	1,394
1952	Fourteen	985	1,534

		Basic Price	With Purchase Tax
	De Ville	1,050	1,634
	Leda	(export only)	
1954 (June)	Fourteen	998	1,412
	Dauphin	2,830	4,010
1954 (October)	Sprite	760	1,078
1955	Sprite	866	1,228

LEA-FRANCIS

		Basic Price	With Purchase Tax
1946 September	Twelve Saloon	750	959
	Fourteen Saloon	750	959
1948 September	Fourteen Saloon & Coupé	998	1,275
	Fourteen Utility	895	1,144
	Fourteen Sports	998	1,275
1950 November	Fourteen	1,080	1,380
	Eighteen	1,330	1,700
	Eighteen (2½-litre) Sports	1,090	1,393
1953 April	Fourteen	1,240	1,930
	Eighteen	1,520	2,365
	Eighteen (2½-litre) Sports	1,254	1,952
1954 April	Fourteen	890	1,261
	Eighteen	1,380	1,956
	Eighteen (2½-litre) Sports	1,240	1,757

LLOYD

		Basic Price	With Purchase Tax
1950		375	480

METROPOLITAN

		Basic Price	With Purchase Tax
1956	Hardtop	475	714
	Convertible	483	725

MORRIS

		Basic Price	With Purchase Tax
1946	Eight 4-door	255	327
	Ten	295	278
1950	Minor	299	383
	Oxford	427	546
	Six	525	672
1952	Minor	373	582
	Oxford	510	795
	Six	640	997
1956	Minor	401	603
	Cowley II	532	799
	Oxford II	565	849
	Isis	607	912

RILEY

		Basic Price	With Purchase Tax
1946	1½ litre	555	710
	2½ litre	880	1,125
1948	1½ litre	675	863
	2½ litre	880	1,125
1950	1½ litre	714	913
	2½ litre	958	1,225
1952	1½ litre	860	1,339
	2½ litre	1,055	1,643
1954	Pathfinder	875	1,241

SINGER

		Basic Price	With Purchase Tax
1947 November	Nine Roadster	400	512
	Super Ten	475	608
	Super Twelve	600	768
1949 July	Nine Roadster	450	576
	SM1500	625	799
1952 July	4AB Roadster	485	756
	SM1500	725	1,129
1953 January	SM1500 Roadster	520	810
	SM1500	703	1,095
1955 May	Roadster	510	723
	Hunter	688	975
1955 December	Hunter S	612	919
	Hunter	688	1,032
	Hunter 75	811	1,218
June 1956*	Hunter Special	530	796
	Hunter de luxe	575	864
*after Rootes takeover			

STANDARD

		Basic Price	With Purchase Tax
1946	Eight saloon	295	378
	Eight tourer	295	378
	Eight drophead	300	384
	Twelve & Fourteen saloon	450	576
	Twelve & Fourteen drophead	470	601
1948	Twelve saloon	495	576
	Twelve drophead	520	665
	Fourteen saloon	525	672
	Fourteen drophead	550	702
	Vanguard	425	544
1952	Vanguard	590	919
	Estate car	655	1,020
1954	Eight	339	481
	Ten	409	581
	Estate	460	653
	Vanguard Diesel	735	1,042
1956	Family Eight	379	570
	Super Eight	405	609
	Family Ten	385	579
	Super Ten (with Standrive)	435	654
	Companion Estate	485	729
	Vanguard III	599	900
	Vanguard Sportsman	820	1,231
	Estate	765	1,149

SUNBEAM-TALBOT

		Basic Price	With Purchase Tax
1946	10 Saloon	535	684
	10 Drophead	570	729
	10 Tourer	505	646
	2 litre Saloon	625	799
	2 litre Drophead	660	844

		Basic Price	With Purchase Tax				Basic Price	With Purchase Tax
	2 litre Tourer	595	761	1952	Renown Saloon		925	1,440
					Renown Limousine		925	1,440
1948	80 Saloon	695	889		Mayflower		450	702
	80 Drophead	745	953					
	90 Saloon	775	991	1954	Renown Saloon		775	1,099
	90 Drophead	825	1,055		TR2		625	886
1952	90 Saloon	865	1,347					
	90 Drophead	895	1,394		**WOLSELEY**			
1954	90 Saloon	825	1,170	1946	Eight		360	461
	90 Drophead	855	1,212	June	Ten		420	537
	Alpine	895	1,269		12/48		490	627
1956	Sunbeam MKIII	835	1,254		14/60		535	684
	Rapier	695	1,045		18/85		590	755
				1950	4/50		550	704
	TRIUMPH			August	6/80		600	767
1946	Saloon	650	831	1952	4/50		660	1,028
	Roadster	625	799	October	6/80		720	1,122
1950	Renown	775	991	1953	4/44		595	844
	Mayflower	370	474	December	6/80		670	950
	TRX Roadster	975	1,247	July 1955	4/44		595	844
					6/90		750	1,064

INDEX